No-Nonsense
Finance

Errold Moody

McGraw-Hill
New York   Chicago   San Francisco   Lisbon
London   Madrid   Mexico City   Milan   New Delhi
San Juan   Seoul   Singapore   Sydney   Toronto

1 2 3 4 5 6 7 8 9 0   DOC/DOC   0 9 8 7 6 5 4

ISBN 0-07-141330-8

Printed and bound by RR Donnelley.

This publication is designed to provide accurate and authoritative information in regard to the subject matter covered. It is sold with the understanding that neither the author nor the publisher is engaged in rendering legal, accounting, or other professional service. If legal advice or other expert assistance is required, the services of a competent professional person should be sought.

—From a Declaration of Principles jointly adopted by a
Committee of the American Bar Association
and a Committee of Publishers

McGraw-Hill books are available at special quantity discounts to use as premiums and sales promotions, or for use in corporate training programs. For more information, please write to the Director of Special Sales, Professional Publishing, McGraw-Hill, Two Penn Plaza, New York, NY 10121-2298. Or contact your local bookstore.

 This book is printed on recycled, acid-free paper containing a minimum of 50% recycled, de-inked fiber.

Acknowledgments

I would like to thank all of the Financial Planners and Planning Organizations who have helped me in the advancement of Integrity and Ethics in the profession over the years:

Since there aren't any, I'd like to acknowledge some very dear friends who have helped me in my life:

Pat and Ted Bazett
Gina O'Byrne
Will Koehler
and my sister, Diane McClelland

I would also like to thank Nancy Corrigan, CFA, for her review and suggestions; Mary Kaufman, Master's in Gerontology, for her insight; and Rosemary Hallum, PhD, for her inspiration. None of their criticisms, however, were warranted. Men do not make mistakes.

A special thank you to Kelli Christiansen, Acquisitions Editor, McGraw-Hill. She is an exceptional person who not only made this book possible but worked diligently in the rewrite for human consumption.

Contents

Forewarned

TRUST NO ONE
DON'T BUY STOCKS FROM A STOCKBROKER
DON'T BUY INSURANCE FROM AN INSURANCE AGENT
DON'T DO FINANCIAL PLANNING WITH A FINANCIAL PLANNER

*T*HIS IS A RATHER UNUSUAL AND ABRUPT way to start a book. But I want everyone to clearly recognize that the bulk of the financial industry is not only lacking in knowledge and skill but, in a large part, has been engaging in deceptive practices for years. The unsuspecting consumer has been led to investments, planning practices, purchases of insurance products, and much more that defy rational thought. Even irrational thought.

You will find the material and insight in the pages that follow is illuminating since it debunks the marketing hype about investment and insurance products: the training, education, knowledge, and ethics of the industry (limited at best); and the sales agents and financial planners that use you as a money pit. You'll learn what the industry does not want you to know. In fact, you'll learn a lot that they don't have a clue about. You will become educated in the fundamentals of planning in many different areas.

I have digested the issues into an understandable format that can be used in real life. But you will have to read and think. If you want something quick, simple, and less than thought provoking, put the book down. Now. You will only hurt your head.

Are these rantings valid? After all, millions of dollars pass through brokers' hands each day. Well, consider this: The fundamentals of investing have never been taught to brokers as part of licensing training. How is it therefore possible that so many become so successful?

Marketing. Lots and lots and lots of very effective marketing. (And, of course, lots and lots of money.) Unfortunately, the gullible media has been taken in as well and has repeated well-worn, but generally incorrect, homilies for years to the unsuspecting public.

Regarding insurance, you certainly need a licensed agent to get the best deal or knowledge on this most difficult area of planning. But using someone you met at your PTA meeting, or while playing golf (fishing is okay), is ludicrous in the extreme. Referrals are one dumb way to design your financial life.

So, you want to use a planner? CFP, CPA, ChFC, NAPFA, FPA, CFC, CMC, POO, small furry animal? Actually, the little furry animal might have more integrity than some of the organizations do. How's that? Don't the planning organizations mandate strict adherence to ethics? Nope. If a planner is not licensed as mandated by law, isn't he reprimanded? Nope. And your financial magazines all know it but don't tell you. Ah, nothing like journalistic integrity.

How's this for an adage?

Don't buy stocks.

That comment, in itself, is sacrilege in our society. It is anathema to just about any article you will read in *Smart Money, Worth,* and literally all the other "financial" publications telling you what the next hot company stock is. Even mating with *The Wall Street Journal* for company insight is generally a fool's game. And so are the chat lines with the likes of the Motley Fool (aptly named).

What's my point? The ability to decipher an analyst's report—even to determine whether the analyst has any integrity—is so far beyond the capability of our little brains that it defies logic. I am not saying that equities are not a good long-term investment, but I am saying that a human's ability to pick a whole mess of them correctly is statistically not possible. Of course you can be lucky. And in the inspiring words of Harry Callahan, "Tell me punk. Do you feel lucky?"

Another adage: Don't die in a Medicaid ward.

There has been a continual assault on reason by various insurance companies, elder care attorneys, planners, and others to find ways to "divest" middle-income families of their monies so they can apply for nursing home care under Medicaid. You never want to die in a Medicaid ward with a bunch of Alzheimer's patients. To suggest substandard care to those that can afford otherwise is unethical and deceptive—and it happens all the time.

And more:

You give $100,000 in cash to your daughter when you die, $115,000 in your IRA to your son. Who got the short end of the stick?

Are security arbitrations fair? Impartial? Does anybody have a clue to what the issues really are?

Dollar-cost averaging is generally a sucker bet.

Bonus annuities are generally an invitation to underperformance.

Fee insurance advice is generally illegal in most states.

Securities attorneys don't know what diversification is (actually, no one has a clue)

Enron employee losses (and others) were caused, in large part, by the SEC, the Department of Labor, and all the way down to the CEO, corporate attorney, and human resources level.

Real estate ownership has a far greater risk than securities.

Standard deviation goes down over time but your risk goes up. Advisers just about always give you false advice about this.

Buy and hold stinks. Think to the terrible markets during 1973 and 1974. Think 2000–2002.

Basic asset allocation is a passive strategy designed by lazy advisors for large fees programmed to generate lackluster returns that can increase risk just when you want to do the opposite.

The Truth Is Out There

Don't despair. It is not my intent to leave you swinging in the wind. I will provide you the insight to a great number of areas that will make you a far more astute investor and insurance purchaser, as well as provide needed insight to the basics of estate planning, long-term care, retirement planning, real estate, and more. Not all the issues will be as simple or clear-cut as some of the supposed experts and journalists suggest it might be. But it will be the real-life essence of what you need to know, how you need to do it, and what risks are involved.

So you have been warned. If you are in the financial services business, you probably won't like the truth, so put this book down before you smudge it. If you think you are the next Peter Lynch, save your money. If you think your golf buddy, coworker, next-door neighbor, or your Mama can properly guide you in the intricacies of these involved issues, then just paint a big target over your belly button and go stand in a room. Sooner or later someone will come in and screw you to the wall.

But if you want the hard truth, pay attention and recognize that you will have to read carefully. You have been warned.

Introduction:
... and Now for Something
Completely Different

I HAVE WRITTEN THIS BOOK for the intelligent, Middle American worker who wants some straight talk about all the areas of finances. No fluff, no flowery prose, just solid information on what—and whom—you need to look at before you get started in any and all financial transactions. It even shows what problems you may encounter when you get a bad agent or product, why the problems happen in the first place (normally because you trusted someone you should never have even talked to), and whether you can recover your losses.

Some of the commentary is not pretty, but I do not pull punches on any issue. Also, I am not going to spend countless—and useless—words on how to become a millionaire. In these pages, you'll find no slick and quick rules on picking stocks, using referrals in picking consultants, understanding how variable annuities will render world peace, or any of the other standard foolishness.

What is presented here is much different because it is simply not lip service. It is what you need to know in order not to get misled or scammed by others—or even accidentally by yourself. It is not a simplistic financial planning book for dummies or an idiot's guide to planning. I have read both types of offerings, and Middle America is not composed of dummies or idiots. You won't end up as a dummy or idiot by reading books like that, but you won't end up very much smarter, either.

I have read hundreds of books and hundreds of thousands of articles on all areas of finances (and fishing, but that's another story). In

this book, I have distilled the best of these principles and incorpo-
rated some of my own planning elements. The result is a concise, objective, comprehensive, and competent compilation of real-life financial
information that can protect you from the adversities and effects of
using bad agents with bad products and a lot of bad information from
not-very-savvy financial gurus with little investment knowledge.

So who am I to offer this commentary? And why do I feel it is
better than the rest? Just about every financial columnist and most of
the authors of *How to Make a Million in the Stock Market in Just Three
Weeks* have no background in the areas they review. Either that, or the
background is simplistic at best. You need someone who has a thorough
knowledge of the subject areas being discussed. That I do. I have a Master of Science in Financial Planning with a major in estate planning,
as well as four other degrees including real estate and law. I have written and taught many investment, insurance, securities, and financial
planning courses.

What about the insurance area, which is certainly one of the most
contentious areas of all planning? I am one of the very few fully licensed
Life and Disability Insurance Analysts in California. There are approximately 40 such analysts in the entire state who are licensed and legally
able to charge a fee for insurance advice and do comprehensive fee financial planning. I have acted as an arbitrator and expert witness on securities cases that specifically address the issues of suitability. I work the
trenches every day as a financial planner for clients. I try to make the system better through increased knowledge and fiduciary responsibility.

There's much more. The point is, though, that nothing in this book
is Ivory Tower babble.

In short, in this book, I will provide the real-life elements to all sorts
of issues that may have confounded you—investments, insurance, estate
planning, basic elements to trusts, and how to truly select an adviser.
(The standard advice to get a referral is ludicrous. Checking the
NASD/SEC for prior violations is effectively useless!). I will even show
you that your never-ending effort to find the best stocks is almost a

complete waste of your time, including the effort spent in reviewing a financial magazine's stock du jour.

The following are some of the crucial issues that will be covered.

Investing

We'll tackle the fundamentals of investing, including alpha, beta, standard deviation, and many more concepts about which you may have felt uncomfortable. You will master this information without reams of statistical formulas that would confound Einstein. (But I will provide some formulas, charts, and mathematics, as necessary, to confirm some statements, because some concepts require further explanation or evidence.)

Each of these basics concepts is presented in generally easy-to-understand formats created from teaching all these subjects for years to people with all levels of investing knowledge and experience. If you have ever seen a bell-shaped curve, you will be able to understand standard deviation. The interesting issue is that alpha, beta, correlation, allocation, standard deviation, diversification, and more have generally never been taught to brokers as part of any licensing training. You will end up knowing more of the fundamentals than many so-called professionals.

Basis

You will learn the importance of tax basis—one of the most crucial issues of tax planning and one of the most overlooked. If you don't understand basis, just about every major asset you will ever buy will ultimately cost you more money than you ever realized. But here is the real gem: For those who leave assets to more than one beneficiary, almost 75 percent of all wills and trusts in the United States are drawn incorrectly and will ultimately lead to animosity lasting for generations. Even if you have just one beneficiary other than a spouse, you could be doing your investments all wrong. Surprise! This concept is also not taught as part of basic education to either securities brokers or insurance agents.

Dollar-Cost Averaging (DCA)

Just about every fund family, brokerage firm, agent, and financial magazine on the planet recommends DCA. You will find out that it has never worked, does not work today, and probably never will into the future. The reality of DCA is that it is a sales technique taught to brokers and agents as a key to investment strategy. It is simply great marketing of a sweepingly bad and misapplied recommendation for people who act emotionally (that is, most people). But there is a unique method called dollar-cost averaging down (DCAD) that is invaluable in a bad market.

Annuities

Fixed annuities are far from the simplistic retirement investment that people are led to believe. Most times you will have no idea what really went on with the purchase and even less of an idea what will happen later on with your money. As for variable annuities, they are a blend of a mutual fund and a standard annuity. Most importantly, variable annuities are generally deceptive offerings of a product that will never work as projected simply because the very entities that you think protect you have allowed pure deception in the marketing material. Yet people dump millions of hard-earned dollars into them because they "trust" their broker or agent. Trust no one—at least till you have done your homework.

Retirement

The simplistic 10-question risk questionnaires used by mutual fund and insurance companies are usually a complete waste of time and actually lead you into doing the wrong thing altogether, particularly when addressing retirement. The right way? Do a budget. If you do not do an extensive budget, you cannot plan a proper retirement. I'll show you how the numbers should work and a number of other issues to address such as the social security offset.

Many people believe that when they retire from a company that offers a pension, they will also get their full social security benefit. That rarely happens, and if that fact is not recognized, it can destroy a retirement budget.

Mutual Fund Analysis

Mutual fund analysis will be reviewed, which won't take long at all. As for buying a five-star fund after a five-minute "analysis," it usually means the purchaser has no clue to the underlying risk or current economic fundamentals. How about turning to the infinite number of investment chat lines (like the Motley Fool) for information? Fuhgetabotit. This is another tough area, but I will show you how to focus your efforts properly.

Pyramid of Investing

The basics for investment success through the standard pyramid of investing will also be covered. You should always invest at the bottom tiers first before you move up to more risky areas. It sounds like common sense, but almost every lost dollar I have seen resulted from the loss of the same common sense.

Asset Allocation

Allocating your assets is not as simple as following the advice in a simplistic article in some money magazine written by an inexperienced financial journalist. Nor does proper asset allocation come from a software program that spews out pretty colored charts uniquely identical for almost all investors. The problem is that the asset allocations practiced

by most brokers, agents, or planners, and suggested by the bulk of journalists, can actually lead to increased risk.

You'll find out what allocation actually is and what you can do to
help yourself. Unfortunately, the process is not easy. It is not just about
picking a bunch of funds and staying the course no matter what. That's
the reason billions of dollars of investment money have been lost in the
last few years.

Insurance

Do you really want or need all those expensive policies with cash value
buildup? I don't think so. Is there an easier way? Yes. Buy something
cheap and do your investing elsewhere. Unfortunately, few insurance
agents have focused on any type of insurance other than term, either
because the commissions were too good on the other products or they
had done no research and didn't know about proper coverage.

Long-Term Care

Long-term care is an issue that impacts us all—if not ourselves, then
our parents. However, the concern is not solely for the patient: Caregivers tend to become both emotionally and physically broken. The
use of a long-term care policy can protect an entire family. You'll
see clearly that you do not buy a LTC policy based on price. You'll
also find out what to look for in a policy, and you'll learn about the
essentials to make your selection easier. In any case, I will quickly dis-
pel the use of Medicaid as a viable planning technique.

Basic Estate Planning

You'll learn about basic estate planning and revocable living trusts,
which are great management tools, and discover how to reduce estate
taxes and probate fees. Once again, there will be a focus on basis, since,

if you miss this, few assets will achieve the desired result and your sons and daughters may end up thinking poorly of you after death. I'll provide a definitive chart on basis that will allow you not only to visually see an example but to put in your own numbers as well.

Real Estate

Are you thinking of buying a rental? How does it compare with the stock market, and is it a comparable investment? You'll get to use a form I developed that will show what you might expect if you plan to invest in this area.

When You Have Been Wronged

This book should provide insight into when you have been wronged. Unfortunately, that insight is not pretty, nor does it even remotely suggest that the odds are in your favor when you are forced into arbitration. You will understand what a *sophisticated investor* is. The text will also examine the concept of *suitability*. Put this all together and you will discover how to, with a good lawyer, proceed in a way that might increase your potential award.

In summary, this book will tell you things you never knew about, specifically about the following:

- How the industry usually looks at you like a money pit
- Why the protections you believe the government and industry organizations set up never truly protect you
- Why learning the fundamentals can provide security for your future or at least make you aware of the risks
- When things go wrong, what you can do to get your money back

If you take the time to really pay attention to each of the subject areas, you will become a more astute consumer, not just an investor, and you'll become far more knowledgeable about many of the financial areas directly impacting your life.

Notes

1. I have assumed that you have read material on annuities, investments, and the like and do not need a complete rehash of, say, what a P/E ratio is, what tax deferred means, and so on. This is not an introductory book. As such, if you have difficulties (hopefully limited) with some of the material, you may wish to reread some of the basic literature on the subjects. I simply start where many of other texts have left off—or where the authors are out to lunch.

2. A lot of the material in these pages has been posted at my Web site in one form or another. It will not be as concise, as well written or, probably, as up to date, but it will possibly provide additional statistics, links, and other resources as necessary. For example, when I reference diversification, I make reference to a study, "Have Individual Stocks Become More Volatile? An Empirical Exploration of Idiosyncratic Risk" (with Martin Lettau, Burton Malkiel, and Yexiao Xu), Journal of Finance, February 2001. If you went to my site, used my search engine and typed in **Yexiao**, you get three references; by entering the more well-known **Malkiel**, you get 10 references. Simply click on one and then search for the name in that article or get the link to an independent site.

3. If you are not precise in your search, for example, and entered **long-term care** as your search, you'd end up with at least 127 matches. If you entered your real concern of **ADL**, you'd get a more explicit 14 matches. Much better. But, hey, if you want to stumble aimlessly through hundreds of pages hoping to get lucky, I won't press. It's your life. Do what you want.

4. It is not my intent to take involved subjects—say, standard deviation—and supply a detailed explanation as though this was a college course. I suppose it might look impressive, but not only would you be brain dead (and utterly bored) in the analysis, but it would serve no real-life purpose. My intent with all such subjects is to distill the essence into an understandable format (I hope!) that you could actually teach to your neighbors. Really.

5. Medicare coverage, taxation, interest rates, statistical data, and literally everything else in your life is changing as you read this. The material I have offered was valid at the time of submission but should never be depended upon for your planning without doing some more extensive homework.

6. Although it defies credulity, if you find an error, email me at efm@efmoody.com and I will post corrections at www.efmoody.com.

CHAPTER 1

THE FUNDAMENTALS
OF INVESTING

N O ONE HAS A CLUE when it comes to buying individual stocks.

When it comes down to products and methodology, ethics, and fiduciary responsibility, there is clear evidence of extreme incompetency by just about everyone involved in the selection and use of securities.

I will tell you right up front that this discussion of diversification, risk, suitability, and competency will not sit well with almost any broker or agent across the world. Nor will it be looked upon kindly by any of the brokerage or fund firms, be they full-service firms such as Merrill Lynch and American Express, moderate services such as Schwab, or no service such as most of the Internet trading sites. It also won't sit well with consumers who buy and sell individual securities as the bulk of their portfolio. Planners are generally out to lunch. Attorneys—and that includes securities attorneys—wouldn't know diversification from a porch light. Arbitrators don't understand it. The Securities and Exchange Commission (SEC) usually doesn't have a clue—and they are supposed to protect the consumer. The NASD doesn't seem to know or care. And, you certainly can't expect your next-door neighbor, coworker, or your Mama to understand these concepts, either.

It's fair to say that practically nobody has but a remote understanding of one of the most important fundamentals of investing: what diversification truly is and its application in securities rules. So here it is: Any sale of an individual security must be suitable for the buyer. To wit: The NASD Rule 2310 (formerly Article III, Section 2 of the Rules of Fair Practice) provides, "[i]n recommending to a customer the purchase, sale or exchange of any security, a member shall have reasonable grounds for believing that the recommendation is suitable for such customer upon the basis of facts, if any, disclosed by such customer as to his other security holdings and as to his financial situation and needs."

"Reasonable grounds" means that you—or your agent—certainly must have an understanding of the fundamentals of investing. And New York Stock Exchange (NYSE) Rule 405 (also known as "know thy client") requires that a firm use due diligence to learn the essential facts relative to every customer and every order. Those essential facts include risk, tolerance, suitability, and so forth. But you cannot determine suitability without totally understanding risk. And you cannot understand risk without understanding diversification by the numbers.

Diversification by the Numbers

So, what is diversification? Let's not repeat the standard sophomoric and naïve treatise used by financial planners, journalists, money magazines, the SEC, and all the others as "not putting all your eggs in one basket." Diversification also is not some simplistic computer program, fund company, or Web site that suggests, based on 10 simple "risk" questions, that you should put 60 percent of your money in stocks, 30 percent in bonds, 10 percent in cash, and 5 percent under your pillow.* But there is your problem. Apparently not one of these responsible entities has done a proper analysis of what diversification is by the numbers—and that's the only way to properly reference the issue.

---

*Did you use your calculator?

CAVEAT INVESTOR

Often, you'll see diversification referred to as "not putting all your eggs in one basket." This oversimplification is naïve at best and dangerous at worst.

Putting all your eggs in one basket implies something simple—like putting all your money into different mutual funds or a few different stocks. But diversification goes much deeper than that, and anyone who invests a dime in the markets should know that.

The danger with this simplification of what is really an important investment fundamental is that far too many financial journalists, chatline pundits, and even so-called financial planners allow investors to believe that the risk of investing can simply be "forgiven" with a few strokes of a software program or Ouija board. Diversification must start with a statistical formula clearly identifying the risks of investing, not some overly simple rule of thumb.

Watch out for oversimplifications and dumbing down conceptualizations that don't take this topic seriously. If someone tells you that diversification is about not putting all your eggs in one basket, walk away—no, run away.

Why have so few people conducted any real analysis on diversification? It's because diversification is not taught to brokers, attorneys, almost all financial planners, and certainly not to your neighbor, coworker, or some stranger on the Motley Fool chatline.

I repeat if you do not understand diversification by the numbers, you cannot determine risk. If you cannot determine risk, you cannot establish suitability. If you cannot determine suitability—well, then the investment is not only suspect but generally wrong. Unfortunately, very few people actually read and do research, certainly not to the extent that they (or their advisers) should in order to be adequately informed about risk and reward.[1]

You need some basic definitions to understand the fundamentals. If anyone invests in the market, there is a risk. We shall assume that the market's risk is defined by the Standard & Poor's 500 Index (the S&P 500), though the risk is better shown by all the stocks in the extended market. The Dow Jones Industrial Average (the Dow, or DJIA) has too few stocks (30) to reflect the broad-based market, and, since the S&P 500 is well known and utilized throughout the world, it's an acceptable proxy for the market. This type of risk is also known as *systematic risk*. If you go into the market, systematic risk is one you have to live with, like it or not.

On the other hand, and this is a position that everyone should agree with, if you enter the market with just one stock, the risk is greater than that of the larger S&P 500 index. This is called *unsystematic risk*—the risk that a single company could go bad. While it's possible to win big with just one stock, the additional risk can wreak financial havoc. Even your "best" stocks can go bad. (Do Enron, WorldCom, Tyson, Adelphia, and others ring a bell?) But a complete breakdown of the company is not the only thing that can severely affect the performance of the company's stock. The impact of the war, poor distribution of product, a CEO divorce, the Martha Stewart debacle —any unanticipated event that can detrimentally affect the company—all can lead to an unanticipated drop in value that has not occurred to other companies.

But how much greater, statistically, is unsystematic risk? Two times greater? Fifty times greater? Five hundred times greater? To put it another way, how many stocks do you have to have in a portfolio in order to insulate it from unsystematic risk? In other words, how many stocks do you have to have in a portfolio in order to effectively assume the same risk as the market overall?

If you do not know these numbers, you simply cannot design a proper portfolio of individual securities at any time during your life except by luck. And even though you may use "diversified" mutual funds, if you don't have a grasp of the fundamentals, anything built on top of ignorance is a poor excuse for investing.[2] (Just so we are clear, a diversified mutual fund is not the same thing as having a diversified portfolio.)

Why is this such a contentious issue? Because the fundamentals of diversification are not taught as part of licensing training to brokers or supervisors. I know, since I have taught most of the securities licensing courses to brokers. And while it may be taught in some small measure to some planners and advisors, the true relevance of diversification is rarely, if ever, addressed. Consumers also generally don't have a clue about diversification and its importance in developing a proper risk portfolio, primarily because there is hardly a magazine or journalist that has properly addressed the issue.[3]

The question all boils down to the inability of a human being not only to pick one individual winning stock but also to pick a whole mess of individual stocks and put them altogether into a portfolio that properly identifies risk as well as current economic conditions. Guess what? You can't do this. Guess what? I can't do this. And I'll prove I can't.

In real-world terms, an average person cannot accept unsystematic risk. You are rarely going to be able to pick that one company (or even two or three companies) that will hit big, and hit big consistently (the real key). Conversely, you aren't necessarily going to avoid all the companies that go belly up. Consider all the huge brokerage firms and their MBA analysts that extolled Enron as it fell apart. That said, as you add more securities to your portfolio, you reduce the odds of such unsystematic risk. (Note, however, that diversification does not reduce systematic—or market—risk.) The question, as mentioned above, is, "How many stocks do you need in order to approximate the risk of the market?"

If you have just one stock, your risk (depending on volatility) is generally at least 50 percent greater than that of the market overall. That might seem like a stretch, but once you put the current economics into perspective, you very likely are now shuddering at the current losses of entire portfolios during 2000–2002 at over 50 percent. Why? Because even the most seemingly conservative stocks—those that you trusted for years and years—all can go bad. However, as you add more securities to your holdings, the risk decreases very, very quickly. By the time you have 10 to 15 securities, you have reduced unsystematic risk very

close to that of the S&P 500 (see Figure 1.1).[4] That is the basic definition of diversification: the number of stocks needed to effectively reduce
risk to that of the market.

Ronald Surz and Mitchell Price calculated returns for portfolios
of 15 randomly selected stocks over 132 years through June 1999. The
authors found that among such randomly selected 15-stock baskets, the
typical portfolio strayed as much as 8.1 percentage points a year from
the market's return. Thus, if the market was up 11 percent in a given
year, the typical portfolio might gain as much as 19.1 percent—or as
little as 2.9 percent. That's still a substantial difference from a 500 stock
portfolio of the S&P 500.

So, what if you are careful to pick a group of 15 well-diversified
stocks? The typical tracking error was still 5.4 percent. Some 15-stock
portfolios strayed far more than this amount, while others would track
the market more closely. Even if you held 60 stocks, and even if you were
careful to diversify, the typical tracking error was still 3.5 percentage
points a year. In my past teachings, I had suggested that one needs to
buy at least 13 different stocks in order to properly diversify. Notice the

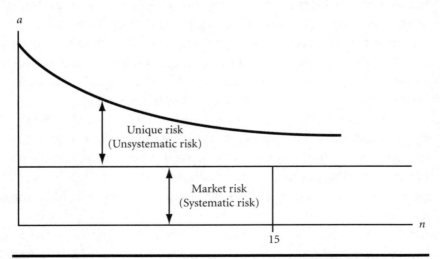

Figure 1.1   Number of securities to approximate risk of market pre-1990s.

word *different.* Different means noncorrelated or randomly correlated securities—those that don't necessarily move in the same amount at the same time or for the same reason as other securities in the portfolio. If you were to buy all your stocks in one category (that is, the same sector or industry), such as auto, steel, rubber, or glass, you really would not be diversified, since they tend to be impacted the same way.

There is a catch to the above, however, that has made the analysis of individual securities even more difficult. Stocks have even become more volatile during the last two decades. Certainly they were during the 1990s once the advent of the computer came along, along with the use of the Internet for analysis (including all those essentially useless chatlines) and the ability to trade instantaneously on 24-hour worldwide exchanges. During this time, market (systematic) risk has stayed roughly the same, though you might think otherwise by day-to-day movements. It's the volatility of individual securities, though, that has gone up. And the correlation between stocks is much greater (which means you need more stocks to attain the same diversification as before).

A 2001 study called "Have Individual Stocks Become More Volatile? An Empirical Exploration of Idiosyncratic Risk" shows that the element of diversification is far more volatile than that previously referenced by Surz and Price. What 15 stocks once were to diversification is now around 50 stocks or more (Figure 1.2). Some studies suggest 100, others 350, and so on. At the level of 100 or 300 or 400 stocks, you're probably down to one or two percentage points of tracking error. (But, then again, who would want to have to research and buy 300 or more stocks by themselves?) Regardless, it takes far more stocks in a portfolio to reduce unsystematic risk than it used to.

In the end, though, the minimum number of stocks to approximate systematic risk is simply beyond the ability of just about anybody to select. Phrased differently, read any chatline you want, visit your friends at cocktail parties, ask your mama, it won't do any good in trying to pick a realistic portfolio.

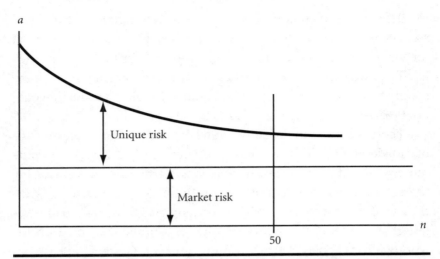

Figure 1.2   Current number of securities to approximate market risk.

The only way to eliminate this tracking error is to own the entire market, preferably through a low-cost index fund that mimics the Wilshire 5000 or the Russell 3000.

In summary, you are not going to beat the system with single securities. So, take your pick: 50 stocks, 100, 200, 350—whatever it is, you don't have a chance to figure out which individual stocks to buy, when, for how much, and how each selection correlates with another. It is that difficult.

Why is this limitation so important? I repeat again, if you do not know diversification by the numbers, you cannot determine risk. If you cannot determine risk, you cannot determine suitability. The real-life application of diversification limits the purchase of individual securities as a significant portfolio to just about no one. In other words, very few individual securities are suitable for the middle-class American consumer.

Suitability and Securities

You have to understand diversification before you can understand risk. Is risk important? You shouldn't have to ask. You must understand risk before you can understand suitability. Is suitability mandatory? It's the law. Every sale of a security must be suitable.

What does that mean? It means that both you and your broker must have reasonable grounds to believe that the investment you are looking at fits your needs—your financial needs, your risk tolerance, your goals, and so on.

Reasonable grounds must include an understanding of the fundamentals of investing. The reality, though, is that brokers, during licensing training, are not taught diversification, asset allocation, alpha, beta, standard deviation, correlation, or many of the other basics needed to comprehend risk and reward. They are not taught this stuff later, either. If you are not thoroughly familiar with those topics, you simply cannot determine suitability. And no one involved in a securities transaction can be considered sophisticated without these fundamentals and the understanding of risk.

The fact is that most investors are far from sophisticated. In fact, research clearly indicates that most investors—not only individuals, but financial institutions, too—do not manage their portfolios effectively. That is, investors do not construct or manage their portfolios in a manner that reflects their attitude toward risk, nor do they recognize the likely financial consequences of disappointing investment performance.[5]

Three critical elements should be central to every rational investor's deliberations:

- **Defining investment objectives clearly and realistically.** This item involves eliminating your emotion—a most difficult issue, I admit—but crucial to sound decision making. You will also need to do a lot of homework (reading) and have the capability of using a financial calculator. If you can't figure out how money works, it may not work very well for you—particularly during retirement.
- **Determining an appropriate asset-mix strategy for achieving these objectives.** Don't accept preprogrammed software that

makes every client the same. For anyone over the age of 50, cal-
culating the appropriate mix demands a formal financial analysis with a budget
- **Adopting operating tactics that will effectively implement the broad strategic plan.** Implementation involves more than simply buying and holding. It covers more than annual rebalancing. It encompasses more than a Monte Carlo analysis that tells you what might happen. Successful implementation requires that a formal program be set up that utilizes the movement of the national and worldwide economy so you can react to what is happening now or to what might happen in the immediate future. Most investment goals are long term. But investors need to have a plan in place now, to address what to do long before any negative circumstances arise, like a loss of 40 percent or more of your money, as happened to many people during the years 2000 to 2002.

Tackling all these issues—before you buy an investment—will go a long way toward helping you reach suitability requirements. But you have to first understand diversification by the numbers through the appropriate studies. It requires a mandatory intensive review to protect your money—and to protect yourself from those who know little about money. I truly feel that one way to validate a sophisticated agent, investor, attorney, or planner is to ask that person to define diversification correctly. If the supposed professional can't do it, she or he is not sophisticated. Then just walk away. Certainly, don't give that person any money.

Beta Is Dead. Long Live Beta

Every major financial Internet site, as well just about all financial books, makes reference to beta. But what is beta? Every investor needs to learn how to determine that figure as well as to avoid the dangers of misusing it through over reliance. Once you learn its derivation as well as its limitations, you can make a decision as to whether or not to use it or to what degree.

And that is exactly what I do. I always look at beta, then I look at all the other important numbers, ratios, alpha (defined later), and numerous articles with specific reference to economics before I make an investment decision.

Beta represents the volatility of a stock or fund as compared with the market in total. The market, as measured by the S&P 500, has a beta of 1.0. A beta higher than 1.0 represents more volatility, while a beta less than 1.0 indicates less volatility. The following is the formula for determining beta:

$$((N) (Sum\ of\ XY)) - ((Sum\ of\ X) (Sum\ of\ Y))$$

Where N = the number of observations
       X = rate of return for the S&P 500 Index
       Y = Rate of return for stock or fund.

Now let's look at this realistically so it actually makes sense. The simpler method to "accurately" determine beta is to merely look at the movement of the stock or fund versus an index over a period of time, say one year. The time period is significant. A short period of time, say three or six months, is statistically insignificant and not going to provide valuable numbers. A long period of time, say most periods over five years, simply incorporates too many variables (called *noise*) and may also not be worthwhile. So the betas you review should be based on one-year, three-year, and five-year periods.

The S&P 500 is the market index normally used for most studies as a reflection of everything that is happening. The S&P 500 actually does not include the entire market—it includes about 80 percent of total market capitalization —but it is generally the acceptable reference for most studies. The whole key to the exercise is to recognize that whatever the market and S&P 500 Index does, it does so by a factor of 1.0. Therefore, no matter what it does—be it a positive return of 3 percent, 12 percent, or 23 percent—it does so by a beta factor of 1.0 when it goes up. Likewise, it does so by a beta factor of 1.0, if it goes down—be it a return of –2 percent, –8 percent, or –16 percent. (Betas don't have to be the same, both up and down for the same security, but most often they are identified in that manner.)

Now let's compare your stock or fund for comparison. Let's say the market (or the S&P 500) goes up 10 percent over a year's time. (As stated, a shorter period of time does not provide enough data and is unreliable. Don't even bother with trying to measure anything less than a year.) Let's say your stock or fund goes up 13 percent. You can simply divide the 13 percent by 10 percent and you get 1.3. That becomes your beta of the fund for that period. What does this figure mean? It means that for every move the market makes, your stock or fund may increase 1.3 times more. (Note that I said "may" increase. Remember, betas reflect volatility, not actual returns.) If the market currently does 5 percent, you might anticipate that your fund would go up 6.5 percent (1.3 × 5 percent). As stated, the beta is not a perfect indication of increase. There's certainly more to analysis, but this calculation is close enough for government work. In real-life terms, a beta greater than 1 is more volatile than the market overall. It is more risky.

What happens if the market goes down? If you have a beta of 1.5, it will be 50 percent more volatile on the way down and would imply a much larger loss than the market overall. How about a stock or fund that is less volatile than the market? Simply put, let's say the market goes up by 6 percent and your fund goes up by just 2 percent. The beta of your fund becomes 2 percent divided by 6 percent, or 0.33. For every movement of the market, your stock or fund goes up a third less. In real-life terms, a beta less than 1.0 is less volatile—that is, more conservative—than the market overall. There are no negative betas (theoretically, yes; realistically, no). Just variations between 0.0 (rare) to up to 3.0+ (above 1.5 is high).

Overall, if you are seeking an aggressive fund with the intent of a higher return (risk versus reward), you may look to a beta greater

CAVEAT INVESTOR

An important caution when using beta: Only compare types of funds that are similar. In other words, don't compare a large-cap fund to a small-cap fund or to a gold fund. Comparing a gold fund beta to the beta of an S&P 500 fund is a ludicrous exercise. You are comparing apples to oranges, and it's a waste of numbers, time and fruit.

Yet I have seen such comparisons by brokers because (and remember this) beta is not taught as part of broker licensing training. Now, if you know you shouldn't compare kumquats to pineapples, don't let your broker, financial planner, or whoever else try to compare the wrong things in order to get you to buy an investment, either.

than 1.0. If you are conservative, you should look for a beta less than 1.0. Of course, you can look for betas as high as 3.0+ in the hopes of making a killing, but that's usually because you have had too much caffeine.

Beta is the first step in reviewing the volatility of a stock or fund and provides a number that compares it against the market overall. Can you use it exclusively? No! In fact, it can be a waste of your time. You must go to the next number called alpha.

Alphas and Other Investment Stuff

Now you are ready to ask yourself, do I just select a fund based on the level of risk I wish to accept? Based on the use of beta by itself (we have taken some latitude in the explanation, but the gist is close enough for our purposes), it looks pretty simple.

It isn't.

Beta is a nice guide but should never be used by itself. The simple and mere selection of a stock or fund by beta alone could lead you to the poorhouse, no matter what the market might do.

You need to use alpha.

Good and Bad Equal Betas = Alpha

Let's assume you were looking at 10 different funds, all with betas of 1.0. Also assume that fund managers are selecting various stocks for their portfolio from a universe of 500 stocks that all have a theoretical beta of 1.0. Say Manager A picks 25 stocks, Manager B picks 25 different stocks, and so on. We'll also say that the market went up by 10 percent. By a slightly skewed definition, therefore, shouldn't each one of these funds provide exactly the same return of 10 percent since they all have the same beta? They won't. Why's that? Because each fund manager thinks the stocks he or she picks are better stocks than those selected by the other managers. Some of these managers will be right. Certain stocks will do better than others, even with the same risk level, and some managers might be able to figure out which of those securities that will outshine their competitors. (Whether they did it by skill or luck, however, would not be known for some time into the future.) Other fund managers will underperform the index because they were incapable (or unlucky or stupid) of picking the better stocks. Therefore, while Manager A earns 13 percent, Manager B, with the same beta, might earn just 8 percent. Obviously, you'd prefer to use Manager A, and alpha helps you determine which manager within a group is doing better.

So how do you figure alpha? You can divide the return of the investment by the return of the index beta. In our example, it would be 13 percent divided by 10 percent, and you get an alpha of +1.3 for that fund. If the manager had returned less than the 10 percent, he would have a negative alpha (see Figure 1.3). Alpha is a reflection that a manager is able to pick better stocks than someone else. Therefore, assuming the managers are working with the same beta, alpha makes your decision simple. The person with the highest positive alpha for the longest period of time at the level of risk (the beta) that you are willing to utilize would appear to be the best selection. (A more statistically correct method is called Jensen's alpha. See my web site for more details. But the essence of the larger positive alpha for a given study is valid.)

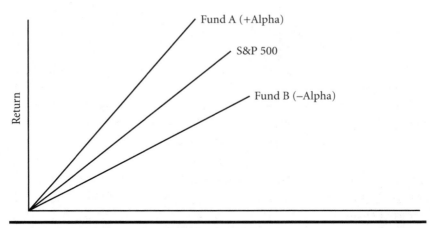

Figure 1.3   Alpha = comparison of funds with beta = 1.

But, wait!

Obviously the positive alpha is good to see. But if it was just looking at a one-year period, the time frame might be too short to justify its
use into the future. You'd like to see at least a three-year alpha—and
maybe even a five-year or longer alpha. The longer the period, the
greater a manager's showing a unique ability to pick better stocks
than others. Does it work all the time? Not really.

Reversion to the Mean

Reversion (regression) to the mean is a tool that will make you take
an objective look at any positive alpha. This concept simply means that
if a return has been higher than the norm for its risk, historical statistics suggest that such higher returns will revert to the lower average
number over time. What was good in one year is not necessarily going
to be good the next year. Now, it is true that some of the hottest-performing stocks might also be good performers the following year. But
once you get beyond this point, the numbers may mean little. In fact,
a study by Micropal showed that the top funds in any five-year period

CAVEAT INVESTOR

Investors should also be aware that managers themselves revert to the mean. Despite numerous year-end articles about hot fund managers who managed to beat the market by double digits, chances are those same managers won't appear on that hot list the next year. Chances are even better that they will appear on the list of failures for turning in below-market returns.

The moral of the story: Don't go chasing after the returns any manager posts over just a one-year period. That performance could be—and usually is—a fluke.

underperformed the S&P 500 Index in the subsequent five-year period.

Consider the performance of the stock market during the past decade. It was way above the historical return of the market of about 10 percent. It had to revert back to some more realistic number. Obviously, the subsequent losses of 2000 forward were more than just an average reversion, but the difficulty in playing a game with stocks and funds is that you have no idea when such a reversion will happen, or by how much, or for how long. Nonetheless, if you plan for a fund manager to retain excessive returns over and above a particular risk level year in and year out, you'd better be prepared for the alpha (and returns) to drop back to reality at some point in the future.

Well, I fibbed a little there. Actually, if you have an active manager outpacing a particular beta, the subsequent return to reality could show a return less than the norm.

Here's the point: Active management entails the buying and selling of stock throughout the year and costs the fund extra fees beyond an index fund. Further, there are manager fees to factor in. For example, look at the costs of the Vanguard 500 Index Fund. It's about 0.20 percent. Now take a look at the average loaded fund fee for large growth stocks. It's closer to 1.5 percent average for the standard loaded funds. Hence, a manager buying and selling stocks in a fund may not only be impacted by reversion to the mean but also underperform the beta utilized because they must account for the extra costs of running the fund.

You must know the beta of a stock or fund so you analyze equal risks. Then you need to review the alphas, only looking for the best in the categories you have selected. But then you have to conduct further review of the fees being charged since the returns have to eventually reflect that offset. Further, understand that most returns greater than the norm may revert back to the mean, anyway. Past performance is no reflection of future results.

Remember as well that this material is not taught to brokers or insurance agents as part of licensing training. Yes, they may learn about some of it as time goes by, but, then again, they probably won't. Even if they do so, they certainly aren't going to tell you about the implications of using a managed fund that we have discussed here (though the new impact from New York's Eliot Spitzer is having an impact).[6]

Standard Deviation—Or, How Figures Can Lie and Liars Can Figure

Standard deviation (also called *volatility*) is a measure of risk. Hopefully you are familiar with the standard bell-shaped curve. This curve, you may recall, is used to indicate the pattern of returns in a graphical fashion: IQs, test results, baseball averages, and much more. The average is in the middle and the sides show how much variation there might be. Figure 1.4 illustrates a typical bell curve.

Everything that happens follows a statistical pattern, with most of the patterns simply falling in the middle of the curve with the lesser odds showing up around the edges. Let's take golf, for example. Almost all of us have played it at one point in our lives, and most people have average ability that is best represented by, say, the three bars in the mid-

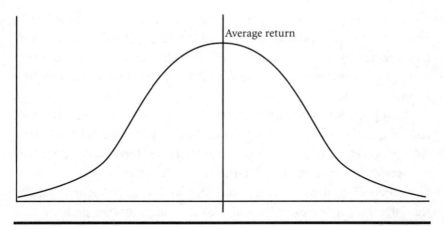

Figure 1.4   Standard deviation.

dle (see Figure 1.5). We'll say that it represents 68 percent of all people that play, and that number also represents one standard deviation.
The average score might be 110, and the two side bars represent plus or

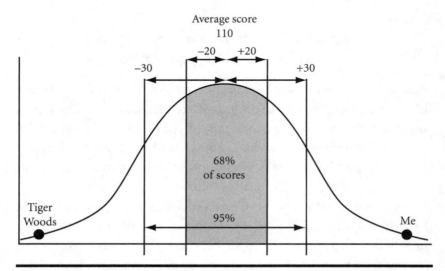

Figure 1.5   Golf standard deviation.

minus 20 percent. That means in 68 percent of the time, people score 110 on average, with scores of 90 and 130 on each side. If you include the next two bars on each side, it would mean that 95 percent of all people are covered by the graph. That is the definition for two standard deviations. It would be a score of 110 average but with, say, a +30 percent or −30 percent difference, or scores as low as 80 or as high as 140 for 95 percent of time. You can keep doing this by adding another two bars that cover 99 percent of the scores/population. And then finally you get to the very extreme left with the likes of Tiger Woods. Or the extreme right, with scores, for people like me, of, say, 150 or more. Guess what? You now know what one, two, and three standard deviations are, and it took less than five minutes.

Put into terms for securities, the average return is around 10 percent, with one standard deviation (68 percent of the time) of 21 percent. That means the low could be as far down as −11 percent (10 percent − 21 percent) to as high as 31 percent (10 percent + 21 percent). It also (generally) references statistics over a period of one year. (If you use periods less than one year, the statistics are effectively meaningless. If you use periods of 10 years or more, too many changes can cloud the numbers. It's preferable to use a minimum of one year to no more than five years.) A graph might look like Figure 1.6, with the shaded area representing 68 percent of all occurrences. The middle point reflects the 10 percent "average" return, and the plus and minus are represented by the extreme ends of the shaded area.

So, believe it or not, you now know what standard deviation means as it relates to securities. It is the return generated over a one-year period, with the pluses and minuses you might expect 68 percent of the time. These pluses and minuses reflect volatility. The greater the standard deviation (SD), the more the volatility and the greater the risk.

Once in a while you may read some commentary regarding two standard deviations (remember that is 95 percent of the time), but I think it fairly rare and usually referenced only in professional articles. Most articles will simply refer to numbers reflecting one standard deviation.

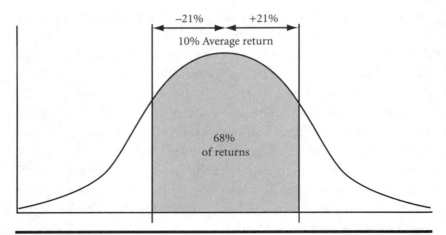

Figure 1.6 Investment standard deviation.

Now, let's consider an example using the stock market. Whenever you view charts that compare similar investments, you want the graph or investment that is not only the highest but also the thinnest. The higher the graph, the greater the return. The thinner the graph, the less the variation in returns.

Let's assume you had two stocks or funds with the same return over a year—say, 9 percent. But one had a standard deviation of 10 percent and the other had a standard deviation of 18 percent. Which one would you want, everything else being equal? You would want the one with the least standard deviation, because it has the least volatility. Figure 1.7 illustrates this example.

For any given return, you want the thinnest graph, representing the least amount of deviation from your anticipated return. But what if you were not even willing to take much risk at all—in other words, you wanted very low volatility? The question becomes, first, are there different standard deviations for different stocks and for different indexes? Yes, there are a whole mess lot of them. Next, are there different standard deviations for assets other than stocks? Yes, a myriad of them. And since there are, the next question is, how do you apply the various stan-

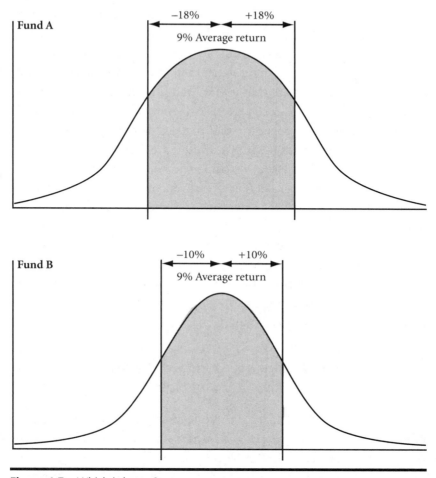

Figure 1.7 Which is better?

dard deviations to get the risk, or volatility, you want? An example will clearly show how to do this.

Let's assume that you were considering the S&P 500 Index and it had a 10 percent average return over time but also had a one-year standard deviation of 21 percent. You definitely like the idea of getting a positive return of 31 percent (10 percent + 21 percent) in one year, but you could not afford a loss of −11 percent (10 percent − 21 percent). You also knew that a bond fund had a lower return of 7 percent over the most recent history and had a standard deviation of 5 percent. (Keep in mind, these are purely hypothetical numbers to make the example more vivid.) The point is that you want a greater return than 7 percent but less volatility than 21 percent. So, you just add various amounts of the two investments together until you get the return you are willing to accept for the deviation with which you are comfortable.

To illustrate (Fig. 1.8), let's assume you had 50 percent of both the S&P 500 Index and the bond fund. The average return is now 9 percent (7 percent + 11 percent = 18 percent/2 = 9 percent) and the standard deviation is 13.0 percent (21 percent + 5 percent = 26 percent/2 = 13.0 percent). Is that what you want? If not, you simply adjust the combinations until you arrive at something that you are willing to accept.

So, is standard deviation that direct and simple? Unfortunately not. The basics of standard deviation go one step further and it clearly reflects a distortion of risk by many planners.

Risk, Variability, Standard Deviation and Buy and Hold

Assume you owned a security with a one-year standard deviation of 30 percent. (Remember, that's how a regular standard deviation is identified.) That's pretty high. But if you potentially held the security for five years, the standard deviation is reduced to "only" 13.42 percent. That's supposedly far more acceptable to investors. How is it derived? You simply divide the annual standard deviation by the square root of the years held—in this case, five years. That number is 2.236. So 30 percent ÷ 2.26 = 13.42 percent. And if you held the security for 10 years, you then would divide 30 percent by 3.16 for a volatility of just 9.48 percent. If you had started with just 20 percent volatility, then a five-year deviation would result in a 8.94 percent volatility and a 10-year deviation of only 6.32 percent. Such a deal!

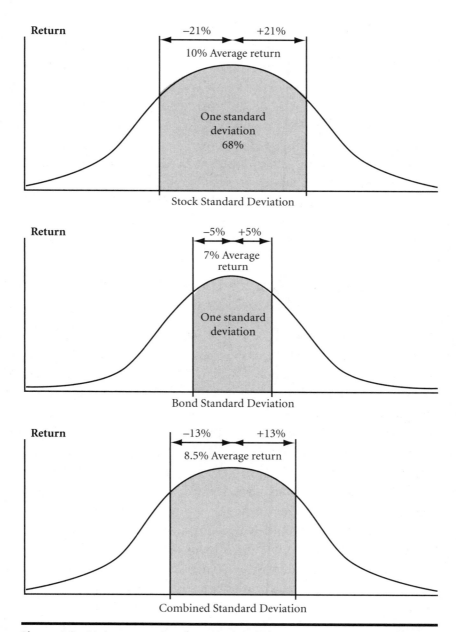

Figure 1.8 Various examples of standard deviation.

Looks great, doesn't it? And investors frequently are told it is great, which is clearly the reason why you want to stay in the market regardless of the singular yearly volatility. Or that buy and hold works so well because risk goes down the longer you hold a security. The statement is false. Read that carefully. It should read that standard deviation goes down. Standard deviation is just one type of risk. It does not represent the risk you are actually taking. The statement you should be hearing is that risk goes up the longer you hold a security. But this concept is one that about which few brokers, planners, and insurance agents know and utilize. It can bury your portfolio with dismal returns. It can bury your retirement. And that is exactly what has been happening for the last few years till just recently.

Risk Going Up the Longer You Hold on to Stocks and Bonds

What is indefensible by planners and brokers is the fact that the issue of increased variability has been addressed for years in certain textbooks, but hardly anyone paid attention. (I did try to suggest that it be included in some instruction for consumers during the 1990s, but no one thought it worthwhile.) Of course, these were professional texts and not the standard drivel generally offered for licensing. Nonetheless, it was a fact requiring formal notice to the public so they wouldn't get caught in the throws of 2000–2002, with the experts telling people to "stay the course" and "the market always comes back". And then watching billions of dollars of retirement money being lost by retirees.

One of the best books of advice for investing is *Investments*, by Zvi Bodie, Alex Kane, and Alan J. Marcus (McGraw-Hill, 1991). The comments in this text addressed a 30 percent standard deviation and that an investor would be "emotionally relieved" that over a five-year period volatility would be reduce to an "acceptable" 13.42 percent. But the text notes that the impact of a one-time standard deviation over the entire portfolio could reduce the amount of the anticipated return by almost 50 percent. Did you miss the number? You could be off your projections by 50 percent!

> Time diversification does not reduce risk. It is true that the per-year average rate of return has a smaller standard deviation for a longer time horizon. It is also true that the uncertainty compounds over a greater number of years. Unfortunately, this latter effect dominates in the sense that the total return becomes more uncertain the longer the investment horizon.

What they mean in simpler terms is that as your portfolio grows, and if something does go wrong, it will affect your portfolio very significantly. A standard deviation in the average return over the five-year period will effect final wealth by a factor of $(1 - .1342)^5$, or .487. (That's the formula. One minus the standard deviation for the time period selected and the resulting number multiplied to the x power, where x represents the number of years in question.) That means that final wealth will be less than one-half its expected value. Do you understand that significance? What you thought you were going to have in the future and on which you base your retirement could be less than 50 percent of what you projected. Try to tell me (or yourself, more importantly) that won't make a difference. Try to say that the devastating losses of 2000–2002 haven't made a difference. Go ahead, try.

The lesson is that no one should use a flat rate of return analysis for just about any computation without taking into account the risks along the way. Investing for more than one holding period means that the amount at risk is growing. This is analogous to an insurer taking on more insurance policies. The fact that these policies are independent of each other does not offset the effect of placing more funds at risk. Focusing on the standard deviation of the rate of return should never obscure the more proper emphasis on the possible dollar values of a portfolio strategy.[6]

You incur more risk the longer time goes on. But you also have already assumed a huge risk if you have put all your money in an investment at

one time; the statistical risk could go against you at any time. For example, I acted as an expert on a case in which the individual had taken all
his investments and invested in the market. (The amount was significant—
$20 million, which consisted totally of stock in his Internet company, a
high risk by itself.) He didn't know what to do and went to one of the
largest investment adviser firms in San Francisco and utilized an adviser
who had an MBA from Harvard. The adviser told him that by keeping an
investment for a long time, the risk would go down. But the adviser offered
nothing showing the huge risk that was being taken simply by having all
assets in the market at one time. So, along comes March 2000 and the market debacle after that. He ended up with less than $2 million. There were
many other mistakes with this portfolio, but that was the biggest. If you
have everything you own at risk in the market at a single point in time,
that may simply be the time when the market blows.

Maybe you can't relate to those numbers—after all, not many of us
have $20 million to invest. But the previous example really is nothing
different than a new retiree taking all her money and putting it into the
market in early 2000. Major losses of 40 percent and more at any income
should make the point very, very clear. You don't have to wait to lose
money if the market changes immediately when you put in a lump sum.

You need to know the elements of standard deviation. But the key
facet is that it is simply a type of specific risk, not risk in toto. Unfortunately, very few investors or professionals recognize that the longer
you hold an investment—or if you have the bulk of your assets in the
market at a single point in time—the odds of a significant loss, while
limited, do exist. And if you don't make appropriate risk offset, you can
lose 40 percent or more of your assets in fast order.

The Mystery of Asset Allocation

A simple definition of asset allocation is needed first. It is a juggling
of various investments—cash, domestic equities, foreign equities, bonds,

real estate, and other assorted investments—to reflect the supposed acceptable theoretical risk/reward profile for a client. Many people tout asset allocation as a simple formula that can be derived from some overly simplistic 10-item questionnaire. That's totally bogus. Asset allocation demands an intensive understanding of myriad interrelated issues. As noted financial expert William Bernstein says, "If you really want to become proficient at asset allocation you are going to have to log off the net, turn off your computer, and go to the bookstore or library and spend several dozen hours reading books."

Well, I have read dozens of books and viewed hundreds of Internet sites on Asset Allocation. Bernstein's point is well taken in that reading is mandatory. But, thereafter, the reference is lacking. There is little formulaic consistency in any of the sources of information. The fund families, advisers, brokerage firms, and software programs almost always suggest different allocations by a wide margin (see Table 1.1). Usually there is no valid reasoning on why one is infinitely better than another—if that actually be the case.

Part of the problem is that most asset allocations are defined by software. But how old is the program? What are the weightings for the stocks versus bonds and why? How far back do the statistics go, what are the weightings for various time frames, if applicable, and why? Generally, no one has a clue to the internal machinations, so there is effectively no way to know if the program is any good. Just because something comes out of a computer does not mean that it is correct, current, or even reflective of what the client should have done.

> If you put tomfoolery into a computer, nothing comes out of it but tomfoolery. But this tomfoolery, having passed through a very expensive machine, is somehow ennobled and no one dares criticize it.
> —Pierre Gallois
> (Yes, I know he is French, but whaddya gonna do?)

So does asset allocation really work? Does it reduce risk? Yes and no. The main point is that, as practiced by 99 44/100 percent of investors

and advisers, it is a focus toward underperformance. Using 40 percent
bond and 15 percent foreign securities as a part of allocation during the
1990s would have produced substandard returns. But what about risk?
Well, the antiquated cornerstones of allocation—stocks—in a very bad
market (2000–2002, for example) will actually increase risk. And it will
increase losses. Those statements are anathema to the industry that has
led you to believe that asset allocation is the next best thing to sliced
bread.

James Martin, CFA, hit the nail on the head when he said the following:

> While I don't dismiss asset allocation, I do dismiss a mindless black
> box computer model trying to optimize what today's proper port-
> folio mix should be. Somehow by dumb luck, or perhaps divine bless-
> ing, I learned that the financial markets are nothing more than a
> confluence of human emotions. And no black box model, no mat-
> ter how many variables are in its multivariate time series, will repli-
> cate and anticipate the collective mind of the market. The problem
> is many advisers view asset allocation as a crutch and a substitute for
> hard work. Or perhaps they simply don't have the confidence in their
> decision making. Wall Street has done a great disservice selling the
> concept of asset allocation to the public along with the prolifera-
> tion of thousands of redundant mutual funds. Mean variance opti-
> mization is a concept applicable only to institutions with indefinite
> life spans, not to individual with finite goals. I argued that modern
> portfolio theory was equally incorrect because its entire backbone
> was supported by the specious assumption that historical cross cor-
> relations between asset classes would hold and repeat. Even back then,
> they [professors] knew that correlations and betas were not stable.
> Hence, trying to build an optimal portfolio using numerous asset
> class is a lesson in futility. It is a constantly moving target. So, we
> design asset allocation strategies based on needs and liquidity con-
> straints, tax efficiency, and that ever subjective "emotional risk tol-

erance." [But] people never get a true understanding of risk until after they have been through it.

You no doubt now have a far greater understanding of the sobering real-life implications of risk—more so, if you have a 401(k) that was left unadjusted during the economic onslaught of the early 2000s.

For those investors who think asset allocation is some simplistic formula, a $29 (even $5000) CD-ROM allocation software package, or simplistic advice from planners or brokers with little to no background in the fundamentals of investing, I invite you to the real world of 2000–2002, with the flawed underpinnings of stay-the-course investing and 40 percent losses—or more.*

It *is* mandatory that asset allocation become part of a lifelong review of the statistical fundamentals of investing. Certain key elements of this concept, however, have been consistently neglected—namely, the focus of local, regional, national, and international economics. Without this type of input, asset allocation tends to be selected in a vacuum.

Also neglected in most treatments of asset allocation is the psychology of the consumer in concert with the real-life elements of life: death, divorce, unemployment, disability, and so on. These problems can take any long-term asset allocation strategy and reduce it to lifelong chaos. As such, the consumer has been, for the most part, misguided in the intricacies and risks of asset allocation.

Allocation Principles

Literally every magazine, fund family, and investment Internet site has at least some commentary about the value—actually the necessity—of utilizing asset allocation as a fundamental of proper investing and for maintaining an acceptable level of risk. They may discuss past stud-

---

* The following is commentary made by American Express in 1999: "Get clear on your personal goals, then buy and hold a diverse portfolio of investments through thick and thin." I'll bet that many of their portfolios were a lot thinner after they had sat in a three-year down market.

ies by the likes of Gary Brinson, founder of the investment firm Brinson Partners. He indicated that about 93.6 percent of a portfolio's gains
(actually variability) are attributable to the classes of securities within
the portfolio; an insignificant amount is attributable to individual stock
selection or market timing. While the figures in this study have been
the subject of some nasty fighting during the last couple years regarding whether the number is 17 percent, 65 percent or whatever, the
approach is valid.

Determining the various randomly correlated assets is the key to
financial success. Stock picking is not the way to financial success. That
said, "93.6 percent tells us nothing about the wisdom of tactical [ongo-
ing] asset allocation and security selection," argues Meir Statman,
Professor of Finance at the University of Santa Clara.

Harry M. Markowitz, winner of the Nobel Prize in Economics,
developed the concept of the *efficient frontier* (Fig. 1.9), which represents the tradeoff between risk and expected return faced by an investor
when forming his portfolio. The *mean variance analysis,* also developed

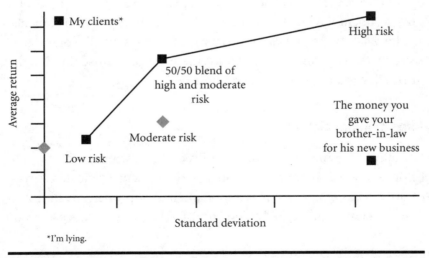

Figure 1.9   This chart makes it easier to compare the risk and return relationship
to these theoretical portfolios.

by Markowitz, requires not only knowledge of the expected return and standard deviation on each asset but also the correlation of returns for each. All of which means that you want various assets that do not all move at the same time, for the same reason, and in the same amount. (Don't worry; you may not yet understand everything about mean variance, nor would you be expected to. But either you or your adviser has to be familiar with the works of Markowitz in order to be considered sophisticated.)

As with numbers, statistics, and financial calculations, asset allocations need to reflect a constantly changing arena of investing—something that is rarely brought to the consumer's attention or even to the adviser's. Beyond anything else you have ever read in any book, you need to focus on that one concept. The shifting sands can cause havoc.

Many advisers and allocations are stiffly defined by some regimented formula that never addresses the issue of economics. Maintaining that narrow focus compounds the problem, because these advisers and allocations do not take into consideration the real-life characteristics of the consumer. For example, note what happens with age-weighted allocations that are bandied about as asset allocation guidelines. [A (pathetic) rule of thumb would be to subtract your age from 80 or 100, and the resulting figure indicates the amount of equities you would need to have in your portfolio.] In colloquial terms, these inane age-based formulas have nothing to do with the personal lives of the retiree. They might work, but almost solely as a result of luck.

On the other side of sophistication, professional asset allocation models tend to be imbued with formulas only the most ardent economist could understand. Such formulaic presentations are static and generally based on old statistics that may have nothing to do with the ever-changing world. If they were so perfect, why did so many money managers with the major brokerage firms lose so much money for clients in 2000–2002?

What I am attempting to do here is to provide some of the fundamentals (with caveats) of asset allocation, as well as new information that needs to be addressed in order to make competent selections of funds and asset classes. It will incorporate some numbers and statistics but, I hope, in a way that will not turn off either the ardent reader or the less-sophisticated investor who wishes to learn more. If you are an investor of any type, the information is mandatory.

But don't expect the norm. Per David Markham, of the Markham Funds, "much of the trillion dollar investment industry is built on half truths, incorrect interpretation, flawed data, unrealistic expectations and absurd contradictions."

First, let me reiterate the issue of asset allocation with individual stocks. As stated previously, the average (even the exceptional) person simply does not possess the skills to figure out a good pharmaceutical company, then a steel company, then a transportation company, and so on, in order to make up a proper portfolio that covers the appropriate risk, correlation, and all the other related areas.

In a more concise format:

Human beings cannot pick stocks. Period.

WILLIAM J. BERNSTEIN

Allocation Recommendations by Brokers

Many brokers have never been taught the fundamentals of investing. Nor have the firms done much to change the lack of competency. In March 1999, John Ramsay, deputy general counsel for NASD regulation, said, "the basic information the brokerage [firm] gets on a [customer] form is usually only enough to make suitable recommendations for the simplest of mutual fund investments. For anything more complicated, an investment adviser would be expected to know much more about the customer." (I disagree even with the ability to pick mutual funds properly.)

I have seen hundreds of these forms and, by themselves, they provide no insight to any level of planning. They will not and cannot provide the foundation to allocation. Clients are required to fill out simplistic forms with questions about income and goals. Fine and dandy. So, tell me, what does aggressive mean? What does conservative mean? What does speculative mean? The problem is, without a formal document specifically identifying the various terms (which does not exist at the private or governmental level), each and every client has a different, and quite probable, invalid perception of what it is that she or he should be doing. Since consumers most likely have never heard of the correct definition of diversification nor the implications of standard deviation, correlation, and other terms, how are they to understand what they are being asked? They have no experience, training, or knowledge to grasp the implications of their answers. And they have no idea whether the investment products or asset allocations ultimately presented are reflective of any valid thought process either.

It would certainly appear logical that if the initial information and client insight are inherently flawed, the resulting hypothesis can be no better, since those trying to decipher the client's input have no more understanding of the fundamentals either.

Furthermore, and an issue completely dismissed by the industry, is the psychological focus of consumers given the market and economic conditions. People do not react rationally to investments (or to many other planning areas either). Because of that irrationality, for decades distinguished professors have been studying human behavior in financial situations. That study, known as *behavioral finance*, has culminated in two recent Nobel awards in economics.*

The average brokers or financial planners might not be aware of these complex financial behavioral theories, covering the gamut from prospect theory, regret and cognitive dissonance, anchoring, mental compartments, overconfidence, over- and underreaction, representa-

---

* Daniel Kahnemann, winner of the 2002 Nobel Prize in Economics, most notably comes to mind. His partner, Amos Tversky, would have gotten one as well, except he died years before and the awards are not given posthumously. That said, you could exhume Tversky right now and he could still give a better strategy on risk and reward than 99 percent of all advisers living today.)

tiveness heuristic, the disjunction effect, gambling behavior and spec-
ulation, perceived irrelevance of history, the availability heuristic,
contagion effects and more. It is not my intent to define each and every
one in this text but to state that while the average broker, planner or
firm was undoubtedly ignorant of the professional studies, they were
far from ignorant of the real-life attitudes, activities, and aberrant
thought processes of the consumer. Why aberrant? Think back to the
euphoria of the '90s. Consumers who had never ventured into mutual
funds were now seriously buying individual issues. Investors who had
never before used the Internet were now spending hours on the Motley Fool and Yahoo! chat lines expecting to find the next WorldCom.
(Okay, that's a bad example.) People who wouldn't use their home
equity line of credit were now using margin accounts to leverage nondiversified equity positions. Consumers who only had certificates of
deposit were now calling their brokers for initial public offerings (IPOs).
Their motives were illogical. Emotional. Unscientific. Greedy. And they
resulted in absolutely no valid allocations whatsoever.

The 1990s represented a time of emotional market-driven hype that
enticed the bulk of the American public into using products and procedures they didn't have a clue to. The view of risk and reward during
that period was completely distorted. You cannot allocate investments
properly without an understanding of the true elements of risk and
reward, and brokerage firms didn't provide any objective material about
these to the consumer. They didn't, because there aren't any. Both the
consumers and the industry counseling them were affected by the same
illogical behavior. Said Robert Shiller, Professor of Economics, Yale University, in his 2001 article, "Bubbles, Human Judgment, and Expert
Opinion": "The kind of errors that people have been making and that
underlie the recent stock market bubble do reflect human shortcomings, but they reflect exactly the kind of shortcomings that can infect
professors, analysts, and trustees thinking just as much as anyone else's.
The current situation in financial markets is just a fertile ground for the
amplification and visualization of the errors."

The point is that from the consumer to brokerage and planning industries to the top of the supposed level of competency of trustees, there has existed an inconsistency in recognizing the inherent emotional shortcomings to investing that was known or should have been known. Such inconsistency skewed the perception of risk and reward. Consumers were effectively preordained to mistake the questions or goals of risk (the ever-subjective "emotional risk tolerance" noted by James Martin) since they were being led by an industry that fared no better.

That said, the industry has accepted the fiduciary duty to do the right thing. Rationalizing that a fiduciary is human and subject to failure is no defense to providing inadequate and unknowledgeable advice to the oblivious consumer who engages in activities and allocations that are wrong.

Asset allocation demands that all parties understand the implications and nuances of each question in order to provide a well-thought-out answer. There is no emotion to investing; it is pure reading and research. That it is practiced in almost a total emotionally charged environment is no excuse to improper and unsuitable asset allocation by the "professional" adviser. Validation of the miscues of allocation is found over the last three-plus years in over 40 percent of losses.

Nothing is essentially gained through this experience with brokers. Certainly not all accounts fared badly. But I repeat a fact: Without instruction in the fundamentals of investing, allocation by brokers may be more imbued with luck than skill.

Managed Accounts

Starting more than a decade ago, the brokerage industry has been embroiled in the controversy of commissions on every trade. The question being asked is, are you, the consumer, being sold the product because it's the right one for you or because it's being sold for a commission?

As time progressed, because of the proliferation of mutual funds, the brokerage industry embarked on a program of flat-fee products called *managed accounts*. A managed account is essentially the same as a public managed mutual fund made available specifically to the clients of the particular brokerage company—Merrill, Prudential, and so on.

Presumably, a client wanting a diversified account could work with the broker who would contact the manager of the fund and pursue the proper risk scenario with asset allocation. But that's not the real world. Consumers were (generally) sold a diversified mutual fund (meaning that it had more than 50 stocks), but that is irrelevant to asset allocation, which is the reduction of risk through several supposedly noncorrelated positions.

That a client is simply charged a fee instead of a commission just to reenter a managed mutual fund is not better asset allocation. It's just a different process to buy into a fund that may not provide any viable risk reduction. Essentially, nothing is gained through this experience.

Fund Families Allocations

Oy! For the past six years I have reviewed the online asset allocation risk questionnaires of Fidelity, *Smart Money*, Vanguard, Prudential, Bank of America and many, many more. The perception is that by answering a few questions in less than 10 minutes, the fund families can determine what percentage of monies should be invested here and there. While these questionnaires have a few more questions than those you answer when opening a brokerage account, the attempt is still pretty lame, poor and pathetic.

Prudential suggested that, for each statement, you should choose the response that most accurately reflects your feelings of or behavior toward risk. Vanguard noted, "your asset allocation decision will also be influenced by your attitude toward investment risk." And so it went with other sites.

What kind of garbage is that? This is not a touchy-feely endeavor. This is planning for your life. As stated previously, an emotional response imbued by your feelings or attitude is fraught with its own illogical risk.

As far as (past) behavior is concerned, this questioning approach is also fatally flawed. I have stated for years that what you may have done or what you would like to do may be diametrically opposed to what you *should* be doing. And that objective, almost universally, must be defined by a definitive budget. By analyzing what you need to do for retirement (or other goal setting) you are able to determine the risk that must be taken to accomplish the goal. Otherwise you are simply guessing. Yet, all of this is supposedly going to be defined by 10 to 15 questions that may take only five minutes to complete.

Listen to this one: "MAXfunds' new 3 Minute Risk Quiz can help. Answer ten online multiple choice questions, and our mutual fund supercomputer will calculate your investor risk profile, and provide you with a detailed allocation plan customized for your risk level based on MAXadvisor's expertly assembled model portfolios." Give me a break. Three minutes and a super computer? Yeah, baby!

For any allocation software, you might get a pretty colored piechart showing the various breakdowns of investments. Nice, pretty pictures. The forms may look valid and are great marketing tools for the sale of funds but they are a real waste of time. For example, let's take a look at three different allocations from three fund families (load and no-load) that get billions of dollars from investors. One form had 8 questions, one had 13. I tried to present myself the same way on each company form. But I had no idea whether I was even close. The questions had no consistency from one company to another.

How is that possible when the emphasis for asset allocation was all for the same person in the same situation? Further, some questions referenced aggressive funds earning 13 percent—and an average return of 9 percent. How in the world can one even remotely consider a 13 percent projected return? It is far above historical norm. And while 9 percent is slightly below the 50-year average, there is literally no one at the time of this writing that remotely thinks 9 percent is possible in the next few years. (I know that the upturn in the market in mid-2003 is greater than 9 percent, but many analysts do not see substantive validation to such returns.)

Anyway, review the varied results shown in Table 1.1.

Table 1.1   Results of Various Fund Families, percent

	Fund A	Fund B	Fund C
Cash	—	—	19
Large-cap	40	44	25
International	5	12	6
Mid-cap	—	16	—
Small-cap	5	—	6
Intermediate bonds	30	8	44
High-yield	10	—	—
Short-term bonds	10	12	—

How is it possible that millions of dollars are earmarked for the marketing of asset allocation and there is zero consistency by three of the major fund families in the United States with billions of dollars under management? Further, the economy was sucking gas big time as I wrote this, yet both Funds A and B suggest you put 50 percent or more into equities. Even Fund C suggests over 30 percent. Sure, some pundits might say that it's a great time to buy when the market is low. But the same thing was stated over the last couple of years as well. Yet during each of the three years preceding year-end 2002, the book value of the S&P 500 Index (with dividends included) declined 9.1 percent, 11.9 percent, and 22.1 percent, respectively. Equity allocation would have brought on larger and larger losses (see also "Rebalancing," below).

(As of December 2003, the market has recently responded favorably. But, as stated above, the allocations by the fund families were made when the market was still tanking. With such inconsistency, why would anyone subsequently use them?)

Financial Advisor Allocations

What about the issue of "financial advisors" and "planners" who charge for services in managing overall portfolio allocation? First, many financial planners are rarely more than closet asset allocators who use computer-generated models that profile what has happened in the past and use that as the sole evidence for the returns of the future. Even the most highly promoted allocation on the Internet—Financial Engines—uses information gleaned from thousands of various past statistical elements. This software incorporates the information into a computer analysis that allows investors to see how good their future economic prospects might be for an allocation program. The program incorporates Monte Carlo simulations, which calculate the odds for success of a specific allocation (see below for further commentary). But the problem is that it cannot incorporate current economic conditions, because the statistical figures aren't known until the situation has passed for about a year.

My point has always been that while statistical evidence is valuable and needs to be analyzed, it is not a precursor to future events (something Morningstar has also conceded in its commentary). Nor does it necessarily take into account recent commentary on, say, the Japanese or Argentinean economies, events in Iraq, Federal Reserve policy, the budget deficit, happenings in North Korea, the recession, or just about anything else. And if you are only living in the past, you are not going to be well prepared for current conditions, never mind the future.

Over the years I have also had the opportunity to look at myriad portfolios from professional advisers. You see the same inconsistency in portfolios as evidenced by the fund family allocations in Table 1.1. How can that be? How is it that CFPs, ChFCs, CFAs, bank trustees, and so on, could have such vastly varied asset allocations while all the time viewing the same market conditions and economics? Well, my first comment is why would you expect consistency? First, there is no substantive *real-life* training for any of the designations on allocation. Actually, what could you expect from a knowledge base that may be no greater in intensity than six months? As far as bank or professional trustees, what qualifications do they possess? (I have no idea; it seems like it is a position to sell trustee services than to have any solid background in investments.) What about CFAs? They do have more direct knowledge of individual securities but the use of managed funds and the purchase and sale of individual securities is statistically not valid for returns above the market average over the long haul, if at all.

Bill Jahnke, Chairman of Comprehensive Wealth Management and a researched critic of passive active management, noted that

> consumers want to believe that the professionals can perform the services they are hired to do. Too often in the domain of financial advisors, even those with CFPs or CPAs, this is not the case. The consulting communities' simple asset allocation policy solution for institutional investors can be challenged on several scores. Why should investors expect that the past relationships between return and short-term volatility are good estimates for the future? Why should institutional investors be overly concerned about market volatility in returns when setting their long-term asset allocation policy? Why shouldn't the asset allocation policy be adjusted if asset class return expectations change?"

Additionally, asset allocators view their primary job as getting a client into an asset allocation solution and advising the client not to abandon the asset allocation solution in volatile markets. But if the fixed asset allocation solution is not right for the client and is inflexible in the face of changing economic opportunities, what is the service worth? Asset allocators claim their advice is designed to benefit the client. But it appears that the advice is really designed to benefit the advisor; the investment process is simplified, and the business risk associated with managing the client's asset allocation is minimized. The asset allocator only needs to provide a package of marketing materials, educate the client on the rewards of diversification, admin-

ister the risk tolerance questionnaire, set up a "normal" asset allocation policy, collect the quarterly fee, and advise the client to "stay
the course" in volatile markets.

Asset allocators claim there is an effort by elements of the financial services industry to undermine their message. They argue that
investors are being bombarded to buy into the hottest-performing
asset classes. Much of the financial planner's efforts are directed at
combating a financial services industry that has found it easier to sell
past successes and hot new ideas than to sell undervalued investments.
It is little wonder that many investors tend to buy high and sell low.

The problem is not, though, a sufficient defense for the allocator
position that investors should "stay the course" regardless of the state
of the economy and asset valuation levels. The view that there is nothing to be gained by an ongoing evaluation of investment opportunities and the positioning of client portfolios in response to those
opportunities is extreme and dangerous. The fact that assessing further
prospects is difficult and subject to error is no defense for not doing it.
Given that most allocated investment solutions are poor interpretations of investment theory and have little to do with meeting financial objectives, the advice to "stay the course" is especially hollow."

As regards financial planners who simply follow the patterns of
institutionalized managers, the consulting community (brokers, planners, and so on) had an answer to these questions: job security for the
person in charge of the pension fund. By keeping the asset allocation
solution close to that of other pension funds, investment performance would not stand out from the crowd. Given that unbridled asset
allocation produces wide swings between good and bad times, it's
better to forgo some upside return if it means getting fired when
the inevitable period of bad luck occurs.

What many financial advisors learned from these topsy-turvy
decades is that portfolio diversification is desirable and trying to
call short-term moves in the market is difficult and a major risk to
business. What has evolved for financial advisors is an investment

solution similar to the one the pension funds came up with a decade or so earlier: Set an asset allocation policy that is middle of the road, but which arguably is consistent with the client's financial objectives, engages in little or no market timing, and concentrates on selecting good investment managers (in this case mutual funds). Usually this involves selecting a number of funds, which provides plenty of diversification. The financial advisor monitors the funds, making substitutions when a fund stumbles badly enough to be an embarrassment.

There are several problems with this model. One of the biggest problems is the cost: 1 percent to the financial advisor, 1 percent or more to the mutual fund, and 1 percent from the fund to the brokerage community. That's 3 percent total, and 3 percent is a big drag on portfolio performance, translating to a 50 percent or more reduction in retirement income for a lot of investors. Another problem is that the asset allocation solution has very little to do with meeting client financial objectives and a lot to do with doing what is currently fashionable. How many financial advisors dare to be underweighted in technology as we enter the new millennium?

To promote their businesses, financial advisors develop marketing and educational programs that appeal to the consumer without painting an accurate picture of the actual limits inherent in investing. Claims about meeting financial objectives and goals have become commonplace in advertising campaigns. Borrowing terms from modern portfolio theory, they introduce consumers to the need to match investment solutions with their risk tolerance, which can be conveniently assessed with a scientifically constructed risk tolerance questionnaire. Consumers are introduced to what they think are sophisticated investment concepts such as the importance of setting an asset allocation policy. Investors are warned about the pitfalls of being a market timer and the need to stay the course when markets are not performing poorly.

This is where reality gives way to illusion. Regardless of what they say, many financial advisors do not even attempt to match investment solutions with the real financial goals of the client. Managing invest-ments in accordance with an investor's risk tolerance sounds good. In practice, however, it proves to be little more than fitting investors into slots where the asset allocation solutions are established mostly for their marketing appeal and low business risk. Instead of focusing on long-term financial goals, the advisors define risk tolerance in terms of an aversion to portfolio volatility.

The education of investors on asset allocation, market timing, and security selection is often misleading and erroneous. At the same time, some of the important determinants of financial success—maintaining an appropriate asset allocation, managing costs, and proper budgeting—are ignored or downplayed. Many financial advisors have no interest in providing active asset allocation services and advertise that they do not engage in market timing. Not only does it have a limited role in determining portfolio performance, as demonstrated by the Brinson studies, but studies have shown that it reduces portfolio returns over time.

Some financial advisors go on to say that market timing is also dangerous. They point to the potential loss in portfolio value that could happen to the client's portfolio if the investor happened to miss being in an asset class when it performed well. If this appears to con-tradict the party line regarding the limited importance of market tim-ing in determining portfolio performance, well, it does.

True, market timing on average decreases investment returns for investors in general, because of the costs associated with the practice. But it is not true that market timing for those engaging in the prac-tice is of limited importance in determining portfolio performance. The more aggressive the market timing, the larger potential there is for a major loss or a major gain in portfolio value. The decision to market time is a very important one and may have big consequences.

Many financial advisors who are unwilling to time the market justify their fees by selecting actively managed mutual funds or individual securities. This inconsistency of providing active security selection while not offering market timing does not appear to trouble them.

For clarification, market timing is not solely the attempt at viewing tea leaves and a 100-day moving average to pick the exact highs and lows. It is, and should be, a constant evaluation and reevaluation of economic events to adjust a portfolio as necessitated by interest rate movements, inverted yield curves, manufacturing, productivity and more. (And it must dovetail with the ever-changing client, who experiences marriage, divorce, remarriage, children, college, divorce, Alcoholics' Anonymous, long-term care, death, and so on.) I have long held this conviction and have taught it in various classes. Admittedly, the issue becomes, how does an adviser actually do the initial allocation correctly and then have the competency to make adjustments via ever-changing economic and market conditions as well as subsequent client issues?

How to Develop an Allocation

The first thing to do when developing an allocation is to come up with a risk profile. The determining factor in this endeavor is a straightforward analysis of how much you need for retirement or other goal. Whatever you might have done or would like to do, or whatever other nonresearched focus that you bring forward to your fiduciary, is irrevelant. My fiduciary duty is to understand the numerical process necessary to objectively define risk and reward. It is my fiduciary duty also to recognize the client emotionalism that skews such objectivity.

Let's make this point real life. Assume you filled out an investment qualification questionnaire in 1995 or 1996, while the market was going gangbusters. The questionnaire asked, how would you feel about losing 20 percent of your investment? What would have been your reaction? Well, most people would react rather nonchalantly, because they "knew" that the market was only going to go up. They had been told so by their broker or planner, TV journalists, barber, gerbil, and so on. The risk was not essentially relevant, because of the market euphoria of continual 20 percent returns, and more. You, as an investor, would probably have indicated that you were unconcerned about the possible loss. It simply was not going to happen. The question did not compute. Consequently, there was a far greater acceptance of risk no matter what offsetting risk statements were presented, if any.

Now fast-forward to our current situation. If you were asked the same question in a recessionary climate, where the market already lost 40 percent or more in a short time, you would have responded to the concept of risk and additional loss in an entirely different way. The thought of yet another 20 percent loss, now that you have recognized exactly what risk and loss actually is, would be anathema to you—and to your pocketbook. Your answer would be entirely different, inasmuch as the element of risk had come full circle. Any investment decisions would reflect a pessimistic attitude. Same companies, same management, same products, same questionnaire, but an entirely different economic environment.

Most people would opt for the most conservative of investments, if any at all. People gauge risk within the context of their limited perception of volatility and returns and without reference to full statistics or a competent analysis of economics. They don't know or understand the necessity. People do not necessarily accept allocations that are in their best interests—or that may even work. They and brokers and planners are led by emotional factors in the selection and continued use of allocations that may have little to do with real life. That's just how the average human animal reacts. But that is *not* how your adviser is supposed to act. That's because that person has assumed a fiduciary obligation. A fiduciary obligation supercedes the excuse of being emotional.

An allocation is partly developed by using a risk questionnaire. But it does not define what the client wants to do or has done in the past.

As regards client changes, it should be obvious that "stuff happens" and allocations need to reflect such variations. If allocations are developed as though you will live the life of Ozzie and Harriet Nelson, fast-forward and you probably will end up closer to the family of Ozzy Osbourne. Flippancy aside, anything may befall you. I have seen client's children die early from disease and accident, early onset of Alzheimer's, all sorts of disabilities, as well as the obvious job losses, college over-expenses, and more. You need to have a Plan B as a backup when stuff goes wrong. And that plan means you need to adjust income and equi-ties consistent with the movement of economics. None of this is easy; it's harder yet when you have few advisers that use much more than software designed for a Methuselah.

Who Can Do Asset Allocation

Gosh darn, here is the biggest problem, because I don't have a clue about those who are putting that much intensity into the real-life analysis of risk and reward. While the various designations provide some insight to allocation, none of it is adequate to address active asset allocation focusing on adjustments to economics. In fact, the Master's program in planning, provided little insight into this competency either. Nor did the CFA classes I took. What did work was a compilation of such mate-rial put into a real-life element combined with reading of the FED mate-rial (and much more) along with a concerted effort of research year after year for at least 20 years.

The research still needs to continue, because as soon as anyone thinks he has gotten it right, the economics, tax laws, and much else all rearranges itself. This intensive and extensive reading demands con-stant attention. Others are undoubtedly doing it, but there is no partic-ular organization of any individuals of any background that rates beyond a scale of 3 out of 10 in this scope of effort. As stated, most financial planners are nothing more than software asset allocators trying to get as much money as possible under a 1 percent to 3 per-cent annualized fee. That's not cynicism, folks. That's just the way it is. You will need to do a lot of interviews and validating what advisers did during the 1980s, the 1990s, and the first three years of 2000. I would

CAVEAT INVESTOR

How to address basic allocations? And what adjustments did I make during the most recent economic scenarios?

Since most of my clients are over age 45, I require a budget in almost all cases. The analysis of the income needed for a lifetime determines what pieces of an allocation (stocks versus bonds) are demanded in order to match the needs. (If you or your adviser cannot do the retirement analysis noted in Chapter 13, you cannot do asset allocation.) The particular funds are cheap, have low turnover, and match directly the focus I want. Okay, what does that mean? Again, it's fairly simple. You generally start with the pyramid of investing. One of the first selections is bonds, which is consistent with current yield and the projected movement of economic interest rates. Normally you can't go wrong with a middle-of-the-road intermediate bond fund (but it is not preordained for all economic scenarios).

You may also want a focus on the stock market, and that starts with the entire market. For that you can consider the S&P 500 Index or the Total Market Index. (I choose to use the S&P 500 but can clearly understand why others might opt for the full market). Well, there you are. You can add in some real estate, generally not more than, say, 5 percent or 10 percent. And maybe have some small cap, some international fund, and some value fund also in the same percentage. But I would tend to keep the extra investments within a 25 percent to 30 percent total. Beyond that, it tends to get ungainly. Again, they are all cheap with low turnover (save for the bond funds). Now, that said, I am not averse to some managed funds, which are buying and selling all the time, but the extra costs, the extra turnover, and the extra time needed to watch the funds limits their exposure.

There you have it. Simple, eh? Nope. During the 1990s, my concern was not if the market would change, but when. Once 2000 started, it looked okay. But then look what happened via the inverted yield curves.

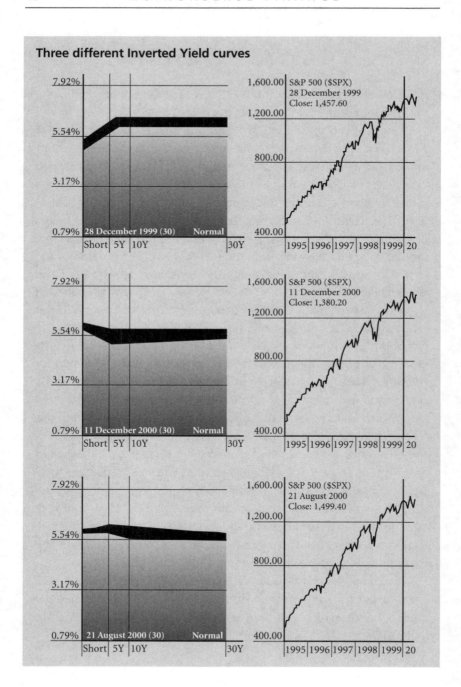

Three different Inverted Yield curves

First chart (top left): Yield curve — 28 December 1999 (30) Normal
Y-axis: 7.92%, 5.54%, 3.17%, 0.79%
X-axis: Short | 5Y | 10Y | 30Y

First chart (top right): S&P 500 ($SPX)
28 December 1999
Close: 1,457.60
Y-axis: 1,600.00, 1,200.00, 800.00, 400.00
X-axis: 1995 | 1996 | 1997 | 1998 | 1999 | 20

Second chart (middle left): Yield curve — 11 December 2000 (30) Normal
Y-axis: 7.92%, 5.54%, 3.17%, 0.79%
X-axis: Short | 5Y | 10Y | 30Y

Second chart (middle right): S&P 500 ($SPX)
11 December 2000
Close: 1,380.20
Y-axis: 1,600.00, 1,200.00, 800.00, 400.00
X-axis: 1995 | 1996 | 1997 | 1998 | 1999 | 20

Third chart (bottom left): Yield curve — 21 August 2000 (30) Normal
Y-axis: 7.92%, 5.54%, 3.17%, 0.79%
X-axis: Short | 5Y | 10Y | 30Y

Third chart (bottom right): S&P 500 ($SPX)
21 August 2000
Close: 1,499.40
Y-axis: 1,600.00, 1,200.00, 800.00, 400.00
X-axis: 1995 | 1996 | 1997 | 1998 | 1999 | 20

A bad scenario was getting worse. So I adjusted the portfolios accordingly, with no more equity investments after March 2000. There were also some deletions of the more volatile funds. In 2001, almost every client was entirely out of equities. Most monies were allocated to the Vanguard short- and medium-term corporate bond funds. Until mid-2003, I was reticent to suggest large equity positions since, what with manufacturing down, huge deficits, and more, why would you want significant exposure to the market right then?

Admittedly, I did not shelter the entire portfolios for loss prior to the mess starting in March 2000. I was willing to ride the momentum curve, at least to some degree. It was a real-life return, albeit riding on a flimsy wave. You have to accept some loss in playing the game. By the same token, the losses were limited due to the allocation adjustments. Clients have slept very well for the last few years as the adjustments to bonds have provided acceptable returns. More than that, they did not continue to lose more and more money in a recessionary market. "Staying the course" may be fine for those with oodles of money. But the average American consumer cannot accept such losses either financially or emotionally.

I have entered many equity positions in late 2003. And eliminated most of the bonds due to a perceived (soon to be real) increase in interest rates. But only because the reading and objective research of economics presented itself. It was not because of marketing.

suggest you review a lot of the individual letters to clients (if, in fact, any were sent) clearly explaining the various market and economic adjustments. More specifically, you need to examine what advisers did after March 2000.

In summary, let's just set the record straight. The entire industry has promoted the element of asset allocation as a meal ticket to be practiced (that's pretty much what they are doing, too—practicing) by generally incompetent agents and planners. These folks are bent on the sale to trusting consumers of millions of shares of unnecessary individual stocks. (In the 1990s, the number of Americans owning stock swelled by 30 million, to more than 80 million, per ICI.) Likewise, they push thousands of redundant mutual funds. (In 1978, there were 505 funds. By 2000, there were well over 8000). In 1980, only 5.7 percent of households (4.6 million) owned funds. In 2001, the figure was 52.0 percent of households (54.8 million). Unfortunately, 99 and 44/100 percent of all the allocations did next to nothing in insulating portfolios from the recent financial and economic debacle. That's not a flagrant statement. It is a fact borne out by the huge losses in retirement and regular accounts nationally.

Bill Jahnke noted that "in focusing on financial services for individual investors, I became convinced that much of the education being given was inaccurate, misleading, and in many cases detrimental to investors financial well being." My own statements dovetail with that outlook, since I have taught courses for years and have had the opportunity to review many educational products. Repeated ad nauseam, without the fundamentals of investing being clearly addressed, you cannot determine risk. If you cannot determine risk, you cannot determine suitability. And if you can't do that stuff, you sure cannot grasp an even more challenging asset allocation intertwined with all the economic variables.

I do not dismiss allocation as regards its risk/reward attempt. But I do dismiss the marketing and exploitation to consumers of a perceived competency that does not exist—certainly one that led the public astray in the 1990s and to the sustained losses of 2000–2002. The standard static portfolio allocation recommendations don't hold up well, certainly in the extreme economics. I admit that the economic malaise of the early 2000s is rare. But it happened before (in 1973–1974), and such situations are apt to happen again in your lifetime. It is a fiduciary's duty to be prepared. Decide where you want to be and who you wish to use.

Summary

You have to understand the fundamentals of investing. If not you, then your adviser must. In reality, this basic understanding has not happened at either extreme. I repeat, repeat, repeat: If you do not understand diversification by the numbers, you cannot determine risk. If you cannot determine risk, you cannot establish suitability.

The attempt to analyze and purchase individual securities for a valid portfolio by the average middle-income consumer is complete folly. The attempt to analyze and purchase individual securities for a valid portfolio by a sophisticated analyst such as Errold Moody is sheer folly as well.

If you need to invest, your plain-vanilla index funds are the way to start, since they come closest to true diversification and have low betas. Which ones to use, and when, are still tough determinations, but at least you avoided the biggest trap by throwing a bunch of singularly risky stocks against a wall to see what sticks.

Notes

1. Two excellent references to check out include the fifth edition of *Investments*, by Zvi Bodie, Alex Kane, and Alan J. Marcus (McGraw-Hill, 2001) and a study called, "Have Individual Stocks Become More Volatile? An Empirical Exploration of Idiosyncratic Risk" by Martin Lettau, Burton Malkiel, and Yexiao Xu, (*Journal of Finance*, February 2001). See also articles by Bill Bernstein and Larry Swedroe in *The Wall Street Journal* and articles in many more informational services. Remember, the point with the references is to validate the material presented and allow you to get the full detail by researching the likes of the material above. My effort is to take the gist of such reading and provide the real-life definition and application.
2. Actually, I would be exceedingly surprised if any reader knew the correct definition of *diversification* for a mutual fund. The first one to email the correct answer gets my newsletter, *Moody's Review*, free for a year.
3. Jonathan Clements has addressed this issue in *The Wall Street Journal*. William Bernstein addresses it in his work, including *The Intelligent Asset Allocator* (McGraw-Hill, 2000), and a few others tackle the topic as well.
4. You might have a problem with the idea that you don't need 300 or 400 securities to effectively reduce risk to that of the market. The following is a little gem that shows exactly how statistics work. How many people do you have to have in a room for there to be a 50/50 chance of two people having the same birthday? It's about 24 (a 54 percent chance). True numbers. Great for parties. Impress your dog.

5. From *Investment Analysis and Portfolio Management*, Fifth Edition, by Jerome Cohen, Edward D. Zinbarg, and Arthur Zeikel, Irwin, 1997.

6. I am not totally averse to using an active fund manager or even against using individual stocks as part of a diversified portfolio. But I demand that the bottom of the investment pyramid be filled with basic index type investments for at least (usually) 66 percent to 75 percent of investable assets (some allowance for age, sophistication level of the investor, and so on). With some of the rest of your portfolio, you can "play" the market with discretionary monies, but it still has to be within risk tolerances. You just can't push the envelope too far, no matter the beta or alpha.

CHAPTER 2

ETHICS IS
YOUR BUSINESS

W HEN I ORIGINALLY SAT DOWN to write this chapter, I must admit
that the element of ethics and personal responsibility seemed
so far removed from the collective consumer and investor conscience
that I wondered just how much good it would do to expose the breaches
of duty throughout the industry. After all, in the financial industry,
much of the success of individuals and firms is attained through at least
vaguely deceptive marketing and practices and, in many instances, a
great lack of competency—though nobody really pays attention as long
as the market keeps going up.

But then, it all started to fall apart. Steven Winn, in a *San Francisco
Chronicle* article (June 6, 2003), commented on "America's epidemic of
lying." He notes that this is a culture that has come to accept and even
expect skewed information at best, outright lies at worst, in everything
from government statements to advertising to art. "We live in a society
of widespread duplicity and deceit. Perhaps in our postmodern world
that is increasingly comfortable with irony, ambiguity, relativism and
doubt, we simply no longer believe it's possible to distinguish fiction
definitively from fact, lies from truth. Deception is so pervasive today
it almost feels authentic to us. Lies, from the skillfully subtle to the blatantly stage-managed, flow around us all the time."

Nevertheless, when such falsehoods directly impact your financial life—essentially all of your life—you need to take a much more cynical and practical look at what is going on around you. As such, it should not come as a total surprise that many companies were cooking the books, accounting firms abetting fraud, CEOs stealing money, brokerage firms paying millions to settle lawsuits, billions lost in 401(k)s, a whole bunch of people pleading the fifth, drinking a fifth, and so on. It is a lot easier to talk about your ethics than to live up to them. It is clear that's what was (and is) going on.

John Bogle, founder of the Vanguard Group, is a vocal critic of corporate fraud and abuse. Before the congregation of the United Methodist Church at Swarthmore, Pennsylvania, on June 1, 2003, he said: "Our capitalistic system—as *all* systems sometimes do—has experienced a profound failure, a failure with a whole variety of root causes, each interacting and reinforcing the other: And the stock market mania; the turn of the millennium; the information age; the notion that our corporations were trees that could grow not only to the sky but beyond; the rise of the imperial chief executive officer; the failure of our auditors and boards of directors, who forgot to whom they owed their loyalty; our regulators and legislators, who actually made things *worse*; the disingenuous hype of Wall Street's stock promoters; the frenzied excitement of the media; the eager and sometimes greedy members of all of us in the investing public, reveling in the easy wealth that seemed like a cornucopia, sitting back and enjoying the ride, at least while it lasted; and the change in our financial institutions from being stock *owners* to being stock *traders*. Too many wrong paths!"

Couple this controversy with a drop in many investors' beloved stocks and precious no-lose planning and investing strategies, and there arose a recognition by most consumers that they didn't have a clue as to how to analyze a stock (or most anything else). They also never knew the risk that they were taking in the first place—and, apparently, neither did their advisors. But these "trusted" advisors said they did, even though they had no background to support it. Federal Reserve Chairman Alan Greenspan was right on the money with his comment of "irrational exuberance."

The discussion of the activities and attitudes of various organizations and individuals in the paragraphs that follow is not intended to be a holier-than-thou diatribe. (Although, in this situation, the Golden Rule is absolutely appropriate.) Look, everyone makes mistakes. None of us is perfect. In fact, some bending of the strictest rules must be considered in the real world. Telling the truth is not always necessary—in fact, there are times to straight out lie for the benefit of others.

The focus in this chapter is on those people who have taken a position of responsibility: financial advisors, money managers, stockbrokers, and other professionals. When they are dishonest about competency, licensing, ethics, and their fiduciary duty, they are doing so to the financial detriment of others—namely, you. The focus of investments and planning is *your* money, and if the people you are using act unethically, incompetently, or just plain stupidly, you have to ask yourself if you are being well served.

I would also need to point out that, while our discussion of ethics is focused on investments, these same issues dovetail with what may be addressed in other financial areas: securities arbitrations, trusts, insurance, retirement, and a host of other interrelated areas. These issues will resurface in later chapters.

I have taught ethics as a continuing education course for professionals and have found it absolutely necessary to define some of the basic ethics terms and uses. In effect, many students are taught that there are no real ethical standards—in essence, they learn that anything goes. People have continually rationalized so many wrongs, by others and themselves, because it suits them, it is in their best interests, it doesn't involve them, or whatever. Per Winn, "Deception is so pervasive today it almost feels authentic to us. Lies, from the skillfully subtle to the blatantly stage-managed, flow around us all the time. Many liars have their own private motives, of self-interest, ambition or self-destructive pathology, for doing what they do." Regardless, because of my personal value system, what I have been taught, and what I teach, it is not okay to get away with anything you want because it suits you. Or that you don't want to get involved. Or that no one has done anything wrong unless they have been caught and convicted (which is where I really get miffed).

Of course, there are legal issues and implications surrounding financial doings, but you need to be absolutely aware that ethics starts where the law leaves off. Do you disagree? President George W. Bush pushed for more integrity in his inaugural address years ago. He suggested (demanded) more personal involvement after September 11, 2001, and, most recently, because of fraud by some companies, he instituted policies and a demand for more fiduciary duty. But, ethics and personal responsibility should not be newly introduced because of terrorism; nor as the result of a particular issue or corporate shenanigans. Ethics must become a part of our nature, and certainly when it comes to your money. Sadly, that hasn't really happened.

Look at Merrill Lynch, Morgan Stanley, Lehman Brothers, and others. Millions of dollars were lost as analysts pushed products that had few or no redeeming qualities. Somewhere along the line, these analysts knew of the violations. But who acted? The analysts committing the wrong? Merrill Lynch officers and directors? The SEC? Nope. It was the attorney general for New York, Eliot Spitzer. The same scenario occurred with Enron. Pursuant to subsequent pleas by President George W. Bush that CEOs should be fully accountable for financial fraud, does that mean only to the level of verifying the accuracy of financial statements and nothing else? (Of course not.) But if implied as such (and it is), does it not send a message to all others that the playing field is wide open for deception and fraud?

What about the ethics and fiduciary responsibility of private companies? Are CEOs exempt from ethical conduct if they are running private companies with no stock offerings? What happens if you are not an officer but just a working stiff like most of us? Do we act responsibly only if we can conclude that the country's safety is at stake? Do we allow people we know—or at least those we have a relationship with—

to commit wrongful acts with impunity? If nothing happens that you perceive as a wrong—or at least if nothing happens to you—has there actually been a wrong committed?

Regardless of the rhetoric and marketing about the strict adherence to ethical standards, the truth is you can do just about anything you want because most organizations will not enforce an ethical violation unless it is preceded by a legal one.

Many planners you trust with your money—and who are extolled by many journalists—are not only rationalizing their ethics but are actually violating the law with at least tacit approval of the organizations supposedly espousing adherence to the highest ethical standards. The point here is that if a person is incompetent—through lack of knowledge, egoism, etc.—yet continues to act as a fiduciary for the interests of others, that person has acted unethically. It's very simple. Very direct. Very truthful. Very distressing.

Moral Egoism and the Veil of Ignorance

The issues mentioned in the paragraphs that follow relate to the Golden Rule—as does most ethical training—but they also provide humane wisdom that can be used for almost any situation, personal or business. They are simple, straightforward, and easily applied. They work. That said, all ethical guidelines work if the individuals are willing to recognize that they have done something wrong and are willing to correct the error. The problem normally is that even when people know they have done something wrong, they are still unwilling to correct the unethical activity.

Moral Egoism/Situational Ethics

Moral egoism is a term used in every class I teach, not just ethics. It means that anyone can justify any action they want because it is in their best interests to do so (it's also called *moral relativism*). It is irrelevant what impact—usually negative—the actions might have on others, because that does not enter into those folks' equation. All the embattled CEOs come immediately to mind when we think about moral egoism.

The same thing happens with *situational ethics*. Each situation that people find themselves in can be viewed differently, and, therefore, a separate set of ethics can be applied. I had the right to speed since I had a special appointment to make. It wasn't wrong to steal from my company since I wasn't being paid enough. Situational ethics is very easy to engage in, and all of us do so in some form every so often. Unfortunately, the more the rationalization is practiced, the less obvious the consequences, the less inclination to do the right thing, and the more others will be adversely impacted, intentionally or otherwise.

These rationalizations are made by many brokers, agents, financial advisors, and the firms they represent. And as mentioned above, it is not only ethics that is in question, but the law as well. Remember, ethics starts where the law leaves off. But let's go one further. There are numerous sales of some financial products that are unethical even though legal.

I also get tired of a great many company leaders who just lie through their teeth about standards or where governmental agencies (such as the SEC) offer a rationale that their power cannot legally stop such inequities and fraud. The consumer should be outraged by any rationale to avoid basic integrity. When people lie about the law, about their licensing, about ethics, it's just a matter of time before they lie about your money.

I am not trying to be an ethics policeman. But there needs to be a more conscious recognition of industry conduct and the limitations of ethics that are applied to the public. There is a direct correlation to your finances.

Veil of Ignorance

Here is the way to force people to be responsible for their actions, assuming they are willing to be somewhat objective: For any action, simply put a *veil of ignorance* between you and the action taking place.

Pretend that the results had absolutely nothing to do with you, anyone close to you, your company, whatever. Just look at the actions as an independent entity and see if the actions are what an ethical person would have done. You would be amazed that, through independent focus, ethical clarity becomes plainly (and painfully) evident. Of course, the trick is to get others to use and recognize its qualities. An unethical person may do and think anything to avoid acting objectively. An ethical person will quickly see the errors. There is nothing sneaky or juvenile about it. Use this technique; it works.

General Ethics Guidelines

Other guidelines on ethics may be developed through asking yourself just a few to perhaps a dozen simple questions about some positions. The following are some questions to ask:

1. Does it seem right?
2. Is it fair just to you, your family, or associates? What about the impact to those not directly associated to you (associates, neighbors, coworkers)?
3. Would you want someone else to perform this action on you, your family, friends, and acquaintances?
4. Would you teach this activity to your children?
5. How would you feel if this action were exposed to others, your spouse, children, parents? If it were exposed to the press?

The National Association of Realtors has devised a list of ethics guidelines that could be applied to any industry and just about any activity. Their guidelines encompass the following concerns:

1. *Questionable or fraudulent practices are not to be condoned.*
2. *Knowingly making a substantial misrepresentation of the likely value of property or an investment to induce a buyer to make a purchase is forbidden.*

3. *No one must knowingly make a false or misleading representation to others.*

4. *The broker (sales agent, licensee) owes his principal full and complete disclosure of all material facts that may, in any way, influence the principal's decision, actions, or willingness to enter into a transaction.*

5. *One may not knowingly make a false or misleading statement or representation, without a reasonable basis for believing its truth.*

The National Association of Personal Financial Advisors (NAPFA) clearly demands its representatives provide comprehensive fee-only planning. Yet there is not a single NAPFA agent that is properly licensed in the state of California and never has been. In 1998, a NAPFA spokesperson stated, "We hope that California doesn't enforce their law since other states may do so as well" (as reported in *Investment Adviser* magazine).

Consumers have every right to expect that the representatives they select are at least ethical; are at least licensed; absolutely have the best interests of the clients in mind; and will abide by the highest fiduciary standards. Unfortunately, that is not happening. New York Attorney General Eliot Spitzer has just touched on the breach of fiduciary duty to consumers. It is pervasive in the industry.

Joseph W. Weiss, Ph.D., Professor of Management, Bentley College, provides some caveats regarding fiduciary responsibility and ethics as follows:

1. The seriousness of the act: Inconsequential harm, particularly on an inconsequential issue, is usually not considered material, though materiality to an issue is clearly open for discussion in various matters. As an example, forgetting to mention break points on a mutual fund investment is normally irrelevant to a loss and should not be considered material to a case. (Though recent lawsuits charged many mutual funds for not reducing commissions as mandated.)

2. Whether, given the circumstances, the person is uncertain about his or her knowledge of a wrongdoing. This bears added scrutiny because of the limited training for brokers and agents. Certainly within the first two years of work, the bulk of brokers and agents simply do not have enough knowledge about investments. As such, the focus is on the responsibility of those who supposedly do know, the supervisors. Once the approximately two-year period is completed, the greater the potential liability is on the broker.

3. If the person was prevented from avoiding the harmful action. However, one needs to review the degree by which someone is restricted from acting ethically.

4. Lastly, by how much the person caused the harmful actions. (In arbitrations, I sometimes indicated that the broker was 50 percent responsible for the loss, though that number could be 25 percent, 10 percent, or whatever, with the remainder of the responsibility being the firm's.)

The key to ethics within the investment industries is the element of knowledge. It has always been my contention that if an agent knew or should have known of the consequences of the act, that person is responsible for his or her actions and is in violation of ethical directives.

Did the Person Know or Should (S)he Have Known?

From limited partnerships to guaranteed retirement investments, financial products have been sold that brokers, agents or planners should have known were not suitable for their clients. Some agents may not have known the possible severe financial losses that their clients might encounter, but they should have guessed. Under the Prudent Man Rule (see the following section), there is no way a rational person, broker-dealer firm, or insurance company could not have seen potential unethical and fraudulent practices. Even if a broker, agent, or planner were unclear about the total risk, most are nonetheless aware that many products are high risk. Therefore they cannot use ignorance as an excuse to suitability standards. They get caught violating ethical standards or laws anyway.

These people must be held accountable for their actions. Manuel Velasquez, in his book *Business Ethics: Concepts and Cases* (Prentice Hall, 1999), says that individuals are morally responsible for their actions, or inactions, and the harmful effects they may cause. This occurs when the person (1) knowingly and freely acted, (2) knew the act would or could have potentially harmful repercussions on others, or (3) knowingly and freely failed to act and the harmful action occurred on others. Brokers, agents, and their supervisors are morally and ethically bound to their clients, even if they are not legally bound. There's little excuse for misleading clients.

I admit the issue of moral responsibility is seldom, if ever, raised, even in arbitrations. But state insurance and securities departments would be well advised to adjust the penalties for violations of law to include the issue that officers of broker-dealer firms had to have known what was going on and failed to stop it. You simply cannot be an officer in the business for years and years and not recognize the irresponsible and unethical activity of subordinates. (But you can, of course, rationalize the activity away by using moral egoism.)

Such irresponsibility isn't just in acts by officers of the firms. At least 85 percent of the reasons people lose money could be alleviated or eliminated through more real-life licensing training. For example, the mandatory use of a financial calculator would quickly eliminate many of the bad products since an ethical agent who had been forced to learn how money works (that's what a financial calculator does) would never knowingly use a product that would not produce the intended results and/or were beyond the risk level of the client. Problem is, this doesn't happen if for no other reason than the training for a financial calculator has never been required for securities or insurance licensees. Will such training become required? Nope, not in my lifetime—at least as I see the industry.

Think about the analysts at Merrill, Goldman Sachs, and others who were fined $1.4 billion because they touted stocks with bad ratings when the market was crashing in 2000 and 2001. In this instance, we are no longer dealing with the potentially naïve. We are dealing with straight out quackery. These folks knew exactly what they were doing. So what happens? The investment houses pay a fine and the analysts still collect millions in salary. (Only a few with the highest visibility were fired or resigned.)

The point is that any person or entity who has dealt with investments (agent, broker, broker-dealer firm, NASD, SEC, and so on) knows full well that proper training and knowledge would have reduced this failure to act responsibly to far less painful results. But the industry won't do it. Nonetheless, is it ethical for those organizations with a mandate to protect the unsuspecting consumer to avoid teaching the fundamentals?

There are exceptions to the rule. Particulary in the case of someone truly ignorant or truly incompetent. But, Velasquez notes, "a person, however, who intentionally prevents him/herself from understanding or knowing that a harmful action will occur is still responsible. Also, a person who negligently fails to inform him/herself about the potentially harmful matter [actions] may still be responsible for the resultant action."

In this day and age of advanced financial education, there are few that are so ignorant of the facts of the real world that they are relieved of the responsibility of their actions. If an agent did not read the material in a limited partnership, is he relieved of the responsibility if a client took on too much risk? Of course not. Due to their fiduciary obligation, they retain the first-line responsibility for risk. And there are very few that, if they were able to pass a licensing exam, do not have the ability to learn the necessary requirements to investment and suitability application.

Prudent Man Rule

In context with these definitions of ethics and ethics guidelines is the issue of what can be expected of an agent, broker, or planner acting with (supposedly) your best interests in mind. (You need to check your state statutes since, when they involve a trustee acting on trust assets, they may indicate the actual securities that can be used. Others indicate the investments for probable income and limited loss. Those issues go beyond the scope of this book.)

W. Scott Simon's book, *The Prudent Investor Act: A Guide to Understanding* (Namborn, 2003), is a must-read whenever someone is given a duty to invest your money (and more). Says Scott: "The Prefatory Note to the Uniform Prudent Investor Act underscores the central importance of Modern Portfolio Theory in investing and its tremendous influence in prompting and shaping the reform of American trust investment law." In other words, those granted with your trust should have a firm understanding of the tradeoffs of risk and reward based upon a minimum of the prevailing methodologies of investment theory.

As an additional comment, if you are going to trust yourself with this endeavor of investing money or most anything else where your financial life is put at risk, you must hold yourself up to these same levels of knowledge and expertise.

Scott notes that, "what's important in modern fiduciary investing is how something is done, not what happened after it was done. While the traditional concept of investment prudence involved static, inflexible rules, the modern concept calls for a dynamic and flexible process in which the fiduciary focuses on the trust portfolio and its purpose."

Standards in certain cases draw upon what a "prudent man" would have done given the same circumstances and by exercising sound discretion—the *prudent man rule*. The actions of the defendant may be compared to those efforts and the defendant judged accordingly. However, once somebody presents himself or herself as an expert, either through some professional designation or degrees attained, or whatever, then that person will be held to the standards of someone of that capability. A CFP, ChFC, CFA, or other professional cannot hide behind simply what a prudent man would have done, because of his or her expert (or, at least, perceived expert) knowledge and ability. In essence, if you are saying you are an expert, that is the level of competence you should be held to.

This takes on additional significance with people who use titles such as Financial Consultant or Adviser, Vice President of Investments, Senior Vice President, and so forth, but have no additional background other than basic licensing. Once you intend to act in a higher capacity—certainly the criteria for brokers, planners and, to a lesser degree, insurance agents—then you have taken on the responsibility and obligation of a fiduciary nonetheless. Unless restricted by state statutes, then the definition and description of fiduciary responsibility in the following section should apply and increase the standards of care substantially.

Fiduciary Responsibility

In the handling of money, and when somebody acts as a corporate or individual trustee, there is a fiduciary responsibility owed to the principal party. *Fiduciary responsibility* is defined as a relationship imposed by law where someone has voluntarily agreed to act in the capacity of a "caretaker" of another's rights, assets, and/or well being. I certainly include the planners, brokers, and the like, who clearly provide "expert" money services. These fiduciaries owe an obligation to carry out the responsibilities with the utmost degree of "good faith, honesty, integrity, loyalty, and undivided service of the beneficiary's interest." Good faith has been interpreted to impose an obligation to act reasonably in order to avoid negligent handling of the beneficiary's interests as well the duty not to favor anyone else's interest over that of the beneficiary.

Think about that when someone gets a commission. There is an unquestioned conflict of interest. But ponder that when someone who is incompetent and/or unlicensed charges a fee for a service that is illegal. There is an unquestioned conflict of interest as well. Whenever an agent finds himself or herself in a position of conflicting interests, that person must disclose the conflict.

The duties of a fiduciary include the following:

1. *Utmost care.* The agent is bound to the higher standard of a professional in the field, which extends the standard of duty to investigate within the means of the profession, and to ensure the maximum protection and information be provided the principal. Utmost care includes a basic knowledge of the fundamentals as well as required licenses.
2. *Integrity.* Defined as the soundness of moral principle and character. It means the agent must act with fidelity and honesty.
3. *Honesty and duty of full disclosure.* This pertains to all material facts, either known, within the knowledge of, or reasonably discoverable by the agent, which could influence in any way the principal's decisions, actions or willingness to enter into a transaction. A duty of full disclosure includes statements to the principal of licensing, at a minimum.
4. *Loyalty.* An obligation to refrain from acquiring any interest adverse to that of a principal without full and complete disclosure of all material facts and obtaining the principal's informed consent. This precludes the agent from personally benefiting from secret profits, competing with the principal, or obtaining an advantage from the agency for personal benefit of any kind.
5. *Duty of good faith.* This includes total truthfulness, absolute integrity, and total fidelity to the principal's interest. The duty of good faith prohibits any advantage over the principal obtained by the slightest misrepresentation, concealment, threat, or adverse pressure of any kind.

Legal Liability

If a person offers professional services to the general public, it is presumed that the person possesses some degree of special skill or knowledge. A professional negligence case imposes a certain level of skill and knowledge on the accused, whether or not he actually possesses that skill or knowledge. This is a standard of minimum professionally acceptable conduct. Though the standards have not been applied until most recently to financial planners, it would appear that the essence for them as well as brokers at least is that the advisor put the client's interest first and act with the best interest of the client in mind.

Trust officers are also held to a higher level of responsibility as an expert. But some trust companies attempt to reduce exposure by putting in an exculpatory clause where they hold themselves only to what a prudent but *inexperienced* man would do. That still does not exclude them from acting recklessly or in bad faith or from willfully breaching their fiduciary duty to the trust beneficiaries. Frankly, this rationale should not hold in valid legal arguments.

Fiduciary duty is an absolute element of a trust service. But as with other such issues, it may be more lip service than anything else. If you want to truly protect your interests, and those of a loved one, consider the use of a trust protector. This concept is described further in Chapter 14, but, in essence, you hire a private individual to look out solely for your rights. Most specifically, the trust protector can force your trust company to toe the line to competency and duty—or otherwise get the violators fired.

Securities and Brokerage Firms

The question initially asked by attorneys, consumers, arbitrators, and others is whether or not a broker acts in a fiduciary capacity in dealing with regular retail customers. In view of the fact that self-regulating organizations, or SROs, impose a requirement upon brokers to provide only suitable investments, it would appear that brokers unquestionably have a fiduciary responsibility to their clients whether they want to accept the responsibility or not. The underlying NYSE Rule 450 of "know thy client" along with the NASD's requirement to brokers for suitable investments demands that brokers always do the right thing for their clients first and foremost in any transaction. The commission or fee is irrespective of whatever the broker may suggest.

If a lower-priced product or one with a lower commission is better for the client, that is one that is to be offered. In the same context, the broker cannot allow a sale requested by the client when he knows that it is unsuitable for the client's purposes. The only time a broker can sell an "unsuitable" product might be when an investor makes an initial suggestion for an investment and the broker subsequently informs the investor, both verbally and in writing, prior to the sale, that the investment does not fit the suitability standards for that particular investor. If the client insists, the sale might still be made. Nonetheless, the sale would still leave the firm, agent, or planner at risk if there were to be subsequent legal proceedings.

Security arbitration panels should therefore impute a fiduciary responsibility on the part of brokers in dealing with a customer's money. Investors "trust" brokers based upon a real or perceived level of honesty, good faith, judgment, and responsibility in looking after the money entrusted to them. The broker, planner, or other agent, in accepting this money, assumes and accepts a responsibility to serve the best interests of the investor. The broker must determine if an investment fits within the customers risk profile, income, age, objectives (assuming they are correct and complete), and so on, and is also within the guidelines for proper diversification. If the consumer has lied to or misled the agent or failed to provide relevant data, this action may possibly lead to a partial or full relief against a claim.

Once again, per Scott Simon:

Among circumstances that a trustee [broker, agent, planner] shall consider in investing and managing trust assets are such of the following:

1. general economic conditions;
2. the possible effect of inflation or deflation;
3. the expected tax consequences of investment decisions or strategies;

4. the role that each investment or course of action plays within the overall trust portfolio;
5. the expected total return from income and the appreciation of capital;
6. other resources of the beneficiaries known to the fiduciary as determined from information provided by the beneficiaries;
6. needs for liquidity, regularity of income and preservation or appreciation of capital; and
7. an asset's special relationship or special value, if any, to the purposes of the trust or to one or more of the beneficiaries.

The following are factors that the trustee (broker, agent, planner) may want to consider when examining investments proposed for portfolios:

1. Expectations concerning the investment's total return, and also the amount and regularity of the income element of that return whenever the beneficial interests or purposes supported by the trust are affected by distinctions between trust accounting income and principal
2. The degree and nature of risks associated with the investment, and the relationship of its volatility characteristics to the diversification needs of the portfolio as a whole
3. The marketability of the investment, and the relation between its liquidity and volatility characteristics and the amount, timing, and certainty of the trust's cash flow or distribution requirements
4. Transaction costs (including tax costs) and special skills associated with the acquisition, holding, management, and later disposition of the particular investment
5. Any special characteristics of the investment that affect its risk-reward tradeoffs and effective return, such as exposure to unlimited tort liability, the presence and utility of tax advantages,

and the maturity dates and possible redemption provisions of debt instruments.

The Rules of Fair Practice set down by the NASD state that a breach of fiduciary duty has occurred if a broker:

1. Recommends speculative securities without finding the customer's financial situation and being assured that the customer can bear the risk
2. Does excessive trading (also known as *churning*) in a customer's account (whether the account is discretionary or not)
3. Does short-term trading (and switching) of mutual funds
4. Sets up fictitious accounts to transact business that would otherwise be prohibited
5. Makes unauthorized transactions or use of funds
6. Recommends purchases that are inconsistent with the customer's ability to pay
7. Makes unauthorized transactions or use of funds
8. Commits fraudulent acts (such as forgery and the omission or misstatement of material facts)

The obligation for fair dealing is not removed through the simple completion of the one-page new account form that's required by brokerage firms. Nor is the liability removed by sending the completed form to the client since clients do not and cannot be expected to know how a particular investment fits within individual and specific investment guidelines. The regulation does, however, relieve the broker of mistakes entered on the form by either party that would be apparent to—and should have been corrected by—the client.

Summary

This chapter is an attempt to provide the framework for further conversation about ethics in real-life elements. It is my contention that unethical activities in the brokerage, insurance, and planning industries will continue relatively unabated due to a lack of insight by the consumer as to what truly is happening. We have, though, in these pages, discussed the key issues that any consumer needs to know in order to adequately address the issues professionally and objectively. In the next chapter, we'll look at issues of trust.

CHAPTER 3

WHO* CAN YOU TRUST?

*T*HE GREATEST PROBLEM CONSUMERS have with finances and money is finding someone they can trust. Right? Wrong! Time and time again consumers lose vast sums of money because they "trusted" someone who had no legitimate background to perform the functions required. And it was primarily the consumer's own fault, because he or she had never done any homework to determine whether the person they considered using had any basic knowledge or competency at all. Those are some harsh comments, but they are universally true.

> While many households will spend a great deal of time shopping for an automobile, the decision of who to trust with their wealth is often made without as much thought.
> DR. JAMES MALLETT, STETSON UNIVERSITY

As a practicing financial consultant and instructor with over 30 years of experience, a securities expert witness, and past arbitrator with several professional organizations including the National Association of Security Dealers, I have had an opportunity to discuss numerous situations and cases with attorneys, public arbitrators, bank managers, security and insurance representatives, and investors and consumers.

---

* Yes, I know it is "whom" but I just couldn't bring myself to use it.

While there is wholesale agreement that many agents and companies are at fault for unsupervised and unethical conduct, the greatest problem is the fact that neither the brokers/agents nor the consumers know very much about what they are doing. And because consumers inherently pick their representatives for reasons totally unrelated to competency, the consensus is that at least 80 percent of the financial problems the consumers complain about would never have happened had they conducted a minimum amount of homework on whom they were using. Unfortunately few consumers do any research whatsoever. No reading, no questioning the adviser, no review of the adviser's qualifications, no nothing.

Getting Referrals

The critical problem with referrals is the same as elsewhere: the inability or unwillingness to do the necessary homework to make the right choice. This is the reason that referrals are so effectively used in the business. Salespeople are told or taught to get referrals from clients to friends, neighbors, relatives, coworkers, or Martians—whomever, because that is a great lead-in. Unfortunately, the subsequent client believes, or wants to believe, that the referred agent has already been critically and thoroughly analyzed and must be of the highest caliber and competency. Invariably most consumers do nothing themselves to check out whether expertise, knowledge, or ability actually exists. The same thing happens to the next person and the next, ad infinitum, as the referrals continue. It ends up that no one did any checking on anyone at all; later those same people wonder how it all went wrong. They end up buying the wrong product at the wrong risk level at the wrong time—and certainly from the wrong person.

Now referrals may work with physicians and certain other professionals (sometimes with CPAs or attorneys, but not all the time), because those people have a degree and other background and training. Even with these professionals, people are finally recognizing that problems with referrals exist. But referrals to financial agents, who often have little to no background or expertise in their subject area, is illogical. It is for these many reasons that I believe that referrals to brokers, insurance agents, financial planners, attorneys, and most other entities is a waste of time unless a comprehensive review of the individual is commenced before any product is purchased or any fee paid. And such review is not calling the SEC/NASD or your state offices to see if any formal arbitrations or lawsuits have been instituted. Only an infinitesimal number of agents have ever been sued or forced to arbitration. (Actually, most consumers do nothing if they have been wronged, so many egregious activities by agents are never reported.) That still says nothing about competency. You need to do a lot more work to assure yourself of some reasonable competency.

Marketing Isn't Homework

Consumers, for the most part, do not have the requisite knowledge to comprehend the vast and ever-changing financial arena. As a result, those who have literally no exposure to objective financial material are considered prime targets not only to scam artists but also to a "well meaning," though still incompetent and unknowledgeable, adviser.

> People are efficient, rational beings who tirelessly act in their own self-interest. They make financial decisions based on reason, not emotion. And naturally, most save money for that proverbial rainy day.
> Right?
> Well, no. In making financial decisions, people are regularly influenced by gut feelings and intuitions. They cooperate with total strangers, gamble away the family paycheck and squander their savings on investments touted by known liars.
> DR. JONATHAN COHEN AND DR. ALAN SANFEY

Of course, the financial industry knows full well that consumers do very little, if any, review. Every company wanting your money, therefore, has spent thousands of dollars, if not millions, to market themselves and their representatives as having superior capabilities (perhaps by bestowing such titles as Financial Consultant or Senior Vice President) and by focusing on the perception of competency. Have they been successful? Obviously.

But such "success" is also measured by the largest fine in brokerage history for consumer fraud: Salomon, $400 million; Merrill Lynch, $200 million; Credit Suisse, $200 million; Morgan Stanley, $125 million; Goldman Sachs, $110 million; Bear Stearns, $80 million; JPMorgan Chase, $80 million; Lehman Brothers, $80 million, UBS AG, $80 million; US Bancorp Piper Jaffray, $32.5 million. And they won't blink an eye to these costs, because their profits are so large. For example, JP

CAVEAT INVESTOR

Admittedly, being well read and knowledgeable, either as an agent/broker or consumer, does not necessarily equate to competency in the financial world. Yet the odds of financial and personal success increase immeasurably when one becomes more knowledgeable through the efforts, most often, of research and reading. True, experience, by itself, can provide knowledge. But caution is advised when focusing too much at this level. I simply ask this: If you could use either a neurosurgeon, age 45, with 20 years experience, who has done much research and work to operate on your daughter, or a witch doctor, age 70, with 50 years experience, which would you choose? Years of experience do not necessarily equate to knowledge or expertise.

Now, I have had pundits say that most people do not equate money, finances, investing, long-term care, insurance, and estate planning, with the same focus and importance as medical care. True, but here is the point: If money is not important enough to at least learn how to try to select competent advisors, then never complain again about getting duped by anyone and losing money. You can't have it both ways.

Morgan Chase & Co. Inc also agreed to pay $25 million to settle a U.S. Securities and Exchange Commission probe into unlawful allocations of initial public offerings. But here is the part that is most galling: The $25-million civil penalty equaled less than 1.4 percent of JP Morgan's net profit of $1.83 billion for the second quarter of 2003. Sure, that will really hurt.

And arriving at that discovery comes from research, which requires that you do a lot of reading. If you do your research thoroughly, and practice the straightforward advice therein, you should be able to avoid most of the disastrous financial entanglements that other people get involved with.

Consumers must recognize this deception and focus on the reality of ability and expertise. For the maximum 6% of adults who do read books on marriage, raising a child, personal finances, investing, etc., and practice the straight forward advice therein, they now should be able to avoid most of the financial entanglements that other people get involved with. They will never be one of the 23,000 that ended up buying the worthless bonds at Lincoln Savings and Loan, they won't buy individual stocks, they won't buy back end loaded funds, they won't be trading commodities when they're 80 years old, they won't buy annuities at a bank, they won't buy a bunch of tech stocks with P/E ratios of 4000 on margin, etc.

Who To Use

So, what are you supposed to do? The answer is shown in Figure 3.1. The left vertical side of the graph represents risk. The bottom horizontal line shows the type of "adviser" that people select for investment advice (or literally any advice).

As you can see, the more somebody uses an adviser who knows little, the greater the odds that something will og grnow, go wrogn, go wrong. And the less homework the individual does, the greater the risk. The selection process is discussed in the paragraphs that follow.

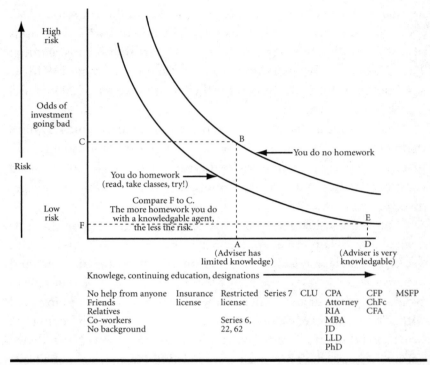

Figure 3.1   Who can you trust?

Using Someone Who Knows How to Use a Financial Calculator

If you wish to avoid reading the rest of this text and still greatly reduce your odds of using an unqualified adviser, by at least 75%, then make sure that whoever you use has and knows how to use a financial calculator. These specialized calculators have the capability of computing present and future values (and much more); they are essential tools for any investment review. Most advisers have never been trained in the use of a financial calculator as part of any basic licensing training—and that includes brokers, insurance agents, attorneys, and anyone else you might turn to for money advice. Even those folks who did learn the basics tend to let a computer program do their calculations for them.

I certainly do recognize the ability of the computers to run vast, errorless calculations in just seconds. But two issues arise. First, wholesale reliance on such programs, which is the norm for financial planning, insurance, and the securities industry and agents, negates any internal judgment by the agent (assuming they could provide such insight). Second, such programs tend to treat all clients alike. That's illogical. Even when people have the same age, income, and more, they undoubtedly have so many unique personal characteristics that distinguish them from one another. Therefore, such planning for everybody, the same way, with standardized software is bound to be nothing more than a superficial process.

I have always used the Hewlett Packard (HP) 12C Financial Calculator for most of my reports. (There are newer and faster calculators out there, but I can't get my old one to die.) I do so because I need to understand what is going into the analysis and what should be coming out. That benefit is best addressed by an instructor at the College for Financial Planning: "I spoke with a number of CFP students who said that they didn't see the value of learning the time value of money on a calculator since they used a computer at work. I agree with you that if you can't use the calculator, you probably don't know what you are talking about. The process of using the calculator helps you learn what result to expect."

I cannot stress that benefit emphatically enough. If you engage someone to do investment, planning, or insurance work who provides you with nothing more than a computer printout and no separate, individual report, why didn't you just buy a computer program yourself? (That said, there is no service or venue that allows even the professionals to compare the products side by side.) While it may not be fair to expect any consumer to try to analyze hundreds of software programs, by the same token, you paid (supposedly) for an individual's competency in the subject matter, not the ability to buy software.

You are committing economic suicide to proceed with someone who doesn't really know how money works.

As for asking friends, relatives, or coworkers for financial advice simply because they are "trusted"? Why? What do they know? Probably less than the person asking. If trust were all that was important when it comes to financial planning, people would use rabbi, minister, or priest to make all their financial decisions—and some do. But the obvious problem (at least I hope it is obvious) is that trust and competency are not the same thing. Individuals should *never* make a selection of an adviser based solely on unsubstantiated trust. They are simply asking for problems and lost money.

Whenever you are getting ready to trust your finances to someone else, you absolutely have to get, in writing, a summary of that person's qualifications: degrees, certifications, resume, and so on. Never sign to be someone's client without at least getting this essential information. Some people may not feel comfortable asking for this information, but those are the very people who will get taken to the cleaners.

Add this simple element to the financial calculator criteria discussed above and you will rarely have any problems with investments in your life because you used only those having the highest competency. Admittedly, that is not a guarantee of success, but it's a lot better than being behind the 8 ball to begin with.

One more note. When it comes to gauging competency, you still need to know whether or not the material you've received on the person is useful or just taking up space. As such, I offer: checking licensing and designations.

Licensing and Designations

The following descriptions concern various professional licenses and designations. The list is not all-encompassing, since there are new designations popping up every day extolling various virtues and knowledge along with a some alphabet soup to impress you (CFP, ChFC, PFP, DEET, and so on). A few are on the up and up, but a lot are designed for home study over a few days and that's about it.

Insurance Agent

To review the inherent knowledge of an insurance agent, you need to examine the criteria necessary to become a licensed insurance salesperson. It is severely limited. Admittedly, the California Department of Insurance substantially increased the licensing requirements starting in 1992 (including a 52-hour course with extensive emphasis on ethics), and all states, to my knowledge, require testing. However, some states require only one day of class, which is effectively useless.

Regardless of the study, the license is really inadequate to properly assist consumers in insurance matters. Often, potential licensees can simply take a course at a training school, where many of the answers to test questions may be provided. (There may be only three or four exams currently given, so it is possible to key in on certain questions.) And much of this knowledge is either theoretical or very basic in nature. Little concrete, useful (that is, real-life) knowledge is normally imparted. As a result, a new licensee may have insufficient, if any, background in this very difficult subject area.

Continuing education is required for about 45 states currently and certainly is a major help in maintaining minimum standards in the industry. (California requires 25 hours of continuing education each year for the first four years and 30 hours each two years thereafter.) However, I submit that consumers would undoubtedly find minimum standards far less than adequate when an agent is designing insurance for major family and business contingencies.

Regardless of continuing education, almost all true professionals in the insurance field will say that insurance is unquestionably one of the most difficult areas to comprehend, not only because of the intricacies of the products themselves but also because of the innumerable variations offered through innumerable companies. Competency in this area requires extensive education and many years of comprehensive experience. One of the better books on insurance, *Life and Health Insurance*, by Kenneth Black and Harold D. Skipper (Prentice-Hall,

CAVEAT INVESTOR

A separate element concerning licensing is rarely identified. Once you become licensed, you are inundated with emails and print litera-ture on every new product that exists. Reviewing that material is almost overwhelming, just like checking out junk mail. But within this literature and email, you are apt to find a few real nuggets of infor-mation and products amidst the reams of useless marketing. I have no reservations in stating that the examination of such material is the only way to stay abreast of this vast, ever-changing subject. It is time consuming, not only because of the amount of reading required but because you need to attend various (sometimes terrible) seminars as well. However, there are no current magazines, subscriptions, or other services of any type that provide such continuing and current insight. If a person advertises herself as having the ability to do comprehensive financial planning, then she had better have an insur-ance license, even if she rarely uses it. It is the only way to stay cur-rent. Further, in most states, it is the only way to be legal.

1999), suggests a minimum five years' experience by agents in order for them to reach an acceptable level of competence. In my experience as a licensed California Life and Disability Insurance Analyst, I think you need up to 10 years' experience before you have an acceptable knowledge base and competency. Insurance really is that hard. And new products and applications are offered almost daily. (For those "in the know," look at what happened years ago with single premium life. Most recently, look at the revised laws regarding split dollar policies. And there are so many variations of indexed annuities that it defies logic.)

From my experience as a past director of advanced planning for one of America's largest and most recognized insurance companies, I can tell you: The major, and sometimes only, focus of a life insurance agency, is to sell insurance. It's not about providing knowledge through in-house education to agents to best serve their clients. The conflict

CAVEAT INVESTOR

Many regulators state that no fiduciary relationship exists between an insurance agent and a client (as per the California Department of Insurance). Instead, there's just a fiduciary relationship between the company and the agent. The company wants to make sure that the potential insureds who are being submitted meet the criteria to make continued payments to the company, that the agent has reviewed the submission carefully and is not aware of any misrepresentation or fraud, and so on. While good agents are also focused on helping the client, it is difficult to serve two masters.

Beyond this is the possible greater master of hefty commissions. It's not of supreme importance to all agents, but this monetary conflict of interest can result in an increased exposure to the consumer. Some insurance companies defend this position of the agent's responsibility to the company by stating that everyone knows the agent is there to sell something, which is generally true. If, therefore, the consumer wants objective advice, he or she should ask the company to send another individual to help give such advice (yeah, sure) or hire someone as an independent consultant. Like who?

Unfortunately, using a CPA or attorney is pretty useless since there is nothing inherent in their training to understand insurance, its application, or, certainly, which product is really best.

Do you think that a harsh comment? Here are statements from the National Underwriter by Blazzard and Hasenauer: "Given that the subject of life insurance is rarely taught in law schools or accounting courses, most lawyers and accountants know little more about insurance than does the general public. When asked by their clients for advice on insurance, then, it is often easier to discourage their purchase than to expose that they are truly ignorant about life insurance and how it works. Even the training that is available on these subjects may be inadequate to provide a level of comfort that lawyers or accountants need in order to recommend a purchase. As things now stand, we know of no reference material that is currently available that would enable an insurance professional or lawyer or accountant to access the technical information that applies to these new insurance products."

of interest through sales commissions (trips and other "amenities") taints the entire process.

It boils down to this: If the person selected to provide financial advice—or even just insurance advice—has only an insurance license, do not use him. Again, don't let the "supposed" experience of the agent be used as a cover-up for lack of education and other background.

Those spouting their 15 years of experience may simply mean that they have taken one year's worth of experience and repeated it 15 times.

In summary, you should never buy insurance advice from someone who is not, at least, an insurance licensee. An unlicensed adviser of any type (a fee-only planner, an attorney, a CPA, Elvis, and so on) does not even maintain minimum skills as identified by mandatory continuing education. And that person is not accountable to any state's Department of Insurance. (No matter how ineffective your state's department may be, it's better to have some authoritative entity working for your benefit than none at all, should something go wrong.) Whether for advice or product, be sure to get someone that has at least five years' worth of experience and the necessary hours of continuing education. Otherwise the skill level is too low and competency is lacking.

All that said, do not universally dismiss all insurance agents simply because the industry and agents have a bad name overall. There are highly knowledgeable and experienced agents—you will just have to do more homework to find them.

Lastly, on the issue of competency, if I wanted direct evidence of a qualified life representative, I would ask that person about no-lapse insurance (this type of insurance is identified in Chapter 11) and if the company provides guaranteed coverage even up to age 120. If the rep is confused, mumbles a lot or invokes the fifth, just walk away and find someone else.

Series 6, 22, 62 Licenses

Three types of securities licenses permit the holder to sell only one type of product, but not all: Series 6, Series 22, and Series 62. Series 6 licenses concern themselves with mutual funds and variable annuities, Series 22 with limited partnerships, and Series 62 with corporate securities. Since the licensing is incomplete, so is the agent, and so is the individual that uses them.

To put a little perspective on the matter, consider the training for the Series 6, on mutual funds. The standard course presented by most training firms takes about two days. Also recognize that more than 11,000 mutual funds now exist. Millions of dollars are sent to funds every day. Anyone would assume that there would be a reasonable amount of time spent in the licensing preparation in analyzing risk and return, the different types of funds, past history, statistics, diversification, alpha, beta, correlation, asset allocation, standard deviation, and so on. Unfortunately, all that is required for the exam is for an instructor to spend approximately 20 or 25 minutes over the entire course and give some very basic definitions on a balanced fund, municipal bonds, growth fund, sector funds, and little else.

In all good conscience, I can tell you that the training I gave was more than adequate to pass the exam but woefully inadequate for even a rudimentary understanding of risk, reward, or, certainly, suitability, the main issue in arbitration. The SEC and NASD periodically comment on the problems in the industry on the part of the brokers, but these agencies must be directly faulted for incomplete and inept services since they require licensees to have essentially nil understanding of securities application. It is risky, to say the least, to use a licensee possessing only this level of (limited) knowledge.

Series 7 License

A stockbroker needs to have a Series 7 license in order to be able to offer a client almost all investment selections: stocks, bonds, options, mutual funds, municipal securities, and so on. Again, this one license is in no way wholly representative of the knowledge that a broker—and certainly a planner—needs to possess in order to plan a consumer's financial future. (There are about 670,000 brokers in the United States.) The coursework for this license is usually taught over a one-week period and requires extensive study. However, while what is taught is necessary for test takers to get a passing grade, it is still woefully inadequate for comprehensive financial analysis. (For example, standard deviation is not even taught, let alone tested.)

This knowledge is also inadequate even if used to advise on the purchase of a singular stock. (Go back to the true definition of diversification for validation.) If a broker has a solid track record of investments and has other substantiated background, and if the client understands exactly what is being purchased and why, then the selection may be acceptable. Otherwise most individuals are simply at risk for being sold something primarily for the benefit of providing the broker a commission.

Be aware that the Series 7 license pertains almost exclusively to investments—not insurance, retirement planning, estate considerations, college funding, or the like. Consumers will have other areas of their lives impacted by an investment decision and they therefore should look elsewhere for knowledgeable advice in these areas.

Some brokerage firms are now touting the fact that their representatives have been trained for financial planning. They have even bestowed various company designations and monikers for such effort. Because much of that training has been done in-house, a person could be forgiven for having serious doubts about its objectivity and the competency relayed to brokers. (Such training is generally product-oriented and merely explains how to sell the stuff.)

Designations, even CFP and ChFC designations, are not degrees. Absent some other extensive education or experience, a person with just this knowledge base is usually insufficiently prepared to perform many planning functions.

That knowledge base is far more limiting for SEC/NASD licensing. The license may be mandatory for an individual to sell a security, but it still represents a relatively small aggregate of knowledge and background on which any major decisions are being made.

John Ramsay, Deputy General Counsel for NASD Regulation, noted in 1999 that the "NASD anticipates that investment professionals will continue to learn on the job—and continuing education is a part of every broker's job." This assumes (illogically) that the material will be comprehensive.

Also note this statement from Cornell University: "A first class brokerage company doesn't necessarily imply a first class stock broker or investment counselor."

So, how well does a Series 7 rep do? According to the Securities Industry Association in 2000, the average broker grossed almost $500,000 (yes, that's half a million) and was able to keep about $200,000 for himself. Feel better now?

Chartered Life Underwriter (CLU)

The Chartered Life Underwriter, or CLU, designation is offered by the American College at Bryn Mawr, Pennsylvania, and is devoted primarily to the use and sales of life insurance. Because those people meeting the bare requirements for the CLU designation are still lacking in the broad scope of knowledge needed by most consumers, you would do better to look for additional education and experience in an adviser if you want help or advice on anything other than insurance. However, if someone needs insurance only, this is a minimum starting point.

CPA, Attorney, MBA, PhD

Individuals holding these designations and degrees should be used for their expertise in specific areas: a Certified Public Accountant (CPA) for taxes, an attorney to(possibly) prepare a buy or sell agreement or estate plan, a person with a Master in Business Administration (MBA) for business and industry matters, and someone with a doctorate for detailed, high-level information and advice in specific areas. However, these professions' background and experience rarely encompass comprehensive areas of investments and financial planning, and the degrees by themselves are inadequate in this area. For example, there is nothing inherent in the study for a law degree that would make one an expert in real estate, stock investments, retirement planning, or even estate planning. (This limitation hasn't stopped anyone from claiming to have such expertise simply because he or she passed the bar.) By the same token, there are no courses in the main body of work for becoming a CPA that would adequately address business, estate, and financial planning. And a crucial area requiring review is an understanding of economics—something not addressed in many of the degrees.

Consumers should not perceive a professional to have an inherent ability in finances solely because she or he has a CPA or attorney designation or license. The expertise just isn't there without advanced training.

Of course, there are degrees that are beneficial: business, finance, economics, and so on. But recognize that there needs to be further knowledge identified if a person is focusing on all-encompassing financial planning. If you think an MBA is the pre-eminent degree for business, consider ex-CEO Jeff Skilling of Enron who had a Harvard MBA. A lot of good that degree did him (or investors).

Registered Investment Adviser (RIA)

Registered Investment Adviser, or RIA, is neither a true designation nor a degree. That title indicates that the individual has registered with the U.S. Securities and Exchange Commission. In the alternative, that person might have had to comply with individual state requirements for registration within that state. The intent of such registration is to be able to charge a fee for securities advice or present himself as an adviser as it relates to investments *only*. Such an individual must provide a prospective client with a document detailing his experience, education, fees, conflicts of interest, and other information a consumer would need to determine competency and objectivity. It is not a reflection of competency, merely a document indicating background.

Many banks, CPAs, attorneys, and other special-interest groups have intensely lobbied against this registration, arguing that they should be exempted from this filing. After all, they claim, they are already highly regulated. That may be true, but they aren't highly regulated when it comes to financial planning. And regulations under financial planning may be more restrictive than regulations in other fields. Furthermore, other planners, including those from major brokerage firms, who do not charge a fee, say that the registration does not apply to them at all. As the advice from those calling themselves financial consultants expanded, the NASD now requires such individuals to become RIAs.

Irrespective of legal requirements and whether an advisor is required to register with the SEC, consumers would be well advised to demand a complete, written document of a financial representative's education, qualifications, and background. Should anyone decline to give this information, walk away. It is imperative to get the best advice from the most qualified advisers, and the written statement is the most all-encompassing document for investment advice. Nonetheless, the document does not address any background to insurance, long term care, estate planning, or the other nuances of comprehensive planning, so many areas of planning do not have to be identified to the prospective client.

I repeat: The RIA registration is not an indication of any true investment ability or expertise. Almost anyone can register. The registration simply forces the individual to comply with documentary evidence of investment background, how they charge, and so forth.

Bank Representative

Most bank salespersons are not employees of the bank but representatives of a separate broker-dealer firm that has made an agreement to sell these investments inside the bank's walls. These representatives rarely have but minimum experience or educational levels (Series 6 and 63 securities licenses, for example). In fact, one of the broker-dealer firms that was offering these services to numerous banks was quoted in a major financial planning magazine as stating that it was only going to do minimal training for their new representatives. Additional training, firm members thought,"wasn't necessary" in order to sell to the clients with whom they would be working.

Furthermore, products purchased at a bank almost universally cost more and/or provide lower returns or have nonexistent or limited track records than other financial products. (Check any of their annuities versus independent offerings.)

Unfortunately, bank customers are prime targets for being sold less-than-ideal financial products, as one representative said, because they are "transactionally oriented." They are used to making "decisions" about taking money out of a CD or savings account, because they may be looking for the highest yield. When a teller indicates that the fellow or gal across the lobby can offer 1/2 percent or more higher yields, many people opt for this package. They rarely discuss the investment, and, just as rarely, they do not understand the financial implications or restrictions of the investment. (Their heirs will.) In fact, such sales had been so easy and so lucrative for so long that many compensation packages for the salespeople had to be changed—commissions generated were several times larger than the salary of the bank manager. Stay away from bank-offered investments.

Certified Financial Planner (CFP) and Adviser; Chartered Financial Consultant (ChFC)

The certification for Certified Financial Planner, or CFP (as of this writing, there are about 40,000 CFPs in number and they are multiplying like rabbits), is earned through the College for Financial Planning. The designation of Chartered Financial Consultant, or ChFC (roughly 37,000), is earned through the American College (12 courses) and is an extension of the CLU designation. The courses are designed, in my opinion, to provide the minimum ability in thorough financial planning.

Be aware: It is possible to study for the CFP exam in as little as six months. *The Wall Street Journal* noted that the education amounted to the same as 15 college credit hours—the same as one semester of college. (It is necessary to pass a singular 10 hour exam to become a CFP. The ChFC is more demanding but still nothing to write home about.) Regardless, keep in mind that these are not degrees and do not encompass the same amount of effort or time involved with attaining a bachelor's degree or certainly a master's degree. (For those of you with college degrees, remember when you had to take 3 hour exams for each of your 5 or 6 classes per semester? That will give you the proper perspective.)

While the CFP and ChFC designations are the necessary prerequisites to get started, they are not panaceas for success. In my mind, they are adequate only to address basic planning issues. Proper insightful planning requires additional background, knowledge, and experience. Caution is advised here as well, since an inappropriate degree lends nothing to the planning process. As proof, consider a Certified Whoever with a Bachelor of Arts in French. Why bother?

Note that there are myriad other "certified" planners—estate, divorce, educational, and mutual fund planners—as well as Certified Fund Specialists, Registered Financial Consultants, ad infinitum with more being added each year. I would be extremely cautious when dealing with any supposed expert with the word *certified* after his name. At a minimum, that "financial professional" needs to have a CFP or ChFC designation. If not, I wouldn't even bother.

If an individual combines a Qualified Planner with the appropriate supplementary education of a business or economics degree, the result might be thorough and competent financial planning. Even these individuals normally do not do all the work themselves. Good finan-

CAVEAT INVESTOR

Some believe that the ChFC designation is almost exclusively oriented to the sale of life insurance and discount their value. A 1990 survey of ChFCs noted that 58 percent said they got their designation, not to become financial planners, but to sell more insurance. By the same token, Certified Financial Planners tend to be inherently weak in life insurance. (In 1995, the College for Financial Planning eliminated its mandatory course in insurance. The subject is supposedly fully included in the overview course. I disagree. Maybe as much as 80 percent is, but that is all. All this while the products and knowledge requirements have increased exponentially.)

New CFPs, therefore, have reduced capability in an area that has become far more complex. Older CFPs who have not maintained current skills in insurance are also extremely limited in competency in that area. Basic individual and family life insurance can be rather straightforward. Nonetheless, the innumerable policy types and various characteristics are enough to drive one to distraction and require considerable knowledge and expertise. Business insurance planning raises the complexity almost exponentially. So does disability, group disability, disability overhead, etc., insurance. And estate planning insurance is involved with the use of irrevocable trusts, Crummey powers, variable policies, and so on.

Even more demanding is the review of existing policies, many of which were improperly sold, overly expensive and never suitable for the true needs of the insured.

You must use someone who at least has a license, for that is the *only* way professionals can stay current on new products. They must also have a minimum of five years of experience—I'd prefer 10 or more. Caution is advised, since insurance can be an absolute minefield.

cial planning incorporates all the other disciplines. In fact, many savvy planners will utilize a CPA, estate planning attorney, and others that have the appropriate background for the situation. A good planner is the hub around which the process works, and she provides the insight and knowledge to complete the plan. But you need a lot more than a designation to complete a good hub. A designation can hold up a few spokes of a wheel but is almost destined to let the wagon fall. In fact, readers can ask themselves just how well their financial wagon held up after 2000. It's impossible to avoid the bumps in real life planning— it's another thing to fall into an investment crevice because the wagonmaster wouldn't change course.

To put some of the value of the one of the designations in perspective, I felt that the attainment of the CFP designation increased my knowledge base by about 75 percent (and I had been teaching real estate for years). It forced me to recognize areas that I never would have addressed without the formal class work (pension plans, life insurance, and so on). Unfortunately, however, the courses were incomplete in providing in-depth, real-life and practical knowledge, and they exposed more questions than answers. Still are.

As stated, don't assume that any designation is all-encompassing. But some of them are a good place to start.

Chartered Financial Analyst (CFA)

The highest level of a designation in direct securities analysis is Chartered Financial Analyst (CFA). It is a three-exam program encompassing economics, statistics, accounting, portfolio management, real estate, and a host of other areas in a demanding format. Its main function is to provide the knowledge to do individual company analysis for portfolios of various types.

Almost all CFAs are used at the institutional level and are rarely seen at the individual brokerage level unless, perhaps, large amounts of investments are involved. Clients with large accounts who wish to purchase individual issues would be well advised to start here. Absent some other background, a broker, CFP, ChFC, CLU does not have even close to the same knowledge base as does a CFA. Clients may also consider this designation when reviewing managers of various funds or wrap accounts. It is not designed for total financial planning, however.

Master of Science in Financial Planning (MSFP); Master of Science in Financial Services (MSFS)

The master's of science, whether in financial planning or financial services, is effectively the highest level of achievement in the financial planning profession to date. (There is one PhD program as of this writing.) The master's provides the "rest" or "bulk" of knowledge the CFP or ChFC misses. The depth of knowledge is at least another 75 percent greater (in my experience) than that obtained through any other designation. Degrees in this area of study may be earned through the College for Financial Planning, American College, and many state and local colleges.

The majors may focus in estate planning, retirement planning, taxes, investments, and several other disciplines. There were relatively few planners with this degree 6 to 10 years ago, but today they are available to clients in almost all metropolitan areas.

Consumers with substantial assets, business needs, complicated estates, or the need to have the most capable advisers available would be well advised to seek a professional with a master's level of competency.

As a personal note, I have found that some consumers say they don't want to drive too far or spend extra time to find someone with greater knowledge or competency. That's fine; if money is not that important, accept someone local of lesser skills, but then never complain again about lack of competency, lost money, inadequate service, etc.

Though all the major designations have been identified (there are many more, with less recognized organizations), the use of someone with a specific one, even a master's degree, does not necessarily guarantee that you will get the best planning. There is far more to proper planning than just the educational background, though that is one of the most important factors. I will address some later, but, remember, while pure technical proficiency is necessary, it is limited in application unless properly applied to the real world. Such an education must be accompanied by at least 10 years of work in all the disciplines (of course, that rarely happens). By the same token, real-world experience in planning is not very useful unless that person also has the necessary technical capability, which is achieved by staying current through intensive reading of national and international economics.

Agent Working on Commissions

Financial planners primarily sell products on which they earn a commission. Inherent in this process is the "conflict of interest" in that an adviser is merely helping a client with free financial advice for the sole purpose of selling a product and earning the commission involved. Industry representatives (and this includes even those individuals with CFP and ChFC designations as well as master's degrees) say that their ethics could never be compromised by any of the products they use and that the consumer would always be best served by the products they recommend.

I generally disagree with the rationalization. So do many consumers who voice concern that the primary motivation of a commissioned-based planner is merely to sell a product. This concern is more than justified. On far too many occasions a client has been sold a product that not only was improper but should never have been purchased in the first place (for example, due to age or lack of sophistication,). The issue is even further compounded by the fact that the numerous products have considerably varying commission structures. Many of the higher-paying products are pushed by securities and insurance firms and are obviously most beneficial to the agent and the company, not to the consumer. (For more detail, see Chapter 10.)

That said, however, you must recognize that some individuals do make the highest effort to put their clients first, regardless of the commissions received. That is further identified by the fact that some products do not pay enough commission to justify the time spent in "sell-ing" the product. For example, a long-term health care policy might cost $1000 and provide a $400 commission. However, if the client is properly counseled, it may take an adviser many hours to properly com-pile and analyze the personal data about the client in order to make a valid presentation of a product. (And these products change frequently and dramatically.) If the adviser charges a fee, the cost could easily be more than the commission earned. And when you look at the cost for a 20-year level term policy for a 30-year-old at $250, the adviser, in my opinion, could not ethically charge a fee higher than the commis-sion generated without getting a client's release.

If you further address business insurance, I doubt that most small business owners would ever pay for the number of hours necessary up front in order to get the proper key person insurance, draft the appropriate buy-sell agreements, and so on, as suggested by a highly competent agent. Notice that I said "highly competent," not a friend or relative. If you wish to pay a commission (or fee for that matter) solely based on the personal attributes of the agent, don't complain how big it was or the fact that the agent went on a free trip at your expense.

Admittedly, however, the commissions on many insurance prod-ucts are ludicrous. I might be able to accept that fact were it not also for the fact that the companies offer unbelievably expensive free trips and incentives that almost totally negate any objectivity to the sale. The insurance business needs to clean house. It unilaterally won't, but in the next 5 to 10 years, you will find extensive state regulations radically changing the entire life business and that of an agent. It's already hap-pening now through suggestions by the National Association of Insur-ance Commissioners (NAIC).

Captive Agent

This is a continuation of the problem addressed previously about agents working on commissions, but it goes further since it comments on the use of only one company (normally the larger insurance companies with major advertising budgets: Prudential, TransAmerica, IDS, and so on) to provide products. In such a situation, the agent is almost universally required to sell the products of that one company only. Policies in these companies are almost always higher in cost and/or provide less coverage than those offered by an independent agent able to select from virtually all the national companies available. Additionally, one company cannot provide products to fit every need for individuals or businesses. The captive agents may therefore have to "force-fit" their products for many situations.

A real-life case illustrates this situation. A client with bad health was seeking to obtain life insurance. Most of these cases should be directed to companies that deal in "rated" or difficult placements. The

CAVEAT EMPTOR

Financial Consultants, Financial Advisers, Wealth Advisers and other nondescript monikers

What do these monikers indicate? Darned if I know. As with other such similar "titles" there are no definitive definitions on what these people are attempting nor that they have the licenses to perform anything.

The use of the term "Financial" implies a capability and competency to perform comprehensive planning, not just investments, not just insurance. What a "Wealth Adviser" is—I don't have a clue. But I submit that its focus is also full planning. As such, all these monikers and more must possess the minimum licensing for both investments and insurance. If they only have one of these licenses, their title is murky at best and deceitful at worst. Walk away.

Do a lot of homework before becoming impressed. Get the reps full written brochure and review it carefully before agreeing to any engagement. If you can't get a written statement on qualifications and background, you are foolish to continue.

odds of coverage with a major firm are very remote, if for no other reason than the underwriters do not have the background or skill to properly analyze such an individual. But the "system" required that the application be filed. Unfortunately, everyone played the game and went through the motions. The end result was preordained. The individual was denied coverage—and it took over two months to come to that conclusion. (What was the liability of the company and agent if the potential insured's health declined—or the individual died —in the interim?)

This issue is also of considerable importance to senior citizens who are being sold other company products (long-term health care policies, as a prime example) that are far from being the best in the business. Extreme caution is recommended to those who wish to use captive company agents.

Fee-Only Planner

Fee-only planners perform financial planning for a fee usually based on an hourly rate, a flat fee, or on a percentage of client's net worth. You should get very objective and comprehensive analysis of a financial position, but that is not guaranteed. Further, these plans may be overly expensive and not very good at all. Some of the reasons are identified below.

As stated previously, many planners buy a computer program to define the allocation of assets, determine life insurance, and to do estate planning and many other functions for a client. But what is the background of the program writer? What formulas are actually used? What assumptions are being made? Per Nobel Laureate William Sharpe, "I have been studying software provided by major mutual fund and software companies and have found that it reflects remarkably few of the lessons learned after decades of the development of financial theory and its implementation by and for large institutional investors." Further, what is the actual input of the planner, if any?

An example further defines the problem. Many years ago I was requested to write an investment course for a CPA group and asked to develop a planning "matrix" that would incorporate any type of client. Simply stated, a CPA planner would then use the basic personal information gathered about a client—say, 45 years old, two children, $50,000 income—merely to look in a box (matrix) where it showed that the client should have 20 percent real estate holdings, 15 percent bonds, 32 percent equities, and so forth. This is not individualized planning. In fact, I don't know what to call it except a waste of time.

Whether you use a fee- or commissioned-based planner, make sure the planner has the ability to use her brains in developing a truly personalized plan. No computer program has yet been developed that can do thorough comprehensive financial planning. (Many have attempted it and all have failed.) The programs are great for crunching numbers, but that is usually the extent of "expertise." Consumers need a report personally developed by the planner and not some paragraphs from a book or program written by someone else with limited expertise.

Costs and Fee Planners

Recognize that the costs may actually be far greater with some fee planners than with selecting a commissionable planner initially. And it all relates to product implementation. Should a fee-only/nonimplementation planner present a very good plan, but without indicating which of the various products to use, the client is still mired in the confusion of which products are any good and where to go to find them. If such a planner sends the client to a "friend" at a local brokerage firm to get the 46 percent of loaded mutual funds the plan suggested or to an insurance agent to purchase the $1,500,000 of insurance, then the client will undoubtedly pay a commission on top of the fee. The cost is far more expensive than just commissions alone. Further, the client may not get the best products but simply what the broker, firm, or insurance agent is pushing that particular month. This type of planning is too expensive and not very good. The individual you hire should be capable of researching the product arena and implementing the essentials of a plan. If not, spend your planning money elsewhere.

Also ask yourself this. Should you pay a fee for advice from someone who has refused to take any licensing courses and continuing education in the area addressed? Or should you work with someone legal who gets a commission who has taken 150-plus hours of continuing education and might have (should have) 10-plus years of experience? True, the commission is an element of concern, but at least the planner knows something to have earned it and is acting legally and ethically.

Recognize further that most forms of planning—retirement, long-term care, estate, and so on—must incorporate insurance—certainly that which you already own. Long-term care planning must incorporate insurance. Estate planning must incorporate insurance since it will be taxed in your estate (if the net assets at death are too great). Irrevocable life insurance trusts are mandatory considerations for some high net worth individuals. Disability insurance is a must consideration, particularly for the self employed. Anyone presenting him- or herself as a financial planner is, ipso facto, presenting themselves as having the competency to perform fundamental financial planning (with the accompanying insurance elements) and is licensed as mandated by the state and the Federal government. If anyone tries to rationalize why they don't have to be licensed, recognize that most are lying. And if you use a liar or incompetent for your financial planning, it probably won't be long before the problems directly affect your pocketbook. In the alternative, many fee-only planners rationalize that they may do an incidental review of insurance needs for a fee—what type of insurance and maybe the amount. Then they refer the clients either to a properly licensed agent, who will complete the plan by selling the insurance for a commission, or to a low-load company (still the wrong product), where the client will need to do the work of purchase. Others note that they can refer clients to low-load insurance products, which is still bogus.

The CFP Board of Standards allows a planner to be fee-only as long as the planner does not receive a commission. That's a smokescreen! If you have to pay a commission to anyone, you didn't get fee-only planning. Further, if you are being sent elsewhere to implement mandatory and fundamental sections of a plan, you probably didn't get a good planner to begin with, irrespective of any designations. As an additional caveat to all readers who have been led to believe that all commissionable products cost more. Au contraire. Do not assume that the low-load products you read about cost less than fully commissioned products. If you are addressing mutual funds, normally they do, but when addressing insurance, there are commissionable life insurance policies that cost much less than low-load products. Further, to my knowledge, there are no no-load or low-load long-term care policies and very few no-load or low-load disability policies. Recognize also that one prerequisite for selecting a company is its longevity and stability in underwriting policies, which may not be true with many low-load companies. Lastly, simply referring a client to a low-load company—when they could have gone there anyway to begin with—is not reflective of personal competency or integrity in helping a client sort through this most difficult of planning areas.

Fee and Commission Planners

Also known as fee-based planners, fee and commission planners provide the plan and do the implementation as well. While the fee for the "plan" would and should be less than that of a fee-only planner, and the implementation possibly better than that addressed previously, the overall cost is possibly still too high because of the commissions the planner will (generally) take on top of any fee. And we still must consider the difficult "conflict of interest."

The final determination of who to use will (must) encompass the issues and concerns listed above. If possible then, the combination of that listed below might yield a knowledgeable and competent individual that could produce acceptable results.

Who Should You Use

Find a planner with a degree in planning—a Master's level preferred. A life and disability license and the skills to use it (Insurance Analyst license or similar is mandatory in California and about 30+ states) and perhaps a Series 7 license. The securities license does not have to be current since no-load mutual funds may be the investment of choice, but some background in the industry is almost compulsory.

Admittedly, the Series 7 training is not adequate in itself, but it beats not having any training at all. Anyone may substitute an MBA in Business or Economics, a CFA, and other recognized designations or degrees for the Series 7 license. They should have registration with the state and/or SEC as a Registered Investment Adviser. (Remember, though, that that designation merely acknowledges legality, not competency.) Other qualifications include an appropriate additional background or degree, such as an economics degree or CPA, and experience with fee planning with implementation for a minimum of 10 years. The years of experience is very important since it can reflect a type of de facto residency program that is missing in the formal educational process.

Sure, this will limit the number of advisers—and it should.

In reference to implementation, the best planner is preferably someone who has had extensive experience in both securities and insurance, perhaps as a previously commissioned agent, who knows the marketplace, and who has the appropriate licenses. He then finds the best product, charges a fee for the work, and negotiates the best fees on other products as applicable. While, as stated, that negotiation normally refers to insurance, you can also negotiate fees on stock purchases (rather moot now due to online trading), and, more importantly, wrap accounts (clients may still pay 3 percent, which is absurd). (Negotiating lower commissions on certain insurance policies may not work since the insurance company will not even consider the effort. In such cases, part of the commission will need to offset the planning charge.)

Clients are paying for the best of service and implementation. The overall cost will invariably be cheaper than any other combination, in some cases costing "nothing."

For example, if a client had $100,000 to invest, a commission-based planner might suggest the use of a mid-load mutual fund. At a 4.5 percent commission, that represents a cost of $4500 for advice, though that might not be deducted on the front end. An annuity might charge a minimum commission of 4 percent (up to 8 percent) or $4000, again not charged on the front end. That said, remember, there is normally no such thing as a free lunch. The commission costs come out of lower returns, higher expenses, surrender charges, and a host of other combinations of fees.

On the other hand, a true fee planner might charge $2500 for all her work (which, for that fee, should be very encompassing and include many other different levels of planning). Assuming the fee planner also decided on the same commissionable annuity, the client would have paid $2500 for competent professional service and received all or part of the commission as an offset to the $2500. I realize that this does not fit the specific guidelines of fee "only" as addressed by most organizations, but the real world has to apply. And here is part of the real world application that defines why commissionable products may be more than appropriate. I had to find a guaranteed annuity for a client. The best was a 4 percent return for five years, A rated company. The no loads I reviewed were TIAA-CREF, Vanguard and Schwab. The returns ranged from 3.05 percent to 3.50 percent. The acceptance of any of these would have violated the fiduciary duty of doing the best for the client. Never assume no load products are always cheaper or provide greater returns, paricularly with insurance products.

Or perhaps the planner would have stated that no investment should be made—that a bank CD or money market fund would be appropriate. Admittedly the client paid a fee to find out they should do nothing, but that might have been determined in the initial review and cost just a couple of hours of work—not the $2000 or so as indicated above. That certainly was a worthwhile expenditure to have avoided purchasing an illiquid, unsuitable investment (for example, a limited partnership or hedge fund) from another adviser. There are not too many planners working this way, primarily because commissioned-based planning makes far more money. However, those that work in this manner are probably the true professionals in the business.

As identified above, the use of some insurance products pays less in commission than the amount of hourly fees that could be charged. The adviser must address this issue and, in my opinion, opt for the lower charge whenever possible.

Monitoring Investments and Planning

That initial investigation into a professional's licenses, degrees, and designations to gauge his or her competency to do a good job is extremely important. Of equal—and perhaps even greater—importance to the consumer, for those with sufficient assets, is their own and their planner's continued monitoring of investments and planning opportunities.

The consumer is put on an annual retainer generally based on the value of the underlying assets, though an hourly fee for work may be utilized as well. This aspect may not seem necessarily new. Almost all brokerage firms are requesting or demanding that managers suggest, implement, and monitor investments. The different element in the statement above is the continuation of financial planning. Most financial planners who continue to work with clients do so under the guise of money managers. But it would seem that the true extra benefit in using them is their continued monitoring—and reporting—of the other financial aspects of the client's life.

Such involvement would include a new budget for retirement purposes, Social Security, Medicare and Medicaid planning, estate revisions, long-term-care issues, business changes, charitable gifting, dying, review of pension plans and other retirement vehicles, real estate, and a host of other issues far beyond the relatively narrow scope of "money management." These issues can be elicited by the planner due to, or hopefully because of, the total involvement of the planner in the client's ongoing everyday life. Unfortunately, this planning involvement has not been utilized extensively to date probably because:

1. the clients do not understand the value of the service,
2. few planners have the knowledge and ability to provide this broad scope of activity,
3. or, MANY planners had been able to "get away" with charging exorbitant management fees during the bull market while the market went continually up.

As more professional planners (MSFP, MSFS) come into being, their worth in this capacity should be invaluable.

Research

Regardless of whom you use or what method is employed, one element assures you will find greater competency by the planner. You as a client need to do an extensive amount of reading and research before engaging any professional. Publications such as *Money* magazine, *The Wall Street Journal*, and *Kiplinger's Personal Finance* magazine are good sources that will provide some insight—though you can never be sure what material is absolutely accurate or viable.

The more knowledge a client possesses and the more intelligently he or she can discuss critical issues with the adviser, the more beneficial the meeting and process will be. Everything else being equal, there is less risk in any venture the more the consumer tries to understand the fundamentals of what the adviser is doing.

There are no guarantees of success, even when you use an adviser with the highest qualifications, but if you, as a consumer, read and do objective research, you should do immeasurably better than the majority of consumers who use guesswork and emotional investing.

Notes

1. For example, in the heyday of the 1990s, people would email me as to why I had not included information at my site on how to buy IPOs. They had not done any homework and yet were willing to dive into something they clearly did not comprehend solely because they heard some little news tidbit on some TV show. I did not even bother to respond. As Joseph Heller said, "It is neither possible nor necessary to educate people who never question anything." That said, there is, nonetheless, a duty to protect those that do not have the capability to grasp the fundamentals—the mentally incapable, the infirm, some elderly, The Simpsons, etc.
2. In 2000, a teenager fraudulently used the Internet to pump up a stock price and was caught by the SEC. He had to give back hundreds of thousands of dollars in fines but was allowed to keep a couple hundred thousand because the SEC didn't think it could make a good case and settled. The commissioner said he thought the punishment was adequate. The kid's father said his son hadn't done anything wrong—as he eyed the new car his kid had bought him.
3. You do know what the meaning for *is* is, don't you?
4. Note that that is not the case with insurance agents. Even the California Department of Insurance states that everyone knows the agent is there to sell life insurance and not necessarily nor certainly legally to act in your best interests.
5. Minimum information includes full name, address, phone number, employer, Social Security number, citizenship, acknowledgment that the customer is of legal age, spouse's name and employer (if any), and investment objective. Other information varies as to firm but might include bank and personal references, previous brokerage accounts, and if the account was solicited, referred, walk in, and so on.
6. As an instructor in most continuing education classes, I have found most licensees have very limited skills, even in the basic products. That said, they are slowly getting better. But since state insurance departments know little about non-physical insurance, it will only go so far. On the other side, there are some very intensive independent courses that offer exceptional knowledge, and I have tried to teach all subjects at that level.
7. I subsequently avoided all management positions in the insurance industry due to the continued deception to the public and singular emphasis on sales to the exclusion of literally anything else. You simply cannot imagine how entrenched the sales orientation is. In fact, it is but a very few companies that have even developed any ethical standards for their agents (managers and staff included). Some life executives have even stated that it is almost impossible to impose such standards since the sales atmosphere is so pervasive. (The

same goes for the brokerage industry.) Agents are told to sell so much universal or variable insurance per quarter in order to retain their desk. Or they should sell so many policies to get the free trips to South America, Australia, New Jersey, or wherever. Or if they make "salesperson of the year," they will get moved to the corner office (someone else has to move out) and get a special office assistant to handle the load. While such techniques may be "acceptable" and even desirable in the sales of automobiles, refrigerators, and nonfinancial commodities, they are far from acceptable where a family's or business's existence is at stake.

8. Many planners in California do "comprehensive" fee-only planning and the implementation of no-load mutual funds. But they rarely can get involved with life insurance, because they would be violating the law. (Anyone in the state of California offering insurance advice for a fee must be licensed as a Life and Disability Insurance Analyst. This requires five years licensing in insurance, the completion of approximately 115 hours of continuing education and the passing of an extensive exam. There are about 30 other states nationally that have similar requirements/licenses.) My June 1998 review of the 57 NAPFA fee-only members in California showed that not one of the representatives possessed the Life and Disability Insurance Analyst license as required by the state. Same in 2002. They cannot review a client's insurance—one of the most numbing areas of planning. Hence, they cannot present themselves as comprehensive planners. I am the only fully licensed and legal CFP in all of California that offers comprehensive fee planning. Therefore, the bulk of the fee-only planners are acting illegally and unethically in analyzing life insurance or recommending product. This does not mean that using an agent or analyst gets you the best product or advice either. But at least they are properly licensed and are required to take the mandatory continuing education in the field. Some states have laws on rebating. Florida and California are the only states currently allowing insurance rebating. Actually, in the alternative, instead of rebating on a large policy, the planner could negotiate the premiums directly with the insurer. It saves a lot of the hassles and paperwork later.

9. I know some readers will find these comments too cynical, but fundamental real life knowledge is inherently suspect with any of the designations. Think of this: Would you hire a physician who has only one semester of education to operate on you or a loved one? And no residency training? That's a precursor to disaster. There is no difference in using agents of limited knowledge to deal with your financial life. Using an adviser with little more that a semester's worth of insight into a vast array of financial issues is completely illogical and fraught with risk.

CHAPTER 4

THE CORNERSTONES
OF INVESTING

*T*HE BULK OF THE INVESTMENT INDUSTRY is generally mired in the philosophy that you set up your asset allocation with the intent of holding the portfolio through thick and thin. This thinking has been preached by major Web sites, brokerage firms, advisers, and many others—both gurus and friends and neighbors—as the cornerstone of proper investing.

In some cases, the buy-and-hold approach may work. Will it work in all cases? No. Further, you don't know which time period will be the one during which buy and hold will or will not work. For example, did you foresee that in 1990 the market would be so strong for a full decade? Did you know of the devastation that would occur in 2000–2002? Of course not, to both questions.

Staying the course most recently would have brought on enormous losses and enormous emotional strife. How have you felt after losing 40 to 60 percent of your money since the markets crashed while you held on? Did you sleep well? Did your spouse say anything? Did you have to change your retirement plans or other spending habits? Did you have to take out a loan to buy this book? The point I have said repeatedly in the material so far is that there is a huge difference between the theoretical aspect of investing (and most anything else) and its real-life application.

Actually, in the real world, buy and hold is one of the biggest sucker bets foisted on the unsuspecting public by unknowing agents and adjunct professors dealing with unlimited time frames. (Maybe dollar-cost averaging comes first on the list of sucker bets.) I have already addressed the knowledge, or lack thereof, of agents when it comes to the fundamentals of investing (see Chapters 2 and 3), and won't beat a dead horse. But references about unlimited time frames that pertain primarily to pension funds and the like that go on forever—unlike humans who retire, die, divorce, breed, and do other strange things that defy specific time frames—are really unrealistic. The claim that long-term, buy-and-hold investing is the best way to go is fundamentally flawed. As John Maynard Keynes said, "In the long run, we're all dead."

Human beings are not unemotional animals that live forever. As such, we do strange things (myself excluded) that defy logic. The Pet Rock is a fine example. Rap music is another. And then there are the Reality TV shows. Therefore, we need to adjust our lives—specifically our financial lives—when something strange happens or when something goes wrong (and right as well). The suggestion that you can develop an allocation that can prosper effectively through any economic debacle (that is, the buy-and-hold theory) has never been a valid long-term, real-world strategy.

You might think I am writing this with the benefit of hindsight just to look good after the recent financial debacle. Au contraire. In everything I have taught since the 1980s, every report for clients, everything I have done, I have made clear the unbridled focus on the mess of the 1973 and 1974 market crash and the various other reasons why buy and hold works better on paper than it does in real life.

Consider this: The S&P 500 started to drop at the beginning of 1973. But note that it did not maintain a high of 130 or better consistently until November 1978. Table 4.1 illustrates that terrible decade.

Table 4.1   The 1970s Market

1972.12	130.140	1974.12	81.639	1976.12	138.838
1973.01	128.200	1975.01	92.023	1977.01	132.274
1973.02	123.681	1975.02	97.892	1977.02	129.863
1973.03	123.781	1975.03	100.376	1977.03	128.497
1973.04	119.041	1975.04	105.494	1977.04	129.032
1973.05	117.105	1975.05	110.520	1977.05	126.502
1973.06	116.636	1975.06	115.795	1977.06	132.754
1973.07	121.380	1975.07	108.338	1977.07	130.706
1973.08	117.241	1975.08	106.434	1977.08	128.849
1973.09	122.246	1975.09	103.114	1977.09	129.049
1973.10	122.448	1975.10	109.851	1977.10	124.022
1973.11	108.868	1975.11	112.948	1977.11	127.944
1973.12	111.024	1975.12	112.032	1977.12	128.902
1974.01	110.227	1976.01	125.671	1978.01	121.501
1974.02	110.147	1976.02	124.612	1978.02	119.037
1974.03	107.892	1976.03	128.811	1978.03	122.538
1974.04	104.023	1976.04	127.808	1978.04	133.596
1974.05	100.879	1976.05	126.387	1978.05	134.824
1974.06	99.734	1976.06	131.989	1978.06	132.967
1974.07	92.335	1976.07	131.356	1978.07	140.720
1974.08	84.360	1976.08	131.115	1978.08	144.955
1974.09	74.644	1976.09	134.504	1978.09	144.491
1974.10	87.191	1976.10	131.999	1978.10	131.894
1974.11	82.931	1976.11	131.460	1978.11	134.726

Investing is definitely for the long term (where goals are properly identified). You must commit yourself to an investment strategy for most of your life—and even longer, if you wish to cover some of your beneficiaries. But if you commit yourself to static formula holdings, you are apt to commit yourself to the poorhouse.

History provides interesting insights in terms of changes in economics. Those who do not learn from the past are doomed to repeat it. (I just made that up—it's bound to be a hit.) But a major problem is that the public is led to believe a distorted view of buy and hold made up entirely by those that are too young to have read about history. A few years ago, a lot of people listened to some 30-year-old pretty boys on TV telling the gullible, and sometimes naïve and greedy, public that economic cycles (that is, recessions) were a thing of the past and that our prosperity would continue unabated. Many consumers believed it, and they invested accordingly. But you also had some 40- and 50-year-old people who touted the euphoria without the offsetting (obvious, in my opinion) risk.

Do you want proof? Years ago, one TV show reported on day trading. Obviously the program mentioned risk—but the visual element offset any of the verbal negatives. They interviewed a very attractive, thirtyish, blonde ex-attorney who talked about how much money she was making. No matter what the caveats, people want to feel young, attractive, and financially successful—and that is exactly what the picture presented. Deceitful? Yes. Ethical? Your call. Good programming? Debatable. News? Not a chance.

You have to recognize that comments about the benefits of buy and hold (and other investing strategies, of course) made in the press, on news shows, in financial tabloids, and at chat rooms and cocktail parties are invariably offered by people who actually have very little, if any, insight to what needs to be analyzed for real-life applications. Even when you hear from the supposed experts, they rarely exist in the same economic stratosphere that you do. Hence, you need to take the advice with a grain of salt.

For example, when the likes of the big investors that own their own investment firms (you know their names) suggest you stay the course when the market tanks, you should consider what the real implication for them is if they maintain their portfolios. So their net worth declines—from, say $10 million to $6 million. Big deal. They can still effectively enjoy the same lifestyle they had before. But if you went from a $100,000 nest egg to $60,000, you'd be hurting big time. Buy and hold is not necessarily a valid position for the average consumer who absolutely needs the assets to live on.

The Myth of Market Timing

Are there ways to reduce the exposure when a buy-and-hold plan starts to go awry? One way that has had lots of press is called *market timing*. It's intent is for the investor to pick the highs and lows of the market by viewing a 100- or 200-day moving average that supposedly sends out buy and sell signals perhaps every week. (Or by reading tea leaves, the new color of Madonna's hair, or whatever.) Certainly some types of market timing can work for a period of time—but it has been clearly shown that market timing won't hold up over time.

One analyst noted that a market timer might be able to make a bundle for up to 10 years—and then go broke. A perfect example was the Lowry Market Timing Fund of the 1980s. The fund sent out a study from the Wharton School that stated that had the fund been in existence over the past 50 years or so, it would have provided a return 2.5 times of that of a buy and hold investment. In 1984, the return at was about 9.4 percent. So their market service would have produced a 23.5 percent return. Now, I don't care who you are, that is one whale of a return! So, how did they do going forward? Their system not only was useless, it was detrimental to an investor's financial health. They actually lost money as the market started its move upward. The situation got so bad, the fund went out of business. So much for historical projections brought forward. In the end, the study proved that market timing cannot be sustained over the long haul.

Economic Analysis: The Market Timing Antidote

Are there ways to protect your assets when the market starts a protracted bear market? (The same question may be asked on how to increase assets in a bull market. But considering the events of recent years, protecting one's retirement life is far more important.) Throughout this book I note that you have to look at economics in order to get a feel for whether to stay in or out of the market. That doesn't mean trying to time the market, searching for the highs and lows. *Economic analysis* is an objective, highly researched endeavor that attempts to overlay the market with what is happening with real-world economics. It is an attempt at risk management given economic conditions. While there is, generally, an intent to maximize returns, the true focus is to adjust the portfolio to reflect the real and anticipated impacts caused by varying elements in the economy.

Once in a while a planning or investment text will address economic analysis to some extent, but such a book is usually fixated on varying types of company or market statistical measures: equity risk premium, price-to-earnings ratio, dividend payout, and at least another 100 different measures. I am not saying those ratios are not important, but equally significant are economic conditions that overlay all of the market numbers. For example, take the Iraq War of 2003. A lot of money will be needed for the reconstruction of that Mideast country. There is clear evidence of looming budget deficits with Medicare and Medicaid. There is still extensive unemployment, and a lot of jobs have permanently moved overseas. China won't devalue the Yuan. Europe has fallen flat. France has significant problems (who cares!). Will Japan ever get out of a recession? On the other hand, U.S. productivity has surged (a major factor), the World Bank looks for a respectable global rebound in 2004, inflation is still low, Greenspan is still alive, a weightlifter runs California (ye gods!) and so on. Many brokers are saying this is a great time to get in because the market is so low and is possibly surging. Perhaps, but the same sentiments were offered shortly after March 2000 and continuously thereafter. Who do you believe now? Better yet, why? If you want to gauge the risk and rewards of investments, diversification and asset allocation, it all starts with extensive reading of economics. That requires an intensive review of the material by the various Federal Reserve Boards. If you are not going to read this yourself, find someone who does. It is that important.

Sure, the material and all its implications are not easy to initially understand nor to grasp the interrelationships from one element, say a change in FED interest rate policy and what it may do to mortgage rates.

(Believe it or not, they may not be well correlated.) I never said that investing or planning was easy, no matter what the simplistic money magazines may have you believe. If it was that easy, billions of dollars would never have been lost from 2000 forward because you would have been warned and taught well before such a financial debacle occurred as to what you should have done. I discuss some of that below, but be forewarned that I am now going to debunk one of the greatest marketing gimmicks ever foisted on the American investor.

Dollar-cost Averaging (DCA) and Monthly Investing (MI)

Why were so many investors led down the Garden Path of Marketing, at least as far as the stock market was concerned, during the last few years? One of the reasons is because so many "analysts, brokers and planners" people were touting the infamous *dollar-cost averaging* as the be all and end all of basic investing. DCA has not worked in the past, does not work today and will effectively never work in the future. Well, that will raise a snit right there since literally every securities broker, financial planning firm, financial(?) journalist, whatever, comments on the effective use of investing "X" amount of money each month regardless of economic fluctuations. It is touted in the industry as a conservative method to get into the market.

Statistically, it is universally a foregone conclusion that you will ultimately have less return on your money under DCA as compared to putting money in all at once. Also, the conservative comment is not valid. It is true that it can be conservative but you have no idea if it will be when you start. Further, because it is a psychological orientation to the market, it can also increase risk by a large measure. Did you read that and do you understand the implications and what you should be doing? Bet you don't so that's why the material below puts it into focus. I will first provide the basics of how DCA works and then provide the additional statements.

DCA is generally interpreted to mean paying the same amount into an investment account each month over a 12-month period. I use the term "generally" because DCA is most commonly interpreted incorrectly. DCA starts with a lump sum, say, $12,000. Instead of investing all at once, you spread the investment over time in roughly equal increments of $1000 monthly in order to average out the price. The non-invested money is put into a cash-type account that earns some interest and is used up over the following 11 months of investments.

If you do not have a lump sum, you are simply doing *monthly investing*, which I will call MI. It's just like a 401(k) plan: You invest only as the money becomes available each month. MI will end up doing almost the same thing as DCA, if the monthly investments amounts are the same, but the DCA is a conscious decision to split up money into increments while MI is primarily only investing what you can or want to do that month. If you do not have a lump sum, you ain't doing DCA.

Both DCA and MI are considered a no-brainer form of investing. I guess that's fine, if you don't want to use your brain. But it also can lead to some rather inappropriate (stupid?) investing patterns. DCA/MI can be very risky investing ventures that lead to a lot of bad investments and lost money. More about that later. But, first, the basics.

How DCA/MI Works

With DCA/MI, the same amount of money is put each month into an investment regardless of market volatility and price movement. By investing this way, an investor is unconcerned about the swings of the stock or fund and does not try to find the lowest price on which to buy (normally called *market timing*). The price of the shares average out over time and can still produce an acceptable profit, assuming that the ending value of the shares is higher than the dollar-cost average or monthly investing. That is *not* a guarantee.

For example, assume you have $1200 and put in $100 per month into Fund X, as shown in Table 4.2.

Table 4.2 Yearly Investment in Fund X

Month	Amount Invested	Share Price	Number of Shares Purchased
1	$100	$40	2.5
2	$100	75	1.33
3	$100	100	1
4	$100	66.66	1.5
5	$100	40	2.5
6	$100	25	4
7	$100	33.33	3
8	$100	66.66	1.5
9	$100	80	1.25
10	$100	80	1.25
11	$100	50	2
12	$100	40	2.5

From the data given in Table 4.2, we show a total of $1200 invested for the year, which purchases a total of 24.33 shares. We compute the average share price for the year as follows:

Dollar-cost average / Monthly investing = How much the shares cost / How many shares purchased

= $1200/24.33

= $49.32 per share

Admittedly, the fund in which you are investing is very volatile, which I use to make a point. (Since I have already dismissed the value of using individual stocks for just about all basic investing, I opted to use a mutual fund.) As you can see, while you would have preferred to buy all the shares at $25, you just as easily might have purchased them at $80 or $100. DCA/MI avoids the "problem" in trying to select the best time to buy.

But look at the end prices. Are you really sure you want to buy something that is so volatile that it will give you a stomach ache if you look at it? And may be no higher than the price you started with a year ago? Would you have felt comfortable as you continued investing funds into the market after March 2000 and watch the prices continually degrade? And lose 40 to 60%? I don't think so.

Caveats of Dollar-Cost Averaging and Monthly Investing

DCA and MI are usually touted as "safe," conservative ways to invest. I strongly disagree. The following caveats, using examples with real-life elements, show why they are not the sensible investments that some folks make them out to be.

If you have money to invest as a lump sum, DCA produces a *lower* return than investing the money all at once. Two researchers (Williams and Bacon) have discounted dollar-cost averaging by statistically showing that putting all the funds in at one time outproduces dollar-cost averaging by a factor of 2 to 1. They invested a theoretical sum in 90-day Treasury bills and moved into the S&P 500 over a year's period. They compared these results with the results from investing all the funds at once, starting with different periods from 1926 to 1991.

Williams and Bacon's study revealed that nearly two-thirds of the time, a lump-sum strategy significantly outperformed dollar-cost averaging. The lump-sum approach returned an annualized return of about 12.75 percent, while the dollar-cost averaging returned just 8.50 percent. Reducing the dollar-cost averaging from once a month to three or four times per year also increased the return. This study's findings should not be all that surprising. First, stocks have outperformed money market and bond funds over almost all time frames (and certainly beyond 10 years). Also, with interest rates being so low in many time frames (as they are today), it is difficult to get a decent annual return with the bulk of funds sitting in 1.5 percent bank accounts.

Moshe Milevsky and Steven Pollard did a study that focuses on vari-ability rather than returns. They proved that DCA would have a greater risk overall and would clearly be less efficient. "Because of the higher standard deviation with dollar cost averaging, you would have higher odds of ending up with less money overall."

Part of the lengthy report offered this conclusion: "Amongst the general public, DCA appears to be an axiom of prudent investing. In contrast to this widespread practice, financial economists have shunned this strategy and repeatedly demonstrated its irrationality. And mean variance inefficiency." Nevertheless, the vast amount of B/D firms, finan-cial planners, mutual funds, Santa Claus, and your mama all get misty-eyed with DCA. But either they don't have the foggiest idea as to what is really going on or they are just playing the emotional element of investing. This emotion is called the "fear of regret"—the problem of watching your funds potentially lose money right off the bat. Rather than face that possibility, DCA simply tells you "not to worry." Well, it's not that simple.

> DCA's delaying tactics are nothing more than thinly disguised attempts to time the market. And delaying investing like that actually decreases your chances of success. Dollar cost averaging with a lump sum is an attempt to "split the baby," and that has historically been a losing strategy.
>
> FRANK ARMSTRONG

Another significant caveat is that many investors using DCA or MI don't bother to watch the investments after they start. They may not rebalance the investments. Normally, investments should be revised at least once per year. (Charles Schwab suggests that revisions can be made up to once every five years—to which I say, not a chance!) While it is true that, over time, stocks outproduce other investments, you need to pay attention to what is going on. You have to, because managers may have changed, the fund may have changed identity (from, say a large-cap one to a mid-cap), and, most importantly, the economics may have changed. For example, you don't want to end up in another 1970s' marketplace, where stocks performed absolutely terribly for some time— as much as a 45 percent loss in 1973–1974. (Or did you not learn your lesson and actually end up in the same scenario for 2000–2002?) If you just let your money sit, as many magazines and advisers recommended, you would have watched your net worth drop—lots.

Then, as now, there is literally no person that can tell me they could stomach a 40 percent+ loss without having sleepless nights. That's the absurdity with many magazines saying, "don't worry, just ride it out. It will come back." Well, what happens if the market has been driven down during a period when you weren't paying attention and just when you needed money for your kids education or some medical emergency or you had just retired? DCA/MI doesn't help you there. The reality is literally every newscast through early 2003 has had interviews with retirees that have lost up to 60 percent+ of their retirement funds and were having to rethink when to retire, where, how much they can spend and so on. I think that younger consumers are also facing some very tough financial situations as well—you just don't hear about them as much. Mindless DCA or MI is not good investing.

The following is a real-life story that addresses two problems at once: no continued involvement in the investment process and the use of a single stock under DCA/MI. My sister's husband, George, worked at Digital for many years. He bought Digital stock frequently at special Digital prices, using DCA/MI all the time. The stock went from around $20 a share up to a peak of $200.

No one paid any attention when it went up, except to note how much money they "made," and unfortunately they didn't pay any attention when it went down—and down and down. Well, you get the point. George died of a massive heart attack many years ago. I had to value the stock at the date of death. It was $54 per share. (Value Line rating service rated it a D at that point.) That's almost a 75 percent drop. It went farther down from there to $16 a share, though it went up somewhat later on. My sister Mary was "out" over $80,000 because no one paid any attention to the economy or the potential, or lack thereof, of the company. Past research shows that a company that goes that far down, generally goes down for a reason (it sucks) and will seldom reach its previous stature. Digital never got back to the old glory days—it was sold.

Many individuals are still doing this today, using single-issue stock that comprises almost all of their fortunes and purchased through no-brainer DCA/MI at work. (Fortunately, this practice has gone down immeasurably since the Enron fiasco, but it still takes place.) It's obvious what happened in the Digital situation—a direct contradiction to diversification and a direct contradiction to following economics. There was no monitoring of the investment and not a clue to economics. The real-life aspect for my sister is that the losses sustained by the use of DCA/MI could not be offset in her lifetime.

Note that DCA/MI means you invest during all periods. It looks "great" as the market is going up, as it did in the 1990s. But how did it fare from 2000 to 2002 when the market decided to tank? The point is that you do not invest when the economics are terrible.

This is where all the sophomoric teachings go astray. If you are unconcerned about your money—or believe those who say you can leave you money in "forever" or rebalance every three or five years (Schwab)—then you may be destined for emotional distress and financial insecurity. Starting in mid 2000 and through the early part of 2003, I opted to keep almost all new monies *out* of equities. For those needing or wanting to do something other than what a 1.3 percent that a bank account would provide, I invested mainly in short- and medium-term no load bond funds. Whatever the returns were, they sure beat losing money for two years. And the clients were (obviously) happy and slept well.

There was is just no way that any astute person could demonstrate to me a viable position to put any significant money into the stock market during that period. (An astute person is someone who knows diversification by the numbers. Well, that just about excludes everybody on TV and all that write articles.) There was no viable written evidence that the market was primed for a movement upwards after the tech crash. For those suggesting otherwise, you must also have read the reports from the FED. These are required reading for critical analysis of the market. I admit that few advisers read these, and even fewer consumers. But that is what investing is really like, not one hour a night at the Motley Fool chat rooms. I don't care if you have a lump sum or are doing miscellaneous amounts over time—say for 401(k)'s and even IRA's. If the economy is just plain against the market and going down further, it is complete folly to throw money into losing propositions.

But is there any viability to some form of DCA? Yes—in a down market. See what I have to say about that in the section "Dollar-Cost Averaging Down: The Simple Way to Avoid Losses."

In summation, if you have a lump sum and are totally naïve to the marketplace, DCA may lower the psychological and statistical risk of investing but it almost unquestionably will result in lower returns. That's a risk in itself.

Both DCA and MI are hands-off/no-brainer investments that, left unchecked, could also lead to irresponsible investment decisions.

If you are well read, specifically in reference to economics, the use of DCA and MI is not particularly valid. Statistically, DCA has not worked in the past, does not work today, and will never work effectively in the future.

Yield Curve and the Impact on Economics and the Market

Yield and the *yield curve* are important topics that are tied in closely to economic analysis. The following paragraphs explain some basics about economic rates that you should understand.

Short-term rates are lower than long term rates. That's because the longer the maturity, the greater the risk, because so much more can go wrong.

At times the yield curve is inverted. An *inverted yield curve* means that the short-term rates are higher than long-term rates. When this happens, there is tremendous uncertainty in the economy. Something has to change big time for the trend to be reversed and the economy running smoothly.

Inverted Yield Curve Charts

An inverted yield curve eventually must return to normal: Either long-term rates must increase or short-term rates must decrease. Regardless, this type of a yield curve is an excellent predictor of a possible recession because the economy is in such turmoil (Figs. 4.1, 4.2, 4.3).

That is exactly what happened several years ago at the beginning of 2000. I commented on this at length at my site and noted that we were in store for a significant economic and market uncertainty. So, did you see any warning of an inverted yield curve and rocky economic times ahead highlighted in your company's 401(k) educational material? In the local newspaper? By your adviser or broker? The answer is, systematically, no. Hence, the reason so much money was lost by so many people.

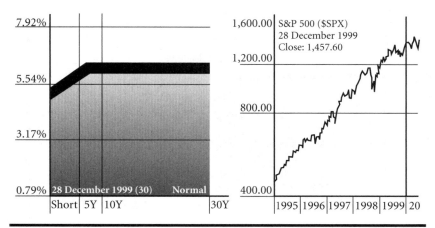

Figure 4.1   Yield curve for December 28, 1999.

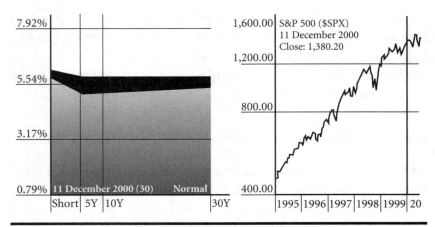

Figure 4.2   Yield curve for December 11, 2000.

Clearly, yield is not the only datum that has to be addressed and analyzed in order to get a good picture of the economy. Among the other factors to consider are productivity, unemployment rate, trade deficit, the Federal Reserve Beige Book (reports about economic conditions, published eight times per year), and GDP. Each factor needs to be examined with the others, to get some feel for the direction of the

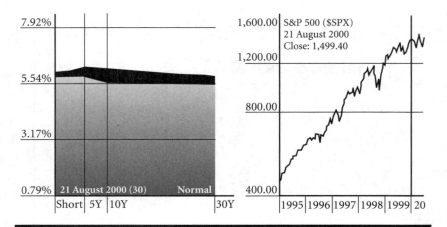

Figure 4.3   Yield curve for August 21, 2000.

economy. Then, and only then, do you start to match it with the standard statistical data about which you can find lots of information in every textbook and every Web site on investing. It's hard and intensive reading that few attempt. But if you do not master the fundamentals, you simply cannot do allocation correctly.

Asset Allocation

Many people tout *asset allocation* as a simple formula that can be derived from some 10-question sophomoric questionnaire. Absolute bunk! Determining allocation cannot be done without a budget and asset analysis in almost all cases—certainly for those age 50 and up—and it should never be done without the inclusion of economic data. There's a lot more to asset allocation than plugging some numbers into a software program. Asset allocation must be adjusted as an individual's situation changes, and it can be difficult to pin down the correct allocation for any one person. Life keeps changing. You adjust as necessary. The same thing happens with your investments.

Asset allocation is not an easy concept to grasp. Thoroughly understanding it will take time. To reach that point, you may need to spend money and hire someone who does understand the nuances. But here is the point. Have you lost 30 percent, 40 percent, 50 percent or more since 2000? Did you lose it yourself or did you use an adviser? The use of dollar cost averaging down and a bit of homework would have saved investors billions of dollars. And an understanding of essential economics will help you get back in to the markets with at least a bit of confidence.

Monte Carlo Simulations: Let's Be Careful Out There

An equally important statistical gauge to future prosperity (or not) is a technique called *Monte Carlo simulation*. Like standard deviation, which we discussed in Chapter 1, Monte Carlo is a fundamental that must be recognized for its implications to future growth.

The name Monte Carlo may be synonymous with the statistical odds of success such as happens in gambling. A Monte Carlo simulation is a statistical technique by which a quantity is calculated repeatedly, using randomly selected "what-if" scenarios for each calculation. The results approximate the full range of possible outcomes, and the likelihood of each happening, as shown in Figure 4.4.

In Figure 4.4, the solid line represents a return in the future from a fixed-rate investment. All the other lines represent the returns that you might expect from an equities investment. It represents a 6.12 percent average return, with a standard deviation of 8 percent. It means that in 95 percent of the time, the returns will fall between –9.18 percent and +22.82 percent. The chart may look like a rat's nest, but clearly lots of various outcomes can be projected. You can see that over 25-, 30-, and 35-year periods

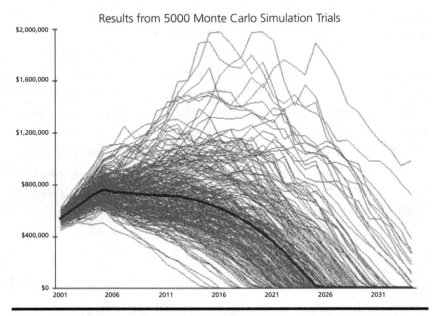

Figure 4.4   Monte Carlo retirement simulation.

many opportunities exist for making huge amounts of money—as well as running out of money in a short time frame. Now, of course, the extreme limits would be very rare occurrences, but the odds do exist and, hence, those situations must be dealt with should the economic scenarios present themselves (as they did in 1973/74 and in 2000 and 2002).

These limits we see in Monte Carlo simulations are the same extremes we see in standard deviation. Extreme gains might be possible, which is why so many people buy lottery tickets, and extreme losses are also possible. Human nature being what it is, however, few people ever dwell on their chances to incur big losses. Most of us just don't perceive ourselves as so unlucky or incompetent to select investments that would tank. This thinking is, of course, a fallacy, which I will prove shortly.

These extreme odds of investment statistical history are not evident in standard linear spreadsheet analysis using, say, an 8 percent return over a 25-year period. (See the retirement section in Chapter 13 for a full analysis of the fallacy of this type of planning.) Without the aid of Monte Carlo simulation or a similar analysis, a spreadsheet model will only reveal a single outcome, generally the most likely or average scenario. Specifically, it avoids the possibility of the losses that can occur.

Let's take a look how Monte Carlo will impact retirement spending and assets. Once again, purely linear projections are quite useless, because the odds exist that a bad market can reduce the asset base to zero well before an actuarial lifetime, and those projections rarely uncover those odds.

Figure 4.5 shows 8.49 percent returns, with a standard deviation of 6.2 percent. The software ran 5000 different combinations of returns. You can see that the possibility is there for very high returns as well as an asset base going to zero in a relatively short time frame.

Does anyone care? Are planners incorporating Monte Carlo simulations in their projections, specifically as it may relate to retirement?

A survey in late 2000 by a Financial Planning Interactive poll noted: "The majority of financial planners prefer standard asset allocation over Monte Carlo simulation when structuring a client's portfolio. In short, 60

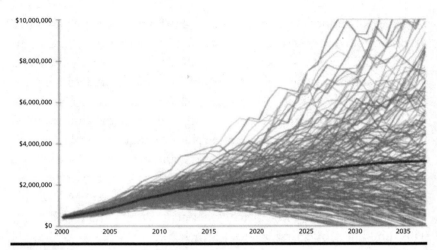

Figure 4.5   Monte Carlo simulation results.

percent of respondents said they use standard asset allocation and 13 percent said they prefer Monte Carlo. Thirty-one respondents, or 26 percent, said they use both methods."

If 60 percent of planners are simply using standard asset allocation packages without addressing the real issue of randomness and, more significantly, of a potential negative return, they are ignoring a significant caveat to long-term investing by not reflecting that you may have far less money than anticipated. Retirees should know and recognize that the projections of basic software allocations (almost all calculators on the Web) may not even come close to providing factual projections because they omit what can go wrong. Further, and an item that will be discussed more fully, few asset allocation projections actually tell you what to do—or, worse, they provide static advice that will wreak havoc with your investments and your life.

Limitations of Monte Carlo Simulations

A Monte Carlo simulation is unquestionably a viable investing tool. But it needs to be able to address what is happening to the market right now or what might happen to the market in the future based on economics and what you need to do about the situation. Without that capability, Monte Carlo is, perhaps, nothing more than a theoretical treatise on random numbers with little or no real-life application. Suppose a planner runs a Monte Carlo simulation that indicates that something negative might happen but offers no indication or insight into how to limit the financial impact. The simulation provides the consumer little benefit.

Some allocators effectively dismiss the importance of pointing out negative possibilities and how to handle them. They state, as they do at almost all Web sites, that you should simply "stay the course" because the market has "always" come back. Well, that is true overall, but it doesn't have to come back in your lifetime. Asset allocation and buy and hold doesn't necessarily hold water when it comes to the real lives and real life spans of most investors.

All that said, I tend to use a static projection of, say 7 percent, when I do my various analyses, though I also provide a couple of ranges of both returns and anticipated inflation (see Chapter 13 for more insight). However, every single report I create also contains cautions regarding the kinds of losses suffered during the market crash of 1973–1974 (and now 2000–2002). Every investor should be able to understand and recognize this period, because it reflects Monte Carlo returns at its worst. In just that short two-year period of 73/74, investors lost over 45 percent. In 1973 a loss of 17.37 percent was posted, and 1974 posted a loss of 29.72 percent. The statement that the market will always comes back misses the real-life emotional element in that there is hardly a person alive who could stomach a 45 percent loss of hard-earned assets in such a short period of time and still be able to sleep at night. Or still retain a marriage or other personal relationships; or provide for adequate distributions to beneficiaries if they should die before the market rebounds; or possibly retain a business; provide monies for your child's education; or retire well or even at all.

True, the market came back. But consider this: If you retired in 1972, you would have lost a significant portion of your retirement funds immediately and would, subsequently, never have been able to live the lifestyle you anticipated. Why's that? Because you were continually draining your retirement account by your annual budget and leaving far fewer funds to appreciate into the future. The impact would not have been quite as severe if it happened in the last 10 years of your retirement, but it would be severe nonetheless and would cause financial havoc.

What if you had stayed the course? Well, it took about 12 years to break even after that stock market crash, finally returning what you could have earned on present value had you just invested in Treasuries. By staying the course you would have suffered great emotional and psychological pain and financial devastation. Admittedly, the resurgence of the current market cannot be dismissed and utilized. But if you had already lost 40% or more of your funds and had already spent several thousands of dollars of your principal in 2000–2002, it will take a VERY long time to get back to where you were. Such optimism is not justified by the analysis of company profits.

Monte Carlo simulations are important to clients since they illustrate a real-world element (losses) far removed from most of the 1985–2000 market heyday. But Monte Carlo has its limitations. What is needed is not only to recognize that no software with Monte Carlo or any other type of computer projection tells you when to make portfolio adjustments necessary to alleviate the kind of losses that no reasonable person could sustain (and certainly losses that would devastate retirees). Learning after the fact that you lost 45 percent+ and that a Monte Carlo simulation was correct in showing that things could really be bad is irrelevant. You do need to recognize that severe losses happen. More importantly, you need the insight to know what to do either before the downslide happens or certainly while the market is in its initial stage of turning down significantly.

Dollar-Cost Averaging Down:
The Simple Way to Avoid Losses

Sometimes no defense is available for massive overnight drops in the market. Sudden and sharp drops in the stock market, such as the notorious October 1987 decline, are usually anomalies. Normally, sufficient and adequate notice of impending problems is given in national and international economic bulletins by the Federal Reserve. So, if you conduct regular economic analysis and do your homework, you can see clues that changes in the markets lie ahead (for example, the inverted yield curve).

If you are not reading the economic criteria from the Federal Reserve, your financial adviser must. There is no excuse, no rationalization, no nothing for the lack of reading. It is fundamental to investment success. Economic analysis is key.

Dollar-cost averaging is a term that's bandied about ad nauseam as the Holy Grail of investment success. As addressed above, the term is misdefined and generally doesn't work. Nevertheless, what I call *dollar-cost averaging down*, or DCAD, is an excellent tool to use in a down market. This technique is rarely used, which is unfortunate, as it could have saved retirees billions of dollars over the last few years. (Actually a journalist said of my material "you could have saved Enron employees billions of dollars"!) How does DCAD work? It starts with basic asset allocation. (For more on asset allocation and the investment pyramid, see Chapter 6.)

Asset allocation needs to be conceived in terms of an *investment pyramid*. (For more on this pyramid, see Chapter 6.) Let's assume that you have put conservative assets at the bottom, or foundation, of your investment pyramid, and more aggressive assets at the top. Now, suppose you have watched, or read, the economic situation slowly deteriorate so that it is working against you. Finally, you determine that the downturn you are experiencing is not necessarily a correction. (Note: A correction is a down move no more than about 10 percent to 15 percent. Personally, I tend to focus on 10 percent.) Rather than the more mild correction, such a downward slide may signal a recession.

You must not panic and react emotionally. You must not sell everything. But as things turn worse, you should start to sell your smaller, more risky investments first, perhaps after the initial 10 percent loss, as the markets head downward toward 15 percent. As the market drop continues from 15 percent to 20 percent, you have economic cause to adjust your portfolio further. Maybe you should sell all your risky assets. And if markets continue below losses of 20 percent, you should take a long, hard look at where the market may go so that you do not suffer any more than a 25 percent overall loss in equities for whatever time remains before a recovery. This is the basis of DCAD.

With regular dollar-cost averaging, or DCA, investors are taught to invest a set amount on, say, a regular, monthly basis irrespective of the market's movement up or down. Supposedly, the purchase of stocks at the lowest price is a purchase at a bargain sale. Oh, really? Admittedly, the market does not slide often as precipitously as it did in 1973–1974 or 2000–2002, but when it does, the money that continues to be invested drops in value more and more. And each subsequent investment also drops more and more. It is a fool's game to continue to drop more money into a losing venture—by that I mean an economy that is sliding further into recession.

DCAD, on the other hand, helps you reduce your exposure when markets slide, keeping the level of risk at an acceptable level in order to limit your losses. (Take specific note to my words, "level of risk." You are not trying to time the market for returns. You are adjusting the assets to reflect higher and lower risk, as applicable.) You not only reduce your holdings of equities (and more), but you also do not invest more monies into the sinking economy and market. I certainly admit it takes more time, energy, and reading for this effort. But I ask you, wouldn't it be worth it compared to a 40 percent, 50 percent, or more loss?

There is no hard and fast rule about when to adjust your portfolio since there are innumerable variables from person to person and from situation to situation. But the concept of averaging down your holdings during down markets is valid. That technique will not shelter against all losses—nothing really does. But it does provide a logical way to limit exposure to the kind of horrifying losses we saw in the 1973–1974 markets. It's what I did starting after March 2000, when technology bit the dust. And it kept my clients from the subsequent significant losses and emotional strife.

DCAD surely would have worked for almost all 401(k) and other retirement plans from mid 2000 forward. It would have saved retirees billions of dollars. Admittedly, the main problem when it comes to reducing exposure is understanding the implications of economics and its impact on the market. (I never said this was going to be easy.) But DCAD is about as straightforward a procedure as you are apt to find anyplace.

Rebalancing

One thing you should know about *rebalancing* is that it actually can increase risk. This section dovetails with a lot of the comments about static asset allocation, Dollar Cost Averaging and other unintelligent rules of thumb when used fatuously (big word). In essence, this technique involves adjusting your portfolio each year (although other longer time frames may be valid) back to the same allocation percentage that you started with at the beginning of the year.

True, a client's *personal* risk scenario might have changed during the course of a year (for example, because of death or divorce) and the allocation needs to be adjusted accordingly to reflect the new situation. But my example will address no such personal adjustments—simply the fact that the internal positions have gone up and down. For example, assume you started with an allocation of 70 percent stocks and 30 percent bonds. Over the year, the stocks went down to 50 percent of the value you bought it at, which is a situation similar to the ones we have seen most recently. Rebalancing simply would have you sell some of the bonds and buy 20 percent more equities to balance out the "proper" allocation back to 70/30. The philosophy is that you are buying back certain investments at a lower cost—in this case, the equities—and that they will increase in value in short order. The theory can look statistically sound when you look at returns over long periods of time. Unfortunately, the volatility in the real-life interim can make theory look ugly.

Here is the real-life essence. As stated, asset allocation generally starts with some software models. The software is based on historical averages. And, historically, equities have provided the bulk of the returns (as compared to bonds or other assets for example). Also note that computer software has not been around that long. So, it has tended, in some of the internal formulas, to rely more heavily on the more recent history of the 1980s and 1990s, where everything blossomed. Further, software does not monitor economics, the budget deficit, the Iraq War, or any of the real-life elements impacting the current movements of the market. My point being, once again, that rebalancing, as practiced by the bulk of planners and advisers, will utilize the formulaic static approach.

Admittedly, a 20 percent or more loss in such a short time is unusual. But with the billions of dollars of losses sustained by Middle America most recently, I submit that such poor, inadequate, and ineffective counseling without an adequate reflection of past history (for example, 1973–1974) is the reason for the majority of sorrows. Yes, some losses are almost preordained with such a drop, but the sustained position was unnecessary.

Consider the accumulated losses of the S&P 500 over the three years, as shown in Table 4.3 (including dividends).

Table 4.3   Losses of the S&P 500

Year	Losses
2000	9.1%
2001	11.9%
2002	22.1%

Say you started with $100,000 in the S&P 500 at the beginning of 2000. You lost 9 percent (round numbers) in 2000. Now you are at $91,000. Next year, you lose 12 percent and are down to $80,000. And you are still told to stay in the market *because it will come back*. In fact, if you were doing rebalancing, you would be putting *more* money into a market and an economy that was sucking gas big time. But we'll just leave it at $80,000 at the beginning of 2002. But now you are down *another* 22 percent at the end of 2002 to $62,500. So in three years, you are down about 40 percent overall in your equities.

Do you know what percentage you have to earn to get back to break even? You would need 61.6 percent. I hate to tell you folks, but the odds of high returns similar to the 1990s, just to get you back to where you started with, just ain't gonna happen. We are in a new period where growth is anticipated to be much lower (though I recognize the significant returns as of late 2003). We are not going to have another market loss in 2003—that would have been four years in a row and it has been seven decades since that happened. That said, it did happen before and there is no reason to suggest that it could not happen again. It's just pure numbers. It is a statistical fact. That an adviser was not taught past history, the ability to interpret the data, or the understanding of why it was so important does not release the adviser from the fiduciary duty of addressing such obstacles.

But the losses are even worse with rebalancing. It's not just the fact that money was left to continually lose. It is the fact that, if someone rebalanced a portfolio to maintain a specific risk profile, then more money was introduced into the market while the world fell apart.

Let's review another portfolio of 70 percent stocks and 30 percent bonds starting in 2000. The 70 percent of equities might have half of that in large-cap funds, 20 percent in small-cap funds, and 15 percent in something else. The same with the bond section. But I will just use the S&P 500 for the equities.

Let's assume there was $100,000 total in the portfolio at the beginning of 2000, with $70,000 in equities. At the end of 2000, stocks were down 9.1 percent. So the equity side dropped $6370. I'll assume the bond side stayed stable. The essence was that the equity side was now too low and you would have had to *buy* another $6370 of stocks/funds to get back up to the 70/30 split. So, now what happens in 2001? The S&P loses another 12 percent—and as should be obvious, so does the inclusion of the new $6370. Now the equity side is now down by $8400. Because you are using the standard rebalancing format, you have to buy $8400 more stock/funds to build yourself up again. Now go through 2002. The S&P dropped another 22 percent, and your $70,000 is now down another $15,400. You go out and buy another $15,400 of stock/funds to get back to the position of equity and risk that your adviser had indicated was necessary or appropriate for your financial situation.

Does this make any rational sense? Why would anyone put more money into an inherently bad economy? Simple. That person had been led to believe that the best allocation was one that stayed the course (no change) or to rebalance (normally) at the end of one year (if that). But it should be perfectly clear that if you do so in an economy that is tanking, your risk of loss gets *greater*, because you are committing funds at the worst possible time.

Now pundits will say that it is impossible to know when the economy is bad. I'll admit that it is not easy, that it takes a lot of reading, that it requires a background greater than some simplistic designation, certainly far more than the nil insight by brokers, that you have to read material from the FED and so on. So be it—some things are simply hard to do. If you were attempting to do this by yourself and did not commit the necessary effort, there's not much I can say except, "sorry you lost so much money." That you were not unlike hundreds of thousands of others may grant you some solace but it won't help your pocketbook. Asset allocation is not easy simply because the market does not react perfectly with theory. Yes, over many a year—perhaps far longer than you will live—the volatility will smooth out. But in the shorter time frame, life can stink.

You will find that very few advisers did little but follow industry marketing of staying the course, basic rebalancing, and static allocation. Some advisers did make adjustments, and those folks will be able to provide written documentation of what was done and why. Verbal documentation is not acceptable. Find out why they made the adjustments and perhaps they can lead you forward.

Summary

While asset allocation and buy and hold are of questionable real-life value, economic analysis, Monte Carlo simulations, and dollar-cost averaging down are tools that can have proven benefits, especially when it comes to limiting losses in down markets. But you can't limit losses in any market if you don't do your homework. Standard deviation, risk, suitability, economic analysis—all of these concepts are key in protecting you from losing your retirement assets. Of course, you also have to know how to structure a portfolio that matches all of your needs. That is the subject we'll turn to next.

CHAPTER 5

BASIS

*B*ASIS IS ONE OF THE KEY ELEMENTS of financial planning, investments, real estate, estate considerations, and 401(k) plans that literally impacts *every* major asset or investment you will purchase in your entire life. Once in a while it is addressed in some classes or textbooks but the text rarely brings the real life element into play. And when you analyze the following commentary, it will also be clear why the vast majority of trusts and wills are universally drawn up incorrectly, since the distributions of NET property are not necessarily what the deceased really wanted. Once again I repeat—never do any planning including estate documents with anyone without assuring yourself that they have personal competency with a financial calculator. NEVER!

The reason that this is important is this—does any difference in money cause problems between family members? Oh, golly gee, of course not. Am I kidding??? According to AARP, of people over 50, 20% said that a will or lack of one had caused hard feelings among family members. Most involved money but 47% fought over jewelry and heirlooms, 43% over a house, 31% about other real estate and 11% about investments. Most thought a particular division of property was probably brought on by one of the kids to benefit them at the expense of another. The distribution of assets upon death is one of the most contentious issues any family can face. While the apparent problem looks like value of the asset being transferred, it is even worse when you calculate the net value after taxes.

Let me give you a quick basics of basis. I'll just do gains here. Assume you bought a stock for $25. It appreciated to $100 in six months and you sold it. How are you taxed? The original $25 was already taxed so only the $75 gain will be taxed. And if the gain was made in less than a year, it is taxed as ordinary income. If you were in the 30% bracket (including state tax), $22.50 will be spent on taxes. The net amount left would be $77.50. If the gain took longer than a year, it is taxed at 20% (or lower in some cases) so you only "lose" $15 to taxes and net $85.00. Now, I cannot demonstrate everything that I do in a regular class since it gets too involved. But I have provided sufficient notes and the essence should be clear enough with the table below. First, in order to do this, I need to make clear some facts and assumptions. In 2003, the amount a single person can gift/leave to beneficiaries is $1,000,000. No estate taxes are imposed on amounts less than that. The maximum deduction is going up to an unlimited amount in 2010. The example I use has eight investments. I will pretend that dad can leave an $800,000 estate tax free (it just makes it easier to use $100,000 for each of eight children). Dad has set up accounts with certain kids as different beneficiaries on specific accounts or has directed the assets to be distributed by will/trust. But neither he nor anyone else, quite obviously, has checked whether equal net amounts, after income tax, will actually result. Third, all income tax, where applicable, is a flat 30% and all capital gains is 20%.

Child/Asset Inherited	Investment Detail—each currently valued at $100,000	Net to Dad while alive	Net after tax received by beneficiary upon dad's death
Jim—Standard Annuity	$25,000 initial investment by Dad. $75,000 tax deferred growth	$77,500— see A.	$77,500—see B.

(continued on next page)

Child/Asset Inherited	Investment Detail—each currently valued at $100,000	Net to Dad while alive	Net after tax received by beneficiary upon dad's death
Susie—Life Insurance	$25,000 initial investment in a universal life policy. Cash value at $50,000	$50,000 no tax. See C.	$100,000. See D.
Bob—Fully tax deferred retirement accounts. 403(b), 401(k), IRA etc.	$25,000 was "invested," but never taxed.	Entire amount would be taxable leaving $70,000	Bob receives the same tax treatment as dad and nets $70,000. See E.
Mary—Non-deductible IRA	$25,000 initial investment. $75,000 tax deferred growth	$77,500. See F.	$77,500. See G.
Brad—ROTH IRA	$25,000 invested	Assuming certain requirements are met, the full $100,000 is not taxed	Brad receives the full $100,000 with no tax. See H.
Ellen—Mutual fund NOT in a retirement account	$25,000 invested but with $2,000 in dividends and $3,000 in capital gains distributions over the years.	$86,000. See I.	$100,000. See J.
Fido—Real estate (assume small rental)	$25,000 invested.	Say $81,000 but you will need to see note K.	$100,000. See L.
Muffy— Personal home	$25,000 invested	$85,000. See note M.	$100,000. See N.

A. (Standard Annuity) If dad were to sell out the entire $100,000, the first $25,000 has already been taxed. The $75,000 of earnings is reduced by the 30% income tax to equal $57,500. Add in the original $25,000 for a total of $77,500.

As additional commentary, if dad had taken out various amounts over different times (say $10,000 in one year, $22,371 in the next year and so on), all monies up to the tax deferred amount of $75,000 would have been taxed as ordinary income. Only when the last $25,000 is removed is there no tax since it has already been taxed.

Lastly, if dad had taken out the entire amount over his actuarial lifetime, part would have been taxable and part would have been a return of his original investment. Assume he got $1,000 per month. Perhaps $750 would have been taxed and the other $250 not taxed.

B. Jim receives the same tax treatment as dad. As such, his $100,000 is impacted by taxes. Admittedly, it is not necessary that Jim actually take the money out and he could leave it to grow. But the taxes are imbedded in the account and they need to be addressed.

C. (Life Insurance) You are able to take a loan on most policies without incurring tax IF the policy remains intact. I have made that assumption. However, if dad let the policy lapse, the earnings, over the initial investment, become taxable as ordinary income. $50,000 total cash minus $25,000 in premium payments would have created a $25,000 taxable event at the 30% assumed ordinary income tax bracket.

D. Susie got the full policy since no loans had been taken out. It is NOT taxed. If dad had actually had an existing $25,000 loan, Susie would have received a net $75,000 ($100,000 – $25,000).

Think about this without even proceeding further. Do some people have just two kids and own just an annuity and life insurance? Absolutely! Does dad think he has treated each equally? Absolutely, and it is his intent to make sure no one is treated differently. But Jim just found out that Susie will end up netting $22,500 more. Does Jim care? Of course not. Money never is an issue when a parent dies. Are you kidding! If the difference was just $50, Jim would still be 'bent'. Differences of just a few dollars between siblings can lead to animosity between families for years.

Let's also assume that Jim wants Susie to give him money to equalize the estate. After all, "it's what dad wanted". Susie would have to give Jim $11,250. Well, it may happen but let's get real. Susie's husband never liked Jim (maybe Susie didn't either). Or Jim is an alcoholic, bum, whatever. But even if Susie did give Jim the money, did it end up equal? No. You can only give $11,000 to each person per year (though it is indexed by inflation). If you give more than that, you have to file a report to the IRS. She will have to pay a CPA for the completion of the report. And Susie will have to reduce her lifetime exemption by $250. The amount is insignificant, but the process and emotional turmoil can be enormous.

This whole scenario is a huge mess that dad obviously never intended. But good intentions won't help his children now. And these two families could be at each other's throats for years. And one or both will never forgive dad for his thoughtlessness.

E. (Tax Deferred Retirement Plan) Obviously Bob is madder than Jim and is even more mad at dad because he has received $30,000 less than Susie. Just imagine the emotion. (As a separate commentary, some of these retirement accounts can include some taxable positions, but that is beyond the scope of this work.)

F. A non-deductible IRA works the same way as a standard annuity. You don't get a deduction for the contribution but the earnings grow tax free. (See note A above.)

G. As with a standard annuity, the tax repercussions are the same for the beneficiary as for the original owner.

H. ROTH IRA's were designed to negate any taxes as well as requirements for distribution later in life. Many people use these and they are not unusual.

I. (Mutual Fund) Most people might think that the amount that becomes taxable is the $100,000 minus the original invested amount of $25,000. Not so. Dividends are normally distributed to a fund. But even if the dividends are reinvested, they are taxable (called constructive receipt). How do you know how much they are? You will get a 1099 each year. Capital gains are only distributed once per year. Taxes will be applied, though some might be long term capital gains and some short term capital gains. You also know the amount by the 1099.

As a second part to the computation, assume you hold a fund for over a year. You get long term capital gains rates at 20% (sometimes even lower, but I will not delve into that further). The 20% would be applied to the $70,000 leaving $56,000 net. Add in the $30,000 already taxed for a total of $86,000.

J. Ever heard of a step up in basis at death? Certain assets—but generally none in a non-taxable retirement account—are allowed by the IRS to increase the taxable basis upon the date of death. (There are certain exceptions but they are wwaaaaayyyyyy beyond the scope of this text.) So Ellen gets the full mutual fund with a new basis of $100,000 and can sell it all with NO tax.

K. (Rental Real Estate) This is a little involved. Rental real estate must be depreciated. But you can't depreciate the full $25,000 purchase price since part of the purchase price includes land. Land cannot be depreciated (and as with every thing else in the tax code, there are exceptions). Assume land was $5,000 and the remaining $20,000 was depreciated down to $10,000. That means the new basis is the $10,000 for the building plus $15,000 for the land. Subtract from the $100,000 sales price and tax the remaining $85,000 gain at 20% long term capital gains. That leaves a net $68,000. Add in the $15,000 basis for a total of $81,000.

L. A full step up in basis at the date of death to $100,000.

M. A personal home retains its existing basis—there is no depreciation allowed. (The basis can be adjusted if you add major improvements, but that is beyond the scope of this material.) The appreciation of $75,000 is taxed at long term capital gains rates for a 'loss' of taxes of $15,000. Total net received is $85,000.

N. A full step up in basis at the date of death to $100,000. Not bad for a pussy cat.

Summary

Look at all the assets and you will clearly note that none is unique or unusual. And while an individual dad/mom might not have all, many would have combinations of several of these. But here is the added part of the problem. Annuities, IRA's—in fact all of these assets—may have named beneficiaries by contract. As such, they may never be controlled by a will or trust since the assets have already passed to the named beneficiary. Here is my point. Assume you own a life insurance contract. You named a beneficiary on the policy. Say it goes to your daughter. Later on you attempt to make me the beneficiary through your will (bless you). But it will make no difference (darn) since a will cannot override the contract. Do annuities "require" named beneficiaries? How about 403(b), 401(k)s, IRAs? Can you name your son as a joint tenant on your home, rental condo, mutual fund? Yes, yes and yes— all can have named beneficiaries. And unless someone (the attorney preparing the will or trust) identifies each and every asset separately with its specific basis and tax ramifications, there will invariably be different net assets to each beneficiary that can leave a legacy of animosity for generations.

Someone better do some homework and someone better get a calculator.

Never do any financial or estate planning with anyone who does not have competency with a financial calculator. And every adviser should address basis at some point in the investment selection process. You need to take this issue to your attorney and request a table be set up in the same manner as above. If they cannot do this simplistically, walk away. You may also ask this of your planner. Surprisingly, the essential concept will probably be unfamiliar since there has never been a real life application applied in all the instruction I have seen so far. But if they can't do it so it makes sense, walk away. Keep looking for an adviser.

CHAPTER 6

THE PYRAMID OF INVESTING

*I*N THE LAST CHAPTER, we focused on the cornerstones of investing. We also touched on the pyramid of investing. The pyramid is a useful tool (used too rarely), which helps investors focus on those assets that should form the foundation of their portfolios and all the way up to those assets which should comprise only a small portions, if any, of their portfolios.

This pyramid (see Figure 6.1) was designed for the average middle-income American family. Certain categories may change over time in terms of appropriateness, but the overall structure provides a good, basic guideline for creating a portfolio. I'm sure that some analysts or financial advisers may wish to upgrade or downgrade some elements in an individual's particular pyramid based on current standard deviation, the Sharpe Ratio or other volatility or risk/return formulas, but, for the most part, the pyramid offers, at the very least, a good starting point.

Some caveats are associated with each of the areas within the pyramid. We will take a look at the various categories in this chapter, and you should review them carefully in order to understand the nuances of the various assets that make up the pyramid. Additionally, there are slight variations in the investment mix for various age groups: More

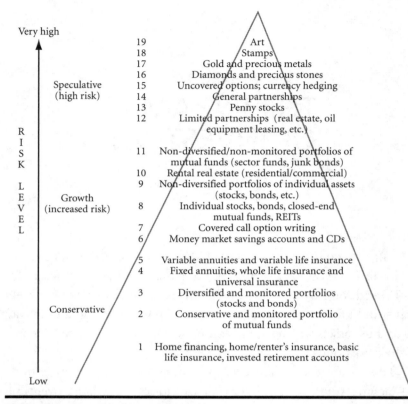

Very high

	19	Art
	18	Stamps
Speculative	17	Gold and precious metals
(high risk)	16	Diamonds and precious stones
	15	Uncovered options; currency hedging
	14	General partnerships
	13	Penny stocks
	12	Limited partnerships (real estate, oil equipment leasing, etc.)

	11	Non-diversified/non-monitored portfolios of mutual funds (sector funds, junk bonds)
	10	Rental real estate (residential/commercial)
Growth	9	Non-diversified portfolios of individual assets (stocks, bonds, etc.)
(increased risk)	8	Individual stocks, bonds, closed-end mutual funds, REITs
	7	Covered call option writing
	6	Money market savings accounts and CDs

	5	Variable annuities and variable life insurance
	4	Fixed annuities, whole life insurance and universal insurance
	3	Diversified and monitored portfolios (stocks and bonds)
Conservative	2	Conservative and monitored portfolio of mutual funds
	1	Home financing, home/renter's insurance, basic life insurance, invested retirement accounts

RISK LEVEL

Low

Figure 6.1 Pyramid of investing.

aggressive portfolios (heavy on stock) are usually recommended for those who are younger or single, while more conservative (more bonds) portfolios are generally recommended for retirees.

That mixture or allocation is not cast in stone, however, and depends on many variables. One of the most significant variables I have already touched upon is an economic downturn, such as the one in the year 2000 and beyond. You don't expose yourself to horrendous market and economic conditions if all you are going to do is lose money.

As mentioned previously, investing at any level must start with a comprehensive, real-life budget (especially as you get closer to retirement) that addresses the individual's current and future needs. For example, suppose you need a lot of income during retirement and you have not amassed sufficient savings. You may have to take on "extra" risk, and adjust your personal pyramid, after age 65 to retain the lifestyle you want. All that said, you still need to take into account what can really go wrong, even in a properly diversified equities portfolio, and adjust your holdings as necessary. If you do not, then even your best investment pyramid can tumble.

The intent of the pyramid is to visually emphasize the basic risk-reward parameters of investing in various securities. *You should not invest in the more risky ventures until and unless you have covered the less risky areas first.* Clearly, you do not incorporate gold, precious metals, uncovered option writing, hedge funds or the use of single-issue securities into your portfolio until the more conservative issues have been addressed first, such as having enough insurance for your family and using basic index mutual funds. If you violate this basic rule, you are probably headed for an insecure future. Unfortunately, people often mistakenly believe they can safely put more risky assets into their investing portfolios before covering the bottom area of the pyramid.[1]

The Bottom of the Pyramid: The Foundation of Your Portfolio

At the bottom of the pyramid of investing, we see "Home, Basic Life Insurance Policies, and Invested Retirement Accounts." Let's first examine owning a home.

Home Ownership

Most people look forward to owning a home. Today, 68 percent of all American families own homes—the largest percentage ever. This number is an increase from 64 percent a decade ago. In late 2002, U.S. existing home sales were up 6.1 percent since October 2001, while the median home price rose 7.2 percent, to $161,800. That increase was due to the high-flying 1990s and the market euphoria that provided extra cash in consumer's pockets. It was also driven by the lower interest rates.

But a severe backlash has also occurred. As more layoffs have ensued, more people have lost the sources of income needed to continue to pay the mortgage. More mortgages than ever are now being foreclosed, and more homes repossessed.

Part of the problem is that mortgages were being doled out right and left—even if the borrowers weren't creditworthy. And, too, homeowners were overly optimistic about their financial well being as a result of the euphoria (or "irrational exuberance," take your pick) that swept the nation. As a result, people simply took on mortgages they couldn't handle. But they needn't have.

Let's assume you have an opportunity for a $150,000 mortgage, with a 15-year amortization at 7 percent. That's $1340 per month, principal and interest. Not a bad loan. And, let's say it looks good because you can pay off the loan faster than a 30-year mortgage and save thousands of dollars in interest. Sounds good. But, remember that each and every month, a payment of $1340 is due.

Assume instead that same loan amortized over 30 years. The monthly payment is $992. That's roughly a $350 per month "savings." If, for instance, you lost your job, would that $350 difference have saved your house from foreclosure? Or provided some relief from other financial issues? Or kept you from dipping into your savings account or rainy-day fund to pay your bills? Pick whatever scenario you want—there are countless ones. The fact is that overextending yourself on your mortgage (or other bills, for that matter) is the surest step to toppling the pyramid of investing.

Of course, detractors (that is, people who would argue against extending a mortgage) note that far more interest would be paid over 30 years than 15 years. True, but does it really matter? If the issue is paying off the loan faster, you could simply take the 30-year loan and pay an extra $350 per month with the mortgage payment whenever the extra cash was available. You effectively accomplish the same thing as taking out a 15-year mortgage, but you have the luxury of not being required to pay the extra money when your pocketbook is light. Additionally, having that extra $350 a month opens up all sorts of other planning and investment opportunities.[2]

Insurance Policies

We will examine basic life insurance policies separately in Chapter 11. But certain issues beyond life insurance require some explanation. In particular, disability insurance bears emphasis, because the statistical odds of becoming disabled during your working years are far greater than the odds of dying.

Disability Policies.   Table 6.1 details the odds of a person having at least one long-term disability that lasts three months or longer before that person reaches age 65. As you can see, the older you get, the more the odds are against you that a long-term disability will befall you.

Table 6.1   Odds of Long-Term Disability

Age	Probability of Long-Term Disability
25	44 to 1
30	42 to 1
35	41 to 1
40	39 to 1
45	36 to 1
50	33 to 1
55	27 to 1

Long-term disability of three or more months certainly would affect your finances, your psyche, your family, and a host of other things.

But the initial disability might not be the worst of it, or the end. According to the Table of Actuaries, the older you get, the slimmer your chances of recovery. Table 6.2 shows how many people have recovered, died, or remained disabled for five years after the onset of a disability.

Table 6.2 Recovery Rates from a Disability

Age at Onset of Disability	Recovered	Died	Still Disbled
24	44.1%	9.7	46.2
35	34.0	12.3	53.7
45	21.5	19.9	58.6
55	11.8	28.5	59.7

Overall, 18.7 percent of the working-age population ages 18 to 64 (32.1 million people) report a disability. Of these, severe disabilities have been reported by 8.7 percent (14.9 million); nonsevere disabilities account for the other 10 percent (17.2 million). Almost 20 percent of people ages 15 to 64 report some level of disability. Nearly two-thirds of all work disabilities are severe.

Per the Unum Provident Life and Accident Insurance Company, the leading cause of long-term disability (more than 90 days) for working-age Americans was cancer, according to claims submitted during 2001. Rounding out the Top 5 List for long-term disability (LTD) causes are pregnancy complications, back and cardiovascular conditions, and depression.[3]

Leading the list of Top 5 causes of short-term disability (STD) workplace absence for 2001 was pregnancy (normal), followed by complications from pregnancy, injuries (excluding back), back conditions, and digestive/intestinal conditions. See Table 6.3 for the causes of claims and the percentage received for each cause.

According to the *Disability Management Sourcebook*, the number of people between the ages of 17 and 44 with severe disabilities has

Table 6.3 Disability Claims

Long-term Disability	Cancer: 13%
	Complications from Pregnancy: 12%
	Back problems: 11 %
	Cardiovascular: 9%
	Depression: 5%
Short-term Disability	Normal Pregnancy: 9%
	Pregnancy with Complications: 9%
	Injuries (Excluding Back): 9%
	Digestive/Intestinal: 8%

increased 400 percent over the past 25 years. One in seven people will become disabled for five years or more before they reach age 65.

If so many people can suffer from long- or short-term disability, recovery rates are so dismal, and the effects of not being able to work have such an obvious effect on personal finances, why don't more people own disability coverage? Well, outside of employer coverage—which may be simply short term of less than one year—people simply do not like to be reminded of this type of morbidity. It's one thing to think about death—many couples at least feel some obligation for their spouse and, certainly, their children, and prepare a will and get life insurance accordingly. Furthermore, life insurance is relatively "cheap." Not so with disability insurance. It is expensive simply because the odds are so much greater for something going wrong—and the costs for care can go on for years and years, far outpacing the one-time cost for life insurance.

Also, the disability insurance contracts are a bear to read and understand. After all, when you are dead, you are dead. But disabilities come in many shades, and insurance companies come up with all sorts of legalese, nuances, and hoops to jump through that make it difficult for you to validate a problem. Then you have some companies that, supposedly, do not cover disability because they say things like the person is, in fact, not disabled and actually is at least able to work part time.

(UnumProvident, the largest provider of disability coverage in the United States, recently got tagged by some states for improprieties in denying coverage.) Nonetheless, although disability insurance is a hard sell, people would be well advised to cover for this contingency before moving on to other areas of the pyramid of investing.

Home Insurance Policies.   There are seven basic kinds of home insurance policies, and they are pretty much the same regardless of where you live, except for Texas. They tend to be defined by the perils they cover[4]:

> **HO-1: Basic homeowners.** This policy covers your dwelling and personal property against losses from 11 types of perils: fire or lightning; windstorm or hail; explosion; riot or civil commotion; aircraft; vehicles; smoke; vandalism or malicious mischief; theft; damage by glass or safety glazing material that is part of a building; and volcanic eruption.
>
> **HO-2: Basic homeowners, plus.** This policy covers dwelling and personal property against the basic 11 perils plus the following six more: falling objects; weight of ice, snow, or sleet; three categories of water-related damage from home utilities or appliances; and electrical surge damage.
>
> **HO-3: Extended or special homeowners.** This policy covers the 17 perils stated previously plus any other peril not specified in your policy, except for flood, earthquake, war, and nuclear accident.
>
> **HO-4: Renters coverage.** This policy covers only personal property from the 17 perils listed previously.
>
> **HO-5: All-risk coverage for building and personal property.** This policy form isn't sold very often anymore.
>
> **HO-6. Condominium coverage.** This policy covers personal property from the 17 perils listed previously along with certain building items in which the unit owner might have an insurance interest.

HO-8: Basic older home. This policy covers dwelling and personal property from the 11 perils covered in basic homeowners policies. It differs from HO-1 in that it covers repairs or actual cash values, not rebuilding costs. This type of policy is appropriate for a home whose historic or architectural aspects make its replacement cost significantly higher than its market value.

Policy Usage.   The chances of using your homeowners insurance are about 1 in 88, which are less than the odds of using your auto insurance, at about 1 in 47. In both cases, however, I suggest you consider higher liability coverage—probably $1,000,000—since exposure has been going up and up as attorneys have sued more and more.

As far as long-term care insurance is concerned, the odds for use are about 2 in 5. Admittedly, the elderly usually use these policies, but not always. For example, I have a friend who has early onset Alzheimer's at age 50. Long-term care coverage is essential for her. Further, about 40% of all patients in nursing homes are under the age of 60.

It's not possible to cover for every contingency, and some risk has to be assumed simply because you are alive. But coverage at the bottom of the investment pyramid is almost mandatory before you move up the ladder to more risky situations such as buying stocks.

Moving Up the Pyramid: Tax-Sheltered Growth

All that said, once you get beyond basic insurance coverage, you will need to address the various savings and growth elements that will be a part of your investment pyramid. (Savings does not mean putting money under your mattress. That's a waste of money and is discussed later.) There are many tax-sheltered opportunities that middle-income consumers can utilize before engaging in other investment products like variable annuities and variable life insurance.

For example, Individual Retirement Accounts, or IRAs, have been traditional investment vehicles that can offer tax-sheltered savings and even tax deductions, depending on income, in many different products. If your income is too high to qualify for a regular IRA, the Roth IRA allows tax-sheltered growth with no subsequent taxes. Such a deal! The downside has been the amounts that can be contributed, but those limits are expanding under current laws. Roth IRAs should be looked at closely as viable investments, since they offer an almost unlimited exposure to just about every worthwhile fund in existence.

Other tax-sheltered investment opportunities to look at generally include 401(k) plans or tax-sheltered annuities for nonprofits. The advantage of the 401(k) is that many companies provide some matching contribution, although the number has been declining recently because of poor company revenues. Hewitt Associates indicates that about 74 percent of employees with such plans participate in them. Well, for plans that still have some type of matching funds, employees should be participating close to 100 percent, at least to the amount that the company matches, because it's nigh onto impossible to make 100 percent on your money this easily. That said, literally every employee involved in such plans has been impacted negatively by the collapse of individual companies like Enron,[5] the market crash, and the subsequent huge losses sustained in their 401(k) plans.

The collapse of Enron affected 401(k) plans of its employees as well as others whose investments were tied up in funds that held Enron stock. Many Enron employees had company stock that made up the bulk of their 401(k) plans. Of course, that was bad diversification, but the fact is, many people didn't understand their 401(k) plans to begin with. Nor were they provided information that could help them.

In fact, just 22 percent of 141 companies surveyed by the Profit Sharing/401(k) Council of America said that they provided investment advice. Whether education is offered or not, plan administrators and employers have a duty to clearly inform employees that they could lose substantial funds for their retirement. Obviously, just trying to get employees to participate is not sufficient. Nor is simply showing a projected growth rate of x dollars in a 401(k) plan without noting that offsetting losses that could be sustained without the appropriate diversi-fication. The proper instruction involves some of the fundamentals of investing such as standard deviation and DCAD. You just can't provide an offset to the conventional defined-benefit plan (where the employer takes the risk) without adequate instructions on the internal machina-tions. It's irresponsible. It's unethical.

Unfortunately, even when employers and plan administrators offer "education," it is usually simplistic and inadequate at best and does not address such clear issues as single stock ownership. A 2002 *New York Times* article noted that investors in 401(k) plans hold an average of 32 percent of their assets in company stock when it is offered as an employer match or employee investment option. In reality, this means that most investors are way overexposed in their company's stock.

Most 401(k) plans have come a long way in terms of the kind of assets they can help generate for investors. But plan administrators have got a long way to go in terms of providing clear insightful and real-life knowledge to investors. New laws have been instituted that allow dissemination of more "education" to employees, but I am highly sus-pect it will be of much value. Without the fundamentals taught by instructors who themselves have not been taught the fundamentals, lit-tle benefit may befall employees.

The same comments are reflective of tax-sheltered annuities, offered through school districts, hospitals, and the like. Unlike 401(k) plans, TSAs employers do not offer any additional contributions. Like employ-ees investing in 401(k) plans, employees of nonprofits, I have found, are no better at investing than anyone else.

Such lack of knowledge, resulting in the loss of substantial retire-ment funds because of the recent recession and market decline, has rad-ically altered retirement plans. The Center for Retirement Research has noted a 2 percent rise in labor force participation among the elderly in 2002. That rise was usually directly attributable to shrinking retire-ment accounts. Retirees are having to go back to work because their retirement funds just aren't what they thought they would be. Tax-sheltered accounts—actually, any investment, no matter where I put it on the pyramid—still require the investor to undergo a formal thought process as to what an investment is and how it works in the first place. Just investing in something, someplace, without an insight (here I go again) to economics, can be fraught with risk.

Mutual Funds: A Key Part of the Pyramid

By definition, mutual funds are generally diversified (roughly having at least 50 randomly correlated stocks), but many people still miss the point of diversification. As we have discussed, diversification is not the same as asset allocation. For example, a gold fund may have 50 to 100 stocks and is diversified because it has spread the risk among a number of gold stocks. Nonetheless, it still has a higher level of risk than the market overall, because it is all still in gold. Mutual funds can help you build a portfolio that is well diversified across various asset classes, but you have to recognize the risks of the types of fund as well.

If you want a conservative fund, you might select a fund with a beta of 1.0 or less. For a more risky fund, you would look for a fund with a beta of more than 1.0. And always watch the standard deviation since it is a good reflection of risk and volatility. You need to continually monitor your portfolio by conducting consistent economic analysis and Monte Carlo simulation in order to gauge the markets. Monitoring is not just looking at your portfolio and rebalancing once per year. Once a year doesn't cut it when the market tanks.

Diversified Individual Stock and Bond Portfolios

The use of individual stocks and bonds is more risky than mutual funds, particularly if you attempt to do the selection yourself. You can tell that individual securities are more complex simply by their placement in the investment pyramid—above mutual funds, IRAs, 401(k) plans, insurance, and so on. Individual stock and bond portfolios must be actively monitored, because the selection process is flawed from the outset, as we discussed earlier in the book. (As William Bernstein says, "Human beings cannot pick stocks. Period.")

If you do use individual stocks as part of your investment pyramid, you must know how many stocks you need to have in a portfolio in order to insulate it due to unsystematic risk. If you don't know the answer, the risk of this area can almost be exponential.

I have taught diversification for years and I still feel totally out of my element in attempting to pick just the right 50 or so stocks for a portfolio. Theoretically, it is possible to do so. Realistically, though, I just don't think many investors should even bother to attempt to diversify their portfolios to that extent on their own. For more on diversification, see Chapter 1.

Fixed Annuities and Basic Life Insurance

Next up on the pyramid of investing are fixed annuities and basic life insurance. Fixed-annuity policies earn income on a tax-deferred basis (possibly tax free with certain insurance policy loans, though the simplistic term policies may work nicely for many), and are essentially risk free as regards the guarantee of payment later on.[6]

Fixed annuities, though, have been shown to be more risky than properly utilized mutual funds, since, even with tax deferral, returns are reduced by inflation and access to annuities may be severely reduced by surrender fees and a 10 percent penalty tax if removed from a policy prior to age $59\frac{1}{2}$. Further, annuity payouts may be absolutely dismal and are subject to ordinary income tax.

Variable Annuities

Variable-annuity policies can possibly provide a higher return than other fixed investments since they use mutual funds generally geared

CAVEAT INVESTOR

One major insurance company got sued because the interest paid upon annuitization was zero! For this reason you really have to do some homework before you ever select an annuity payment, certainly for life. And you better know how to use a financial calculator. A lot of elderly consumers are blinded by the statement that you can get payments for life with an annuity. That's true, but if you are going to earn less than you would with a staggered bunch of Treasury instruments, you have actually hurt your retirement by going backward.

In terms of cash value life insurance, the caveats are at least as severe as with fixed annuities. The policy illustrations alone can drive someone to distraction. They are difficult to understand even for those in the business, sometimes based on totally bogus projections and rarely identify the tax repercussions. Yes, they can work to build up funds for retirement, but I'd just opt for either a term policy or a guaranteed policy for life where the cash buildup was effectively irrelevant (no lapse, for example). Many consumers don't understand all the implications regarding insurance, and I point you to Chapter 11 for further understanding.

for growth, but they can involve substantially higher fees than basic funds. They also incur the 10 percent penalty if used before age $59\frac{1}{2}$. Also, many are fixed during the payout period and subject the annuitant to inflation, as described previously. (This means, in effect, that while the annuitant, or policyholder, can count on a payment, the actual value of that payment is diminished because of inflation). Further, variable-annuity contracts are very involved and few agents understand them, let alone consumers.

It's important to note, too, that a lot of brochures that pitch the virtues of variable annuities have nothing to do with real life. By the time you actually do a real-life study, you could actually have less net money in a tax-deferred account than if you had invested in an index fund. I have not included a full study here, primarily because President George W. Bush recently changed the tax laws. Capital gains taxes are now very low, effectively negating the need for variable annuities and the tax-sheltered element except for the very gullible, greedy or just plain stupid. Apparently there are a lot of these. According to the National Association for Variable Annuities, new sales of variable annuities continue to run at a $120 billion annual rate. Oy vey!

Variable Insurance

Variable insurance policies are truly one of the most difficult and misunderstood products on earth, worse than setting up a VCR. First, these products must be sold as insurance, not as investment vehicles. Second, you must remember that you will need to own this policy for the rest of your life or face some potentially severe tax repercussions. Third, if someone uses the allowed 12 percent projected return for variable insurance, there is a 20 percent chance that you will need to put more money into the policy in the later years. Why? Basic Monte Carlo simulations of the kind of crashes we saw in 1973–1974 and 2000–2002 easily reveal that a 12 percent return just doesn't hold up. Frankly, anyone projecting a 12% return on any reasonable investment should be shot. It's not historically supportable. Variable insurance policies can work as investment vehicles, but I tend to opt for pure insurance and buying your investments separately. This is why you'll see this "investment" is above some of the more reliable investments in the pyramid.

Both variable annuities and life insurance focus on the use of mutual funds. But the products do not necessarily incorporate the best funds—certainly the cheapest—and investors still have to monitor their performance. One of my primary beefs with these tools is that you are combining two very different elements—annuities and insurance with mutual funds—and I have never felt that that is the best use of money.

Money Market Accounts and Certificates of Deposit (CDs)

While most consumers think of money market accounts and certificates of deposit, or CDs, as easy, safe investment tools, they actually have been shown to have higher risk than most financial literature would imply.

Because of the significant drop in rates during the last decade—and certainly during 2002 and 2003, the after-tax, after-inflation return on these investment vehicles is minuscule at best—or even negative. Middle-income wage earners are getting essentially nothing for their efforts if they invest in money market accounts or certificates of deposit.

That said, the returns money market accounts and CDs generate may be great, if your equities are getting hammered.

Covered Option Writing

As we move up the pyramid of investing, we come to options. An option is a form of hedging. Let's look at why they are considered conservative, and then let's look at why they can be a sucker bet.

First, a brief explanation of options. A person can buy the rights to a bunch of stocks for little money, called an *option*. If the stock appreciates greatly, the owner of the option (not the stock) can make out big time. If the stock falls in value, the purchaser has not lost as much as if (s)he owned the stock outright. But someone has to sell these options, and most people doing so are the ones already owning the stock (meaning they are *covered*).

Covered option writing simply means that the person selling the option also owns the stock. It is a way of generating more income, though it is not risk free. For example, if you owned 100 shares of IBM, you could write an option and maybe get $200 for doing so. If the stock does not appreciate that much, the owner of the stock gets to keep the $200. Say! Such a deal!

But the kicker that few people address is that if your stock has a low basis and is called away by the owner of the option, you can face significant capital gains taxes. The thing is, if you don't understand all that, you probably should not own large amounts of individual securities. And you shouldn't do covered writing. I personally would require a written statement of the risks and other tax ramifications before doing anything with options. Do not just sign an options agreement simply because you like or trust the broker or planner. Invariably that is the reason why people lose money.

Option writing can work, and in a relatively flat (low-volatility) market a stock owner can pick up additional income. But tell me right now, are we in a flat market? Was the market flat six months ago? Two years ago? You have to have absolutely correct answers to these questions, otherwise option writing is out of your league—and likely out of your broker's league as well.

Rental Real Estate

Ownership of real estate has provided many investors with substantial returns. However, investors must recognize the personal management they usually must provide in running such operations: leasing, maintenance, evictions, unplugging toilets in the middle of the night, and so on. Being a landlord can be profitable, but it also can be extremely labor intensive. Further, the tax laws can change dramatically, as can the economy, severely affecting the investment return potential that can be derived from being a landlord.

In addition, real estate is a nonliquid asset, and the mortgage payments and time to sale can reduce equity to zero. And with the probability of inflation staying low into the future, investors cannot depend on the high appreciation of the 1980s and early 2000s. Investors likely should calculate their potential return with a longer holding period than in recent years.

Though the use of Real Estate Investment Trusts (REITs) does reduce individual exposure, too much real estate, in itself, is not recommended in any individual portfolio. Certain amounts are acceptable, as long as they are in line with the size of the investment pyramid at that point. Just be careful.

Closed-End Funds

Closed-end funds are similar to open-ended managed mutual funds, but they are issued with a generally fixed capitalization. Closed-end funds are bought in the same method as stocks. But the real difficulty in analyzing their possible return is that they tend to be sold at a discount to net asset value (NAV). Unless the track history of closed-end funds is considered, many investors may simply purchase these funds with an incomplete understanding of their risk-return profile. Considering the complexity of these funds, I personally opted out of these investments some time ago.

Sector Mutual Funds

Sector mutual funds must have at least 25 percent of their portfolios invested in a particular area—be it health, communications, technology, or whatever. Having too much money placed in a risky area is ultimately not beneficial to the investor, who rarely understands risk in the first place. Certainly, those funds can perform very well, but the risks are compounded exponentially, if they are not watched carefully. To wit, the dot-com crash of 2000 and the millions of dollars investors lost as a result.

So, how did the many people who invested in technology funds fare after 2000? These can be viable investments, of course (hence the reason that some products can slide up and down the pyramid), but most sector funds have lost 10 percent annually or more the last few years. Sector funds, despite the opportunity for great returns, are not for the faint of heart.

Limited Partnerships

A limited partnership is a grouping of investors (limited partners) who invest money into various investments controlled by the general partner, who manages the partnership. Prior to the tax law change of 1986, many limited partnerships did very well indeed. The purchase of limited amounts of partnerships was generally considered acceptable for middle-income wage earners. However, many firms and agents "forgot" that these were long-term, high-risk, illiquid ventures, and they sold units in excess of an investor's risk tolerance or acceptance level. Many partnerships were sold for the tax benefits, and when the 1986 tax act closed most of these tax offsets, many high-risk partnerships started to default.

You could safely use, say, 5 percent to 10 percent of limited partnerships in a portfolio. But not the 50 percent to 100 percent that was sold by high-commissioned salespeople and brokerage firms. Some partnerships do continue to work and are even viable today, but the risk orientation limits their use.

You usually don't find too many of these investments anymore, so the point may be moot for the average investor. But, if you do want to incorporate limited partnerships into your pyramid, I'd spread the funds into two or three separate categories.

The Top of the Pyramid

At the top of the pyramid of investing, we have general partnerships and commodities. These investment vehicles require a sophistication generally far in excess of the normal middle-income wage earner and, for the most part, should be discouraged. There's far too much risk involved and far too much to go wrong.

Individuals using such investments must have considerable wealth and a thorough understanding of risk—or be fully advised by a knowledgeable adviser. And there ain't many of those, so it's usually best if you just don't bother.

If you have purely discretionary funds—meaning gambling money that you wouldn't care if you lost—fine, go ahead and use these investment vehicles. But many people tend to get too emotional with the

pretty metals and the sparkling gems and go overboard with investments in this area.

Summary

We have looked at a lot of different investment vehicles in this chapter. The
pyramid is a simple way to illustrate how those vehicles should be used and in
what kinds of proportions. Obviously, the higher up you get into the pyramid,
the more narrow the area, and the less you should use those vehicles. In the
end, though, you have to look at the fundamentals—diversification, asset allocation, deviation—before making any investment decisions. And, if you decide
to go to an adviser for help on any of these points, make sure they are creden-
tialed and know how to use a financial calculator.

In the next chapter, we will look at bonds (also a part of the pyramid)
and explain the yield curve—which every investor needs to understand.

Notes

1. Just about every investor I've come across who lost a lot of their wealth did
   so as a result of trusting a financial planner, adviser, or agent who advised
   them to deal with risk before dealing with the more basic elements of the
   investing pyramid. Remember that trust is an issue but competency reins
   supreme. They are not mutually exclusive, but true competency remains generally elusive in most of the financial industries.
2. Others note that a 30-year loan generally has higher points. True. But, in
   my opinion, that may be more than offset by the additional planning opportunities.
3. The list comes from Unum Provident's extensive claims database, the largest
   private database of disability information in the United States.
4. Take a look at Insure.com. All the information there isn't always right (then
   again, neither am I). But they have pretty good stuff overall.
5. It is my strong opinion that employers at all levels (CEOs, attorneys, Human
   Resource personnel, and so on) never understood what investing was all
   about. That they turned over the responsibility to a brokerage or planning
   firm to administer 401(k) programs and products does not release them from
   the fiduciary duty to inform employees of the risks that they were taking in
   the use of defined contribution plans. I repeat, if you do not know diversifi-

cation by the numbers, you are invariably clueless to the fundamentals of investing. Some may remember the default of the old Executive Life and other insurance companies that went belly up years ago and the fact that they had A and A+ Best ratings. But literally all insurance companies have instituted upgrades to their investment portfolios and current A and A+ Best companies should hold up well over time.

6. To show you that such risk has actually occurred, consider what happened for property insurers during the last decade. Remember the monstrous hurricane that swept across mid-Florida years ago? Certainly the insurance companies were well diversified since they had thousands upon thousands of different homes covered. But the storm was so huge, it also decimated huge numbers of these homes, thereby voiding the offset of diversification. Think about all the other calamities these insurers faced during the 1990s. The average yearly losses went from $775 million in 1989 to $3.5 billion as of 1998. Hurricane Andrew in Florida in 1992 cost $16 billion itself! And we have, or course, the Twin Towers tragedy that will cost billions more.

CHAPTER 7
BONDS

*T*RADITIONALLY, BONDS ARE SEEN AS SAFE INVESTMENTS that offer stable, expected returns. In actuality, they are complex investment vehicles and are rarely fully understood.

Historically, bonds have earned less than stocks over time. That said, they can return more than stocks during various time frames—certainly when the market is tanking, and the past few years have shown this to be the case. Additionally, and though there is lots of controversy in the field, some analysts believe that bonds might outperform stocks for many more years to come because of the current problems in our economy and society: budget deficits, terrorism, larger population of the elderly, increased strain on Medicare, and so on. Others also note that because stock returns were so high in the 1990s, there needs to be a period of reversion (regression) to the mean. That means that, irrespective and regardless of the recent bear market, stock market returns for the next few years—some say 10 years or maybe more—will be less than historical averages and perhaps even less than bonds.

The stock market's historical average is about 10 percent, depending on when you start (1925?, 1950?), where you end (2000?, current?), whether dividends were reinvested, and other statistical anomalies that screw up the analysis and make you wonder what a true number is.

In 1984, the 50-year average return on stocks was about 9.4 percent, and I tend to use that rate for generalizing any future returns.

Bonds returned around 6 percent. Bond returns are not even close to historical averages right now, and I also don't think that they will approach that in the near term either. The Fed would have to raise interest rates for bonds to see higher returns (if only because they are so low now). But to suggest Treasury instruments would get as high as 6 percent in the near term (10 years) is beyond reason. By the same token, the suggestion that stocks might earn less than 6 percent is also difficult to accept. That said, I have learned never to allow one's ego or arrogance to step in front of economics.

At the time of this writing, the analysis seems valid, but constant reading is the only way to address any changes and adjust accordingly. It is also prudent to be prepared for all contingencies. Regardless of what returns are anticipated, investors need to recognize the importance of bonds as a generally conservative position located at the bottom of your investment pyramid.

In the pages that follow, we will examine the fundamentals of bonds. They are not the simplistic investments they are generally portrayed as—certainly when you consider the various mortgage funds.

Yield

How much income will you earn on a bond? In other words, what will be the yield of a bond? Income is based on the interest rate, called the *stated rate, nominal rate,* or *coupon rate.* For example, if the coupon rate is stated as 6 percent and the bond has a par value of $1000, the bond will pay $60 per year. (Par value for bonds, for all intents and purposes, is the amount the bond was initially offered for sale to the public, generally $1000. If the value is different, it will be stated on the bond.) This $60 will be paid semiannually—$30 every six months. At some time in the future, the owner of the bond will be paid the $1000 upon the maturity date (when the bond becomes due and payable), though there are caveats.

Many people buy new bonds, but many bonds are also bought and sold on the secondary market, where the price is generally more or less than the original $1000, depending on what has happened in the economy after the bonds were first issued. For example, let's assume you bought a 6 percent bond that was offered new four years ago. Subsequently, however, economic interest rates plummeted (as have most currently) so that new bonds (same rating and maturity) are now being offered paying only 3 percent. Would you pay more or less than $1000 for a bond that is earning 6 percent? It should be obvious: you would pay more since you are getting more income. Your bond would go up in value and is offered at a premium to the original price. Regardless of what is paid for the bond, the owner will still only get back the $1000 at maturity (some caveats apply). But it would be worth it due to the higher current income.

In the alternative, assume interest rates in the economy went up to 9 percent and that is what new bonds are being offered at. Your old bond pays 6 percent. Would someone pay more or less for your bond that earns less? Your bond has decreased in value and is now at a discount to its original value. The buyer pays less than $1000 but will get the $1000 at maturity (or as defined below.) That is as simple as I can make it. A bond's price reacts conversely to the movement in interest rates. It moves like a seesaw (see Figure 7.1).

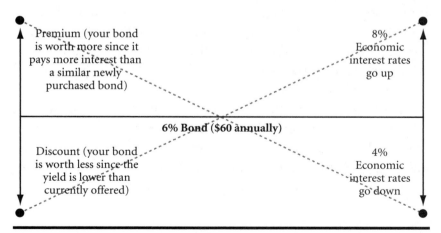

Figure 7.1   Bond prices as impacted by changing economy and interest rates.

Current Yield

Current yield is the interest being returned on a bond divided by the current price. If interest rates in the economy had gone down, the value of a bond would go up. If the price was quoted at 120, it means that the actual price was 1200. But the bond would continue to pay its stated coupon rate, which we will say was 8 percent. The current yield would therefore equal the yield divided by the current price—in this case: $80 ÷ 1200, or 6.67 percent. If interest rates had gone up, the value of bonds would have decreased. An 8 percent bond priced at 83 ($830) would have a current yield of $80 ÷ 830, or 9.64 percent.

Ratings

The lower the quality of the bond, the more volatility it will experience. You no doubt are familiar with the various ratings services of Standard & Poor's, Moody's, Best, and several others that rate bonds from the highest of ratings such as AAA all the way through to D (which stands for "default"). The various rating services do not necessarily analyze the same information. (Explanations of their methodologies can be linked from www.efmoody.com.) So, if there is any confusion whatsoever about the quality of a bond, simply compare the ratings of two or three services and see if the ratings are effectively the same. If you are considering a bond fund rather than individual bonds, the average rating will be identified by the fund itself.

The lower the bond rating and the more fluctuation with interest rates, the greater the price fluctuations. For example, if interest rates change, a lower-quality bond or fund with, say, a C rating, will have significantly greater volatility than that of an A-rated bond or fund, assuming all else being equal (maturity dates, for example).

Maturity

One of the most important issues to consider when buying bonds is how long it will be before you get your money back, or what the *maturity* will be. For example, bonds may be offered with 30-year maturities or with 10-year maturities. The maturity of a bond represents the number of years before the bond comes due.

Everything else being equal, which bond will pay more, a 10-year bond or a 30-year bond? It relates to risk; the greater the risk, the greater the return—supposedly but not necessarily. (See Chapter 4 for a discussion of risk and buy and hold.) If you take a 30-year maturity, you are supposedly not going to get back your originally invested principal for 30 years versus the return of your principal for the shorter period of 10 years. The longer the period of time, the more things that can go wrong; hence, you need to be compensated for this uncertainty. Therefore, the 30-year bond should pay more than the 10-year bond, everything else being equal.

As stated above, interest rates impact the value of a bond. But the price is also reflected by the maturity of the bond. Here is another simple example: If you had a bond with only one day to maturity and interest rates changed, would there be much of an impact or change in the value of the bond? No. The time frame is so short that any value adjustment would be nil. On the other hand, the impact on a 10-year bond is far more pronounced and the change on a 30-year maturity even greater.

You can see that if you have a short-term bond fund, the change in value due to interest rates will be far less than that of a long-term bond portfolio. Also note that there are no maturities, per se, with mutual bond funds and the return of principal will not be the $1000 per bond as identified with individual issues but whatever the fund share is worth at the time you sell. That is another major difference between individual issues and large diversified funds.

Whatever has been said thus far about the maturity of a bond is but a partial truth. (That's a common "mistake" among a lot of people in this business.) Hence, much of the reason for buying certain bonds may be moot. I neglected to indicate that most bonds (save for most Treasury bonds) may never last to maturity. And those that do may offer miserable returns. It all refers to *call dates*.

Call Dates

Assume a corporation or municipality sold $10 million of bonds paying 6 percent several years ago. Rates are now much lower today—say, at 3 percent. The issuers (that is, the corporation or municipality) would love to trade in their old bonds for the new bonds since they would only have to pay half as much per year in interest costs to borrowers. Generally, they can. Most bonds are offered with call dates, the date(s) in the future when they can pay off the old bonds with the intent of offering new bonds with lower interest rates. Call dates are identified with the bonds and are a mandatory element for review by investors.

Let's see how this works with an example. Say that you bought a bond four years ago with a yield of 6 percent and maturing in 30 years. It sounds great, particularly because rates are now much lower. The problem is, the bond had established its first call date at four years after the original offering. Guess what? They will call in the bonds, pay you the $1000 that the bond was worth (sometimes with a slight premium, the terms of which are also noted on the bond), and that's it. Here you were hoping to hold onto a great-yielding bond for many years to come and now, all of a sudden, you got back your money in a financial environment that is far less viable than it was four years ago. Well, tough luck, because that is how the game is played.

You also need to understand the term *risk of reinvestment* and how it applies directly to this situation. You got back your money all right, but now you'd have to take a higher risk with reinvesting in something else in order to approximate the 6 percent return you just lost.

Different companies' bonds may have initial call dates starting in, say, two years, five years, eight years, or whatever. So there is at least some period of time when you will get the interest specified on the bond. This is called your *call protection period*, the period in which you know you will get the stated return before there is a potential of having your principal paid off. But even if you do get past the first call date because nothing has happened with interest rates, complacency is not warranted. The bonds generally will have more call dates—maybe one in seven years, another in 10 years, another in 14 years, and so on. You simply have no idea how long you will keep your bond if interest rates subside in the future.

On the other hand, if interest rates actually rose, there is effectively no reason for a company to call a bond due. As a result, you would be secure in your ownership of the bond. But here is the kicker: If you bought a low-interest, 30-year bond earning, say, 4 percent and rates rose to 6 percent, you'd end up earning 2 percent less for a long period of time. Picking a long-term, low-interest-rate bond at the bottom of an interest rate cycle can be a contract for underperformance.

How do you know what to do given any specific economic situation? Sorry, there's no easy answer. You have to read statistics, history, and a then lot of economics to get a feel for the future.

If you own a bond fund, the risk of single issues is diversified away, because the fund may be made up of more than 50 to 100 bonds. But some of the positives of owning individual bonds go away as well. For instance, you do not have a specific maturity date at all—the funds buy, sell, and let bonds mature all the time, so it goes on forever. Secondly, with individual bonds you know what the yield is: It's stated. Though the principal might change because of interest rate movements, you always get the same income. Not so with bond funds. With the funds, so many bonds are bought, sold, and matured that the yield at any point in time will vary tremendously. There are thousands upon thousands of probabilities that are too numerous to figure out.

All that said, the risk of single issues is usually so severe that most analysts suggest you might need up to $500,000 of individual bonds to get a properly diversified portfolio. That's way out of reach for smaller investors. Most middle-income investors should consider a good bond fund. And when you do, look for low fees. Bonds are bonds. You generally only can get more return from a similar bond fund by taking more risk—hedging, using margin, and the like—and that's not advised at all. Personally, I'd opt for using large, established funds like TIAA-CREF, Vanguard, or the like. They're cheap, and what you see is what you get (no extra hedging techniques, and so forth).[1]

High-Yield Bonds

High-yield bonds require special attention since, at certain times, they can provide exceptional returns at less risk than equities. High-yield bonds generally carry less than Standard & Poor's BBB rating. A BBB rating is the minimum for an investment-grade bond. Any yield lower than that and the bonds are euphemistically called *junk bonds*, or high-yield bonds. Now, a bond carrying a higher-risk rating like BB is not inherently in imminent threat of default. Nor is a B-rated bond. But because these bonds carry a higher risk due to the lower rating, the issuing companies must offer greater returns with them than with bonds with other, higher-rated companies—and obviously much higher returns than Treasuries.

If you drop the ratings even further—say, to a C—the yields have to be very high in order to offset the risk. In late 2002, the average bond maturing in 7 to 10 years yielded around 12 percent. That's at least 8 percent (800 basis points) more than 10-year Treasury notes and close to record levels. The yield is so high because such lower-rated bonds have a much higher default rate, certainly as the economy softens. And default rates did escalate since 2000, to over 9 percent in 2002.

So, why buy high-yield bonds at all? Well, in a down economy they really don't make sense, even with the higher yields. The default rates can be most troublesome. But if the economy is improving, not only will you get a nice return, but some of the companies will actually prosper. Hence, their ratings can go up. And if the ratings go up, so does the price of the bond. You can get very attractive double returns—income plus the appreciation. These bonds may act, in such situations, like investments with a small-cap company, providing high risk in a bad economy, but with the potential of an upside return in an improving economy.

All that said, investors would be foolish to buy individual high-yield bonds. They carry far too much risk. Stick with bond funds like Vanguard. They may have overall ratings of B or BB and give some decent hedge against outright defaults. On the other hand, funds that have lower overall ratings—and higher risks—should provide greater returns in an improving economy, because there is so much latitude for improved ratings. I personally like the higher-rated average B and BB funds.

Municipal or Corporate Bonds?

Should you buy a *municipal bond* that is tax free or a comparably rated *corporate bond*? First of all, if you are in the lowest tax bracket of 15 percent or so, you should not buy municipals, since you will not get significant benefits from the tax relief. Here is how to figure your effective yields between the two types so you can determine which one you want to buy.

Take the municipal bond yield and divide it by 1 minus the taxpayer's tax bracket. For example, suppose the bond has a 6 percent municipal yield (.06) and the investor is in the 30 percent tax bracket (.30). The calculations would be as follows:

$$.06/1 - .30 = .06/.7 = 8.57 \text{ percent}$$

That means, everything else being equal (it never is, though), that an investor would find no difference between buying either a 6 percent tax-free bond or a taxable 8.57 percent bond, since they would both produce the same net return.

Summary

While bonds historically have not outperformed stocks over long periods of time, they sure can provide a haven when the market tanks. And, who knows? They might provide above-average returns for some time to come—maybe, on a risk-adjusted basis, even greater than stocks. In any case, short- and medium-term bond funds are good positions in a volatile market and may even be warranted currently. Nevertheless, always be aware how a bond's principal reacts to moves in interest rates. That is a key element to the use of bonds along with the various call dates.

Notes

1. This assumes normal bonds with the primary caveat being the various types of mortgage funds like GNMAs, FNMAs, and the like.

CHAPTER 8
MUTUAL FUNDS

*D*O YOU WANT TO KNOW HOW to pick a mutual fund? Simple. Go for those with no load, a low-expense ratio, and, generally, low turnover. So what funds meet those criteria? Index funds. That's about it.

As an example of this approach, let's take a look at the Vanguard 500 Index Fund, which mirrors the S&P 500 Index.

It's no load. That saves you commissions. But keep in mind, paying a fee or commission planner or advisor for professional services to help get you into the *right* fund can be valid. Of course, if you use a schmuck and he puts you into the wrong fund at the wrong time, you haven't gained much. By the same token, if you want to save money by doing it yourself but end up buying the wrong index fund, you haven't gained anything either and you can't even blame someone else for the error.

The Vanguard 500 Index Fund has a low expense ratio of 0.18 percent—at least 1 percent lower than the average of equity funds. High expenses make a huge difference in your pocketbook over time. They are certainly a major consideration when market returns are low, which is pretty much what many analysts are currrently expecting. Always review all your costs when selecting a mutual fund.

The Vanguard 500 Index Fund has a turnover ratio of 7.0 percent. That means that ongoing taxes for dividends, interest, and capital gains will be low. (This is a moot issue, however, if the fund is part of a tax-sheltered account.)

Take a look at the industry and then compare funds. You want to look at fees, costs, and turnover ratios in addition to the fund's return, holdings, and manager. Do your homework. Table 8.1 illustrates average returns of mutual funds, plus turnover and expenses.

Table 8.1   Mutual Equity Funds Industry Average

Equity Fund Category (number of funds in grouping)		5 Year Average 1998– 2002	Period One >98–> 99 Average	Period Two >01–> 02 Average	% Change
Large Value (144)	Turnover Ratio	74.0%	70	77.7	11
	Expense Ratio	1.04%	1.02	1.07	5.4
	Net Assets ($Bil)	1.92	2.07	1.74	−15.7
	Annual Return	−.03	8.5	−11.6	
Large Blend (75)	Turnover Ratio	73.7	73.4	72.3	−1.4
	Expense Ratio	1.04	1.03	1.07	3.9
	Net Assets ($Bil)	1.98	2.10	1.77	−16
	Annual Return	−1.3	20.7	−17.3	
Large Growth (182)	Turnover Ratio	97.8	96.4	97.7	1.3
	Expense Ratio	1.18	1.16	1.22	5.2
	Net Assets ($Bil)	2.01	2.10	1.59	−24.3
	Annual Return	−2.8	35.9	−25.1	
Mid Value (27)	Turnover Ratio	79.7	79.4	80.7	1.6
	Expense Ratio	1.22	1.18	1.26	7.2
	Net Assets ($Bil)	.54	.40	.73	83.5
	Annual Return	3.3	4.2	−2.9	
Mid Blend (30)	Turnover Ratio	98.6	91.6	97.5	6.5
	Expense Ratio	1.27	1.27	1.27	0
	Net Assets ($Bil)	.47	.37	.54	47.9
	Annual Return	3.4	16.8	−8.1	

(continued on next page)

Table 8.1 Mutual Equity Funds Industry Average (continued)

Equity Fund Category (number of funds in grouping)		5 Year Average 1998– 2002	Period One >98–> 99 Average	Period Two >01–> 02 Average	% Change
Mid	Turnover Ratio	136.8	128.5	143.4	11.6
Growth	Expense Ratio	1.27	1.28	1.28	0.4
(110)	Net Assets ($Bil)	.84	.81	.72	−10.6
	Annual Return	−1.1	39.3	−25.1	
Small	Turnover Ratio	63.6	57.8	66.3	14.7
Value	Expense Ratio	1.20	1.2	1.18	−2.1
(29)	Net Assets ($Bil)	.34	.26	.41	57.7
	Annual Return	3.4	−.1	4.3	
Small	Turnover Ratio	90.9	86.1	86.9	0.9
Blend	Expense Ratio	1.28	1.30	1.27	−1.9
(34)	Net Assets ($Bil)	.43	.35	.57	63.8
	Annual Return	2.7	3.7	−1.8	
Small	Turnover Ratio	137	136.5	130.8	−4.2
Growth	Expense Ratio	1.39	1.39	1.43	2.5
(120)	Net Assets ($Bil)	.38	.39	.35	−9.1
	Annual Return	−1.1	32.8	−18.8	

Source: Dr. Craig Israelsen, University of Missouri, from Morningstar Principia Pro

Now let's look at the Total International Stock Index Fund from Vanguard. This is a no-load fund with expenses of .37, which is well under the average. It has a turnover rate of 5 percent. Table 8.2 illustrates a comparison of international funds.

Lastly, let's look at the Vanguard Intermediate Term Corporate Fund. This is a no-load bond fund with an expense ratio of .21 percent. That is a material issue of bond funds, since the fees are a direct reduction of the income. You really have to watch this ratio carefully, particularly where the interest rates are low (like now) and are projected to stay that way (like now). The Vanguard fund has a turnover rate of 118 percent. This is not as material as it is with stocks, because there are bonds maturing and being called all the time. They must be replenished. Table 8.3 shows how the Vanguard fund compares with the industry average.

Table 8.2   Mutual International Funds Industry Average

Equity Fund Category (number of funds in grouping)		5 Year Average 1998– 2002	Period One >98–> 99 Average	Period Two >01–> 02 Average	% Change
International Equity Funds					
Large	Turnover Ratio	55.7	51.1	55.3	8.3
Value	Expense Ratio	1.15	1.18	1.12	–5.1
(14)	Net Assets ($Bil)	1.48	1.81	1.27	–29.8
	Annual Return	.8	23.2	–13.5	
Large	Turnover Ratio	84.1	77.5	92	18.6
Blend	Expense Ratio	1.33	1.33	1.35	1.5
(76)	Net Assets ($Bil)	1.00	1.07	.83	–22.5
	Annual Return	–2.5	25.9	–18.4	
Large	Turnover Ratio	89.6	85.7	91.1	6.4
Growth	Expense Ratio	1.47	1.49	1.46	–2.3
(53)	Net Assets ($Bil)	.75	.79	.63	–20.9
	Annual Return	–3.2	29.9	–20.3	

Source: Dr. Craig Israelsen, University of Missouri, from Morningstar Principia Pro

Which index funds, or combination thereof, might do well, given a certain economy and correlation? Well, there's the rub. I point you to the section on asset allocation in Chapter 1 for information and warnings about using standard risk profiles and allocation of all the mutual fund firms and advisers. Selecting just the right fund or combination of funds is really that tough. There's no Holy Grail. There's no magic formula.

But an index fund is where most investors should start. Believe it or not, the selection of an index fund is as simple as this short section describes. If you want to use managed funds exclusively, pay the higher fees and higher taxes, and get potentially lousy advice through a broker, be my guest. That said, I have no problems with a limited amount of loaded mutual funds, but not for an investor's whole portfolio.

Wasn't that simple?

Table 8.3   Mutual Bond Funds Industry Average

Equity Fund Category (number of funds in grouping)		5 Year Average 1998– 2002	Period One >98–> 99 Average	Period Two >01–> 02 Average	% Change
U.S. Intermediate Bond Fund					
High	Turnover Ratio	161.1	148.8	180.1	21
Quality	Expense Ratio	.84	.85	.84	−0.6
(132)	Net Assets ($Bil)	.59	.55	.65	18.2
	Annual Return	6.4	3.3	8.2	
Medium	Turnover Ratio	151.2	122.3	178.7	46.2
Quality	Expense Ratio	.98	.97	1	3.1
(38)	Net Assets ($Bil)	.71	.69	.75	8.8
	Annual Return	4.9	2.7	7.0	
Low	Turnover Ratio	123.5	112.7	148.6	31.9
Quality	Expense Ratio	1.05	1.02	1.07	4.4
(41)	Net Assets ($Bil)	.81	.94	.70	−26.1
	Annual Return	−0.6	2.4	.3	

Source: Dr. Craig Israelsen, University of Missouri, from Morningstar Principia Pro

Summary

Conservative mutual funds make up part of the foundation of the pyramid of investing. Selecting individual mutual funds or a selection of mutual funds can be difficult and time-consuming, and it may not give you the payoff you are looking for. Index funds, though, are a relatively simple alternative. They are simple, they usually have lower fees than other funds, and you don't have to mess with a broker or adviser to invest in them. Nonetheless, you still need to do your homework. Just picking something cheap is a bad investment theory.

CHAPTER 9
REAL ESTATE

*T*HIS CHAPTER WILL PROVIDE A UNIQUE ANALYSIS and comparison of stocks versus real estate. A comparison of these two asset classes may not be perfect, but, if it is done objectively, you will be able to see returns of each, analyze the results, and choose which investment you'd like to use.

Proper analysis requires that you address the 26 points below, make some basic calculations, and have an overall understanding of risk. The list can be used for any property you might consider as an investment. It will provide a total equity rate, which you can then compare to other types of investments, and it is an excellent tool for initial evaluation. But, you *must* put in real-life numbers. No cheating!

Comparative Investment Analysis

A *comparative investment analysis* is the first step in analyzing a real estate investment.

Starting Points

The analysis starts with the following points:

1. Sales price—nonexpendable transaction costs

This is the total price that the property costs.
2. Less Total Loans
   First mortgage, second mortgage, whatever
3. Equity, 1 minus 2

Property Income Analysis

The next step is to evaluate the property income. The following points assist with that analysis:

4. Gross Scheduled Income
   Make sure the rent is reflective of the neighborhood.
5. Less Vacancy and Credit Losses
   Always add in 5 percent to 10 percent, unless there is evidence of something different. But don't use 0 percent as a vacancy rate, even in an exuberant economy. If you have a single rental such as an office or industrial building, be careful in that the vacancy rate can reflect 100 percent, if you lose that tenant.
6. Gross Operating Income, 4 minus 5
7. Operating Expenses
   Be careful if you take these expenses from a Realtor sales form, because the amount shown on the form is apt to be less than the actual one. Owners are notorious for showing fewer expenses than were actually incurred, and there may be deferred maintenance that also doesn't reflect true operating expenses. Several services are available, some on the Internet, that can give you realistic estimates on how much you should anticipate for expenses.
8. Net Operating Income

Taxable Income

You also have to look at taxable income when considering a real estate investment. The following points must be considered:

9. Net Operating Income

10. Less Interest Payments

    If you are taking out a new loan, recognize that almost all your initial payments will be interest, and therefore they normally will be deductible.

11. Less Depreciation

    Rental and commercial real estate have different straight-line depreciation schedules. Also, you cannot (generally) depreciate land.

12. Taxable Income

    If your taxable income here is negative, it can be offset by passive income (where you are not actively engaged in the management of the property. See Passive Activity and At-Risk Rules, IRS Publication 925.). If the owner has 10 percent or more interest and income is under $100,000, $25,000 of loss may be offset against regular income. Otherwise passive loss may not be used and must be carried forward. You can use them when you sell.

Spendable Income

Spendable income can be derived through these points:

13. Net Operating Income

14. Less Principal and Interest Payments

15. GROSS SPENDABLE

16. Less Income Tax (subject to qualifications above)

    If the number is negative, remember that subtracting a negative number becomes positive.

17. Less Capital Improvements

18. NET SPENDABLE ANNUALLY

19. Per Month

Equity Income

Equity income can be derived by reviewing these points:

20. Net Operating Income
21. Less Interest on Loans
22. Less Income Tax
    Subject to qualifications above.
23. NET EQUITY INCOME
24. Net Equity Income Rate
25. Plus Equity Growth Rate
    What is the expected appreciation? Keep the figure realistic.
26. Total Equity Rate

Comparison of Real Estate to Equities

At this point, it is possible to start comparing real estate to equities save for a couple of specific issues with real estate. The first is liquidity. To put it into perspective, we need to define the difference between marketability and liquidity. *Marketability* refers to the value of an asset. *Liquidity* refers to the ability to be able to easily dispose of an asset for the market value. Traded securities are both marketable and liquid. You can simply call up a broker and immediately sell the securities for the value at the time of trade (some caveats obviously apply, but the general picture is valid). On the other hand, while a real estate property may be marketable for, say, $500,000, the ability to immediately liquidate the property is remote. The average time to list, sell, and close a property may be several months. Therefore, with a nonliquid property the return must be offset by the amount of risk that is taken.

True, you might not need the money immediately, but that's not the point. It is the essential requirement to try and compare apples to apples. Hence, the return for a nonliquid asset of any type must be reduced. Can I select what discount to use? No. Each state, county, neighborhood, or block will have its own characteristics, so you will need to make an educated guess. That said, be realistic. Don't get caught in the euphoria of recent real estate returns. Don't do what many equity investors did during the 1990s and use the phenomenal recent returns (20 percent annually for equities during that decade) as a benchmark for returns in the future. Those returns don't last forever.

Sample Real Estate Analysis

Here is a relatively simple example for the analysis of a $1 million property, using rounded numbers, following the criteria we set forth previously.

Starting Points

1. Sales Price: $1,000,000—nonexpendable transaction costs
2. Less Total Loans: $750,000 @ 8 percent for 30 years ($5467 monthly, or $66,000 annually, rounded)
3. Equity: $250,000

Property Income Analysis

4. Gross Scheduled Income: $125,000
5. Less Vacancy and Credit Losses: $10,000
6. Gross Operating Income: $115,000
7. Less Operating Expenses @ 30 percent: $35,000
8. NET OPERATING INCOME: $80,000 (cap rate of 8 percent)

Taxable Income

9. Net Operating Income: $80,000
10. Less Interest Payments (assume $60,000 of $66,600): $60,000
11. Less Depreciation (land at $300,000; Improvements at 39 years): $18,000

12. Taxable Income: $2000 ($80,000 – $60,000 – $18,000)

Spendable Income

13. Net Operating Income: $80,000
14. Less Principal and Interest Payments: $66,000
15. GROSS SPENDABLE: $14,000
16. Less Income Tax (use 30 percent, federal and state) × $2000 Taxable Income: $600
17. Less Capital Improvements: None used
18. NET SPENDABLE ANNUALLY: $13,400
19. Per Month: $1120 (rounded)

Equity Income

20. Net Operating Income: $80,000
21. Less Interest on Loans: $60,000
22. Less Income Tax: $600
23. NET EQUITY INCOME: $19,400
24. Net Equity Income Rate ($19,400/$250,000): 7.8 percent (rounded)
25. Plus Equity Growth Rate: 4.0 (estimated)
26. Total Equity Rate: 11.8 percent

Pretty straightforward, eh? Of course, this begs the issue that you need to have done your homework and been reasonably accurate with net income.

The fun part is the equity growth rate. I know that real estate has once again surfaced as a great investment, but I caution you not to get overly aggressive when it comes to appreciation. Further, real estate also suffers significant cycles, and a future high rate of return is not suggested.

Other Factors to Consider

So, is that it? Can you take the 11.8 percent and compare it against the stock market and make your decision? Nope. As stated above, real estate is an illiquid asset, whereas stock can be liquidated with a phone call. There is, therefore, a significant risk due to illiquidity that must be adjusted into the equation for total equity rate. The problem is that there is no universal number to use to delineate such risk. In my experience with clients in all areas of the nation, getting stuck with a piece of real estate at the wrong economic times is worth at least a 3 percent to 6 percent reduction in anticipated return. Let's assume I use 4 percent to adjust for the lack of liquidity, so that the final return is now 7.8 percent. Does that compare favorably to the stock market's return over the last 50 years? Actually, it's a little lower, since a 10 percent return is pretty commonly accepted as the historic market average. But let's not forget that future stock market returns, according to many analysts, may be no greater than 6 percent to 8 percent. Therefore we are in the ballpark with our real estate investment.

Unfortunately, that's not all we need to look at. I have not addressed the emotional strain of dealing with tenants if you choose to own real estate and rent it out. Some people can handle it. I could not. I had no interest in deadbeat tenants, and no matter how careful you are, you are apt to run into these. Secondly, if you tried to do your own management, you must make the time and commitment. If you can handle a call at 9:00 P.M. on a Saturday night that someone's kid just flushed their pet water buffalo down the toilet, go for it.

Summary

Real estate ownership has been a major fixture of wealth in the United States. However, we're addressing ownership of properties for the middle-class consumer, which entails more personal involvement and emotion than the institutional properties with professional and hands-off management. Sure, it can work for some people, but do the numbers above for comparison and then include the various risk factors I identified. Return rate isn't the only thing to consider when you are looking at real estate investing.

CHAPTER 10

ANNUITIES

I N THIS CHAPTER, we are going to look at annuities, which are one of the most misunderstood, misrepresented products available to consumers. Even many books, magazines, newspapers, and other sources purporting to offer guidance for investing get it wrong. To illustrate, I'll provide commentary from *The Wall Street Journal* on annuity returns that was so wrongheaded that it was hard to believe.[1] In the paragraphs that follow we will explore the basics of annuities, with additional real-life elements that possibly no one else has presented to middle-income consumers.

What Are Annuities?

An *annuity* is a type of retirement product that falls under special IRS guidelines that allow gains of the internal investment to grow tax deferred until you pull them out. Because this deferral is allowed, the rules also impose some stipulations, the main one being that any receipt of funds prior to age 59½ (with some exceptions) is subject not only to ordinary income tax but to a 10 percent penalty as well. Additionally, the total amount is not allowed a step up in basis at the date of death, which is a major drawback, as explained later. While basis should be evidenced in all investment sales, it's rare you will ever hear it in a sales presentation.

The following examples contain numbers solely for the purposes of illustration. If you have trouble following the entire context, just wait for the punch line: the end result with the explanation. Annuities have to be analyzed with numbers, but I have tried to make the illustrations as simple as possible.

Annuity Growth

As a simple example, let's say you put $25,000 into an annuity at 5 percent, compounded monthly. During the first year, it grows by $1279. None of that is currently taxed, as annuities are tax deferred. Over a period of 10 years, the annuity grows to $41,175. You turn 62 and pull it all out. Only the amount over $25,000 (the initial contribution that had already been taxed) is taxed. The excess amount of $16,175—the *appreciation*—is taxed as ordinary income. Assuming you were in the 30 percent tax bracket, you'd be left with $11,322.50 after tax to be added to your initial contribution of $25,000 for a total of $36,322.50. Any good? Did the tax sheltering help? Read on.

Understanding the major selling point to annuities requires a tax comparison against that of a CD. With a CD, all the interest (gains) would be taxed on an annual basis and you have less to compound each year. With an annuity, nothing is taxed annually and more is compounded each and every year. You will have more money at the end with a fixed annuity, even after taxes, assuming certain conditions that will be described later. But what you get may not be worth all the trouble or expense to get it.

Let me first give you some real-life numbers regarding a fixed account. Assume you had $25,000 in a standard taxable CD account earning a guaranteed 6 percent for two years. You were also in the 28 percent tax bracket. At the end of the first year, daily compounding, you'd have $26,545 (all numbers are rounded). But the $1545 of interest would be taxable and therefore you would net only $1112, giving you a true total of $26,112. At the end of the next year, the $26,112 would have grown to $27,726. But $1614 second-year interest would be taxed, leaving $1162 for an actual total at the end of the second year of $27,274.

How would you have done with the annuity? You'd have $28,178. Hey, that's a heck of a deal. But not so fast. That's an incomplete answer—and one I believe also is unethical because you have to adjust the $3178 interest gain for taxes. At a 28 percent bracket, that is a reduction of $890, leaving a true total of $27,288. Table 10.1 illustrates this comparison.

Table 10.1   Annuities and Taxes

	Taxable annually at 28%	Non-taxable annuity
25,000 initial investment at 6% for 2 years (Daily Compounding)	$27,274	$28,178
Net afer tax	$27,274 (already was taxed)	$27,288 (+$14)

Now, did you really gain that much? On the one had, you have a CD that netted $27,274 already taxed, and on the other hand, an annuity that netted $27,288 after tax. You got a lousy net $14 more over two years with the annuity but with the restriction of surrender charges (a possible 10 percent penalty if it were to be withdrawn before age 59½), several emotional meetings with an agent, and more possible unpleasantness.

Admittedly, the difference in the returns grows as you extend the years and, certainly, as you invest more money. But even with this consideration, there is more than meets the eye. Are you comparing annual yields equally? Probably not. And unless you know what goes on, you can actually end up with less money with a tax-sheltered annuity than with taxable cash accounts because an annuity could easily pay you less than the going rate. Read some more.

When you buy an annuity, you normally get a fixed rate guaranteed for some period of time. I like a minimum of a one-year guarantee for short-term positions, and it is possible to get them for longer term if you have a lump sum to invest. If you are investing monthly amounts (generally called *flex plans*), most annuities are offered with minimum guarantee periods normally not exceeding the one year mentioned. Subsequent nonguaranteed years are a potential crapshoot, depending on the movement of national rates. Maybe you will continue to get a good rate, meaning that the rate would be reflective of then-current bond market rates. But not necessarily so. You could get screwed royally with abysmally low yields over which you have no control.

I'll cover that issue, but first let's look at the next real-life element, which is reflective of a large part of the annuity industry.

Bonus Interest

Bonus interest, while not completely a sham, is, generally, a deceptive inducement to get your money while not necessarily providing any long-term benefit.

If you cannot estimate future company returns by getting the company history and then working the numbers through a financial calculator, then you cannot figure out whether the investment is viable. Regardless, the estimates do just that—estimate—so you really have no idea what you will end up with.

A number of companies offer high first-year yields, generally through the use of some bonus interest for the first year. For example, the regular one-year return might be 4 percent. But the company might give you 6 percent, 10 percent, or even more for the first year. How is that possible, and will the policyholder really net more money?

First of all, insurance and annuity companies, at a given point in time, are all buying the bonds as their investments for their portfolios. Same bonds, same returns, same maturities (some latitude taken for purists, but it is close enough). If they give you a big return the first year, higher than the actual yield on the purchased bonds, then they are going to have to reduce the return in later years. And they do. But once they do, they generally keep the lower returns year after year. In other words, if Company A offered a 10 percent first-year return and then offered 3 percent the next nine years, while Company B offered a flat 5 percent return for all 10 years, who would get more money?

Let's assume that $10,000 was originally invested. Company A would produce total returns of $14,352. Company B would give you $16,288. So you really didn't do that well with that "bonus." And the longer you hold the bonus annuity, the less money you generally will net, because the lower interest rate continues to drive down the overall return. Table 10.2 illustrates this phenomenon.

Table 10.2   To Bonus or Not to Bonus?

	Bonus interest of 10% first year and 3% subsequent years	5% for full period	Difference
$10,000 invested in an annuity for 10 years	$14,352	$16,288	$1,936
20 years	$19,288	$26,533	$7,245
30 years	$25,922	$43,219	$17,297

Keep in mind: Not all bonus interest is a sham. Some companies may offer, say, a 1 percent bonus if you have stayed with the company annuity for 7, 10, or 15 years. It is an incentive to get you to leave money with them, offered because a direct expense is incurred by the company if you or other clients switch to another annuity company. But, again, you have to check how rates are applied, because getting a 1 percent bonus on a 3 percent yield may not be worth much. (Although with the ultralow rates of 2003, any better return is good.) However, if you get a good company that doesn't play games, and so many do, staying with the company could be financially worthwhile.[2]

The problem is simply not just those companies that offer bonuses. What I'll mention next is much worse. A company could give a good, current 5 percent first-year guaranteed return and then significantly drop the rates the following nonguaranteed years just because they want to, and irrespective of rates in the economy. You lose even more compared to those who invest in companies that keep returns reflective of current rates. If you don't like it, tough. What do they care? They get a surrender charge if you pull the money before the contract date has expired. The key question is this: Is there any way to know for sure what percentage return will be offered after year 1 unless it is guaranteed?

Nope. You'd have to look at the past history of yields—assuming that the company would provide the data, which almost all would not—to see what had transpired after the first year. You'd also have to check out whether they used portfolio rates, new money, old money, and so on. (I am not going to define these concepts, as they are very convoluted.)

The unfortunate thing is that the bulk of agents who sell annuities have done little to no homework. They simply market the yields. But in most cases it makes little difference whether or not they did look into the subject further, since they usually cannot use a financial calculator to determine the end numbers in any case. (As previously stated, never give money to anyone who cannot use a financial calculator.) So you lose all the way around. You really have to do some homework here, but if you don't know the problem, you don't know what to ask for.

Lastly, even if you did get certain historical information from a company, you'd have to compare each return against annual corporate bonds, Treasury bills, and notes under a spreadsheet analysis to see which was the better deal. In other words, annuities are far from the simple, conservative investments they are advertised as. *Caveat emptor.*

It is for this reason, as well as others, that you can actually end up with less money with a tax-deferred annuity than you would with other investments. If the subsequent annual returns on a flex (monthly) annuity are set so low below economic rates, then you have gained nothing by sticking monies into a clearly underperforming product. It would have been better to use higher taxable returns—even using municipal obligations. Unfortunately, many retirees have been lulled into the use of so-called conservative annuities because the companies marketing them would obviously never mention the real-life ploys and disadvantages.

Two-Tier Annuities

Another gem is called a *two-tier annuity*. This type of investment was used extensively in the 403(b) (teachers) market in the 1980s. To illustrate how one works, suppose a company offers a nice rate each year—7 percent. So after, say, investing $400 for 20 years you have more than $200,000 that you think is all yours. Right? Nope. If you want to take all the money out as a lump sum, the company recalculates the account at a lower return over the 20 years at, say, 5 percent. Table 10.3 illustrates the numbers.

Table 10.3 Returns on Two-Tier Annuities

Monthly Investment and Return	Total Return Two-Tier Return	One-Tier Return
$400 per month/ 20 years, 7% (Accumulation Value)	$208,371 (Looks good but see below to what you can actually get in cash)	
$400 per month @ 5% (Cash value)	$164,413 ($43,957 LESS)	
$400 per month @ 6.25%		$190,390 (What you see is what you get and a lot more than the two-tier lump sum)

Two-tier annuities are not a good deal. Why do consumers buy these? Most likely, it was because the agent didn't tell them how the tiers worked, didn't understand the two-tier methodology, or simply wanted a higher commission. Or maybe consumers didn't do their homework.

Anyway, as the owner of the two-tier annuity in our example, could you get the $208,371 you thought you would? Yes and no. You could get the full $208,371, but you'd be forced to take payments (annuitization) over something like three years, five years, or more. And guess what happens when you are forced into taking money over a period of time? The company can reduce the interest rate to almost anything it wants. Getting 7 percent on the way in does you no good if you are forced into 2 percent or 3 percent on the way out. Are there many of these two-tier annuities now? No, but they are still out there. And you need to be vigilant about doing your homework in order to avoid them.

(I know some of you are getting glassy eyed with these initial numbers and comments. But all this—and more to come—is mandatory for an understanding of these "simple" investments.)

When a Rate Is Not a Rate

In early 2001, a company sent out thousands of brochures—probably hundreds of thousands—touting a five-year 7.25 percent guaranteed return on an annuity. It was a heck of a deal. I had to find out what was going on, though I was pretty sure of the underlying tactics. Well, it was true: Consumers would get a guaranteed 7.25 percent for a five-year period. But then they couldn't get the money. How's that? If they wanted the money after five years, they had to take a five-year forced annuitization where the company guaranteed that the payout rate would be no lower than 2.5 percent. Now, do you understand what happens with forced annuitization? They can market extra-high rates at any time, but they can simply take them away with very low rates later on.

Are You Getting the Best Rate?

When an agent offers or suggests a rate, you may never be sure it is the best rate the company can provide you. This sort of uncertainty has been going on for years. A real-life example shows you that, unless you research what the rates and terms actually are (which rarely happens and is basically an impossibility, anyway), you can get a lower yield and longer term simply because the agent wanted a higher commission. Table 10.4 illustrates the math.

In Table 10.5, we see that commissions play a huge role in annuities. Pay specific attention to the increase in commissions against the lower rates.

Notice what is going on? The agent is obviously presented with several options of interest rates and time frames. But what is really happening is that the company has carved out lower interest rate returns with higher commissions, allowing various agents a selection as to what they offer the client. I have been at several seminars in which a company offers various rates to agents and says they should just pick whatever commissions they want. Though I have never seen any statistics indicating what rate is more prevalent, I think the agent's focus would

Table 10.4 Rates and Yields

Annuity	Guarantee Rate	Guaranteed Period	Agent Commission
A	6.85%	5 years	1.85%
B	7.0%	7 years	1.85%

Table 10.5 Commissions and Return Rates

Annuity	Guarantee Rate	Guaranteed Period	Agent Commission
C	6.52%	6 years	3.25%
D	6.63%	8 years	3.25%
E	5.82%	10	5%

CAVEAT INVESTOR

By way of a real-life example, I once used one of the higher rates / lowest commissions in a referral from an agent on a 1035 exchange (a nontaxable transfer of assets from one company to another) for a poorly performing 403(b) plan. He was getting 50 percent of the commission. Once I discovered the 6.85 percent return, I opted for it without hesitation. But I was soundly rebuked when I told him the commissions were only 1.85 percent. His comment simply was that the client was going to get a good rate anyway with a longer six-year period, lower 6.52 percent rate, and higher 3 percent commission.

I suppose the issue might have been moot, because the difference in returns over a total of five or six years might not have been that much. But it was not moot to me because the client comes first.

I believe this kind of scenario is standard. Agents will go for the higher commissions and rationalize that the client is doing fine anyway. It's a perfect example of moral egoism, situational ethics, and ethical relativism.

be on the higher commission rates, primarily because the consumer has no idea what is going on anyway.

Fiduciary Obligation?

Let me also ask this rhetorical question: If an agent selected the lower rates as the best investment for the client, was it a breach of a *fiduciary obligation* for the agent not to divulge the different rates from which he could have selected? You would think so, but perhaps not. That's because the first fiduciary obligation is due to the insurance company. (It's different from the securities industry, where the client supposedly comes first. Notice I said "supposedly.")

Nonetheless, I think something is really amiss, since an agent might have even tried to place a 10-year rate above 5.82 percent solely for the 5 percent commission. An ethical agent wouldn't do that, but that is not the point here. The fact is, you should be informed about areas you may never have dreamt of and people with whom you really shouldn't deal. This is just one area where consumers have no knowledge of what may be going on.

It's also one where I don't think the practice will change one bit, since there would need to be a wholesale change in the marketing of products. Why won't it change? Because there simply is no consumer backlash against the industry, largely because consumers don't even know what is going on and how it really affects them—and their pocketbooks.

Surrender Charges

Almost all commercial products (meaning products that are sold by agents) that I am aware of use *surrender charges* to recoup costs, if you should decide to leave the company too early. Surrender charges are simply a percentage that is charged against the remaining principal for a period of (normally) 5 to 10 years.

Here is an example. You buy into an annuity and face a seven-year surrender charge of 7, 7, 6, 5, 4, 3, 2, 0 percent if you took out money before the contract expired. If the policyholder decides to exit the annuity, say, in the second year, the owner will be charged a 7 percent fee on the principal. However, almost universally, annuity companies allow a 10 percent withdrawal each year without any surrender charges. They just don't want you to leave early. That's entirely justified since they paid out a lot in costs and commissions to get you into the thing. You need to read the contract carefully to know the fees—though few consumers actually do that. But if you haven't paid attention to the problems addressed above and buy in without doing your homework, you probably will get hammered later on.

Payouts

Great numbers of retirees and preretirees think annuities are great vehicles since, if you opt for a life payout, you cannot outlive the payments. True, but so what? If you give me a dollar when you are born, I can pay you money for your lifetime starting immediately and still make a tidy profit. How? Simple. All I have to do is to pay no interest (and this actually happened with one annuity company that was sued a few years ago). Or, more likely, I can pay you a very small interest rate. So, tell me this: You are age 65, male, in average health, have $100,000 to invest, and will get $523 per month for life. Is that any good? Nope. It's a negative return. You'd only get back $94,140. What about a payout of $600 per month? That's about a 1 percent return. Feel better now?

How in the world did I get those numbers? Were they provided by the annuity company? No and no. The companies may indicate the lowest rate they will pay, but rarely have I seen a policy that indicates what the yield will be on a lifetime payout (some Web site annuities now do). You have to figure the return by estimating a singular number: your actuarial lifetime. And, of course, you must have a financial calculator to do that correctly.

This is how it works. You know the principal, in this case, $100,000. You know the monthly return, in this case, $600 per month. You know the final value is $0 since neither you nor anyone else will get anything back (life annuity). So, the missing ingredient is the time frame. But isn't that impossible to figure out, since you don't know how long you will live? That's what you think.

In reality, there are lifetime actuarial standards that every person can, and should use, in an analysis involving long-term care, estate planning, retirement planning, and almost everything else. Actuarial standards will help determine the time frame.

The standard I use is from the U.S. Department of Health and Human Resources, though there are many others. For those uninitiated with such lifetime tables, let's explain a couple items to make more sense.

You may be aware that the lifetime for a newborn female is about 80 years and a lifetime for a newborn male is about 75 years. There is roughly a five-year difference in actuarial life. (Although men have been gaining in life expectancy faster than women most recently.)

But, assume you are a man already age 65. Does that mean that you only have ten more years to live? Of course not. The longer you live, the longer you have to live. Statistically, other people have died before you, and the ones that are left simply have a separate, remaining actuarial lifetime for that age. In the case of a man, it's about 15 more years. In the case of a woman, it's almost another 20 years. Now, you also add or subtract years depending on heredity, health, lifestyle, income, your main activity for the week is watching fishing videos on ESPN2, and many more factors. (Actually, I learned a lot from Jimmy Houston, but I digress....)

In fact, there are many Internet sites where you can use a checklist of various questions to estimate how long you have left to live. This is, therefore, how you determine what the return might be on an annuity or other unknown payment that uses a remaining lifetime: you estimate your supposed lifetime and add in a fudge factor.

For the calculation above, I used an actuarial lifetime of a 65-year-old man (15 years) plus another five years, for a total of 20 years. The yield can then be calculated at about 3.92 percent. You have to do this calculation for each annuity to determine if the yield is acceptable and makes economic sense. In this day and age, 3.92 percent may be acceptable, considering the current low rates. That said, you are tied to that rate for an estimated 20 years. Further, if you died earlier, say at the standard 15-year expectancy, your return drops to 1.05 percent.

The point is that companies tell you what you will get per month, but not what the return is projected to be. Of course, they could state that they don't know exactly how long you will live. But you won't get life expectancy estimations from them either, and that's the reason someone has to do the calculation. You have to know the approximate yield—how else can you make a objective decision? You really need to do the numbers.

Some journalists suggest that you just compare payouts from various companies and choose the maximum—assuming that they all have the highest rating from the various rating services (S&P, AM Best) as well. That might work, but maybe not. And that's why you need to compare the returns against what you could have made if you bought, say, a bunch of staggered Treasury instruments.

For example, the *staggering* (or *laddering*) might consist of 20 percent of one-year T bills paying, say, 1.75 percent, 20 percent of five-year notes paying 2.25 percent, 20 percent of 10-year notes at 4.25 percent, and so on. Use whatever combination you want and whatever time frames you desire. (The above rates reflect some of the lowest rates due to the recession.) You might also consider the inflation-adjusted bonds.

Admittedly, there is more work to accumulating a portfolio of staggered returns than this. And you face potential commissions, though not if you buy the issues directly. And you can't be sure you will always beat the returns on an annuity should economic interest rates tank (which was exactly the scenario in 2002). But there is a major plus to staggered or laddered bonds. The money is yours. Or, better phrased, you can get to it if you need it.

The point is that once you decide to annuitize (get payments) from an annuity, that's basically all you can get. You can't get your principal, for all intents and purposes. (A very few annuities now offer riders where you can get access to some of your funds. But the cost of the riders will reduce your annual payout. There is no free lunch.)

In our example annuity, you gave $100,000 principal to the insurance company for the guarantee of $600 per month for life. That's it. If you needed $25,000 after one year, tough luck. You gave the company the money, they invested it, and they gave you a contractual return over your lifetime. If you or your spouse become ill, too bad. If you need to make a major repair or fix the house, too bad. If your son needs some emergency money for his child, too bad. If they just opened a new casino, too bad.

CAVEAT INVESTOR

Some articles note that you shouldn't tie up all your money in an annuity. An oft-quoted rule of thumb says that you should not put more than 25 percent in an annuity during retirement. And where did that figure come from? Formal analysis of a retiree's assets and budget? No.

These rule-of-thumb simplistic rules are rarely valid, save by luck, and I find them to be a disservice to the public. Simplistic comments rarely address real life or the effort necessary to do comprehensive retirement planning. In the end, you have to do your own homework, do the calculations, and follow your budget.

Retirees fail to acknowledge that once you retire and get older, *stuff happens.* You invariably need more access to money after you retire than before. Tying up large sums of your assets simply to get payments for a lifetime or for you and your spouse may be exactly the wrong thing to do. Annuities in this case become risky investments, not conservative ones.

The Wall Street Journal Goes Out to Lunch

The Wall Street Journal puts out a lot of good stuff, but in early 2003 they published a totally misleading article on annuities that clearly exposes the fallacy that annuities are simple. It noted: "Suppose a 65-year-old woman invested $100,000 in an immediate-fixed annuity. That would buy her monthly income of $613, according to Berkshire Hathaway's Web site. That's equal to a 7.4 percent yield, far above the 4 percent yield on 10-year Treasury notes."[3] What a lot of garbage. The stated yield has no reflection to reality.

Here is what makes it so bad. It is true that the payment is $613 per month, or $7356 annually. It is true that if you divide $7356 by

$100,000, you get a 7.4 percent "number." But it is not "yield." The bulk of the $7356 received each year is nothing more than a return of part of the $100,000 invested. (That's also how you are taxed on a life annuity.) The annuity payment gives you back part of your original capital on a monthly or annual basis, which is not taxed, along with the interest on the investment, which is taxed. In January 2002, there was not an insurance company anyplace that could offer a life annuity at 7.4 percent. Think about it—if there was, not a soul would have invested in the stock market when you could have gone into this annuity and gotten a guaranteed 7.4 percent return for life.

How do you figure the return? The same way we identified previously, by using a 20-year actuarial lifetime. The return actually is 4.17 percent. That's a 77 percent difference from what the article said. And it's a reflection of the dangers of oversimplification and misinformation.

The article went on to state, "according to Berkshire's Web site, a 75-year-old woman who invested $100,000 in an immediate-fixed annuity would get monthly income of $785, equal to a 9.4 percent yield." They did the same thing again by multiplying $785 by 12 months for $9420, dividing it by $100,000, and saying the yield is 9.4 percent. Hogwash! What was she getting based on an actuarial lifetime of 12.2 years, which is how long a 75-year-old woman statistically might live? The annualized return ends up being 2.3 percent. She would have to live "forever" in order to get a true 9.4 percent return.[4]

It should be clear—and I have repeated this before—that you must know how to utilize a financial calculator. If you did, you'd know the important numbers—the real-life return.

Other Payouts

Annuities can be structured with payouts other than life only. For instance, you could use a joint life survivor payment. A joint life covers for yourself for life and then for a beneficiary for life. Most people tend to think of a spouse as the other beneficiary, but it could be anybody. As should be obvious, the more people you put as payees, the lower the monthly payment each would receive. You figure the return the same way, except you need a chart that identifies a joint life actuarial lifetime. The following paragraphs describe the types of calculations you need to make.

Payouts over a Set Period

For payouts over a set period, assume you are age 65 and want a 5-, 10, 15-, or whatever-year payout. Since you know the time frame, you can easily determine the yield and compare it against other companies' yields. There is no guessing here about how long anyone is going to live; it is the time frame selected that controls the calculation.

Payments over a Life or a Guaranteed Period

For payments over a life or a guaranteed period, you can get a guaranteed payment for, say, 10 years, or if you're still living after that, for life. Assume you had one of these 10-year plans and you died after six years. Your beneficiary gets payments for four more years (10 total) and then the payments cease. But if you happen to live past 10 years, you continue to get payments until you die. The payments are far less than life, only because you have selected a guaranteed minimum period for payments.

Lump-Sum Payments

Lump-sum payments may seem the most obvious solution for many, since you get your money and control the asset as you desire. I think it is a most desirable option, but you still have to do a financial calculation to determine if it is valid.

Sometimes the companies discount the cash flow substantially and present a lump-sum value that is too low. The calculation for a discounted cash flow is beyond the scope of this text, but you need to do it to determine which payment is better—a lump sum now or payments for a period of time? That said, note again how involved a "simple" annuity has become.

Anyway, the first question is whether a lump sum is even available for you. Let's assume you were the beneficiary of an annuity and you were unfamiliar with the contents of the original contract (even many owners are unclear). You will be sent forms by the company asking for the type of payout you want. However, a lump-sum option may be suspiciously absent. That's because the company, obviously, wants to keep control of the assets by annuitizing the principal and may not reference a lump-sum option. On numerous occasions I have had to call companies to find out whether, in fact, a lump sum was available. Such "omission" could be called a breach of the company's fiduciary obligation to clients. Regardless, it simply reflects how business is done and yet another reason to be cautious with annuities.

Summary

The essentially conservative annuity may have been turned on its head by the realities of the business. In this chapter, we have provided the kind of insight you need to protect yourself. Unfortunately, in many of the cases identified, a lot of the information you need to analyze (assuming you could use a financial calculator) is not even known by agents (past history of company yields, for example). And other data needs to be properly researched for the calculations—again beyond the limited background of agents.

You really need to do a lot of homework on the offering company before purchasing an annuity. And the homework involves past history of rates to get some idea of future returns. It is not an easy task even for an agent who makes the effort. And someone must know how to use a financial calculator. But it's your money, so decide how much effort should be expended.

Notes

1. *The Wall Street Journal* is one of the nation's premier financial authorities and it can't even figure out how an annuity works. Furthermore, once notified, they did nothing to correct the errors. As a result, I'm sure that many trusting readers bought something that could never work as presented. It sure shows that even the experts can't figure annuities out.
2. Just so you know, I have used fixed annuities. If you get a good company, fixed annuities work just as intended. The returns can surpass CDs, Treasuries, and other investments and are excellent considerations if economic rates are declining. A few years ago when rates were tanking (and were expected to continue that way, as far as I was concerned when I viewed the economic forecast), I used a 6 percent, five-year guaranteed annuity, five-year surrender.
3. Jonathan Clements, "Answering the Critics: Buying Annuities Makes Sense, but Avoid These Traps," January 22, 2003.
4. The really sad part is that the Berkshire Hathaway site actually tells you what the inherent yield is. *The Wall Street Journal* couldn't decipher the numbers correctly (or perhaps they didn't even read the right numbers from the Web site). They ran no correction. They had no idea what they were talking about. And this from one of the most prestigious financial publications in the world. Now do you see how badly annuities can be misinterpreted by the supposed experts?

CHAPTER 11

INSURANCE

*I*NSURANCE, PROPERLY UTILIZED, IS NOTHING MORE than a pool of money to reimburse those who experience a misfortune. Others simply get the emotional protection for a loss that may never occur. In essence, therefore, you hope to never have to use it.

In this chapter, it is not my intent to reinvent the wheel with every element of insurance. I will simply attempt to keep the focus simple—just the way I endeavor to do so with clients. That said, no matter how simple anybody tries to reanalyze this material, once you see a policy illustration or talk with any company representatives and agents, your eyes will gloss over and, in a matter of seconds, you'll start thinking about how you really would rather watch a tractor pull.

While other areas of personal finance have come under attack for poor standards, there has been a somewhat valiant attempt by the National Association of Insurance Commissioners (NAIC) for higher ethical standards and more conformance nationwide within the insurance industry. Their continued attempts will make the process better over time—though they are still beholden directly to the life insurance companies and reform will only go so far. I am unsure whether any entity, including the Internal Revenue Service, can keep up with the proliferation of products designed to fill financial coffers and, especially, the agency firms that battle each day to retain agents and acquire new ones.

And what is the focus for all these products? Money.

Money is generated through lots of agents getting lots of commissions. That said, don't think that all commissionable agents are bad or that all commissions are exorbitant. Some fee services can hammer you worse than a commission ever could. Actually, it is not just the commissions themselves that are the real trouble—it is the trips, bonuses, and other promotions that insurance agents compete for (often at the expense of consumers) that defy logic. Additionally, the main thrust of literally every product offered to agents is the high commissions to be earned. (At least 60 percent of the material I get focuses heavily on how great the commissions are. It really gets nauseating.) These incentives are clearly one of the main reasons why insurance has such a bad name. It's too much money gunning for too little business by agents with limited expertise on too many products, the bulk of which are not needed or do not work as presented.

What are the other problems? Education and knowledge. The situation is just terrible. States have some form of licensing training, though it varies tremendously. Those in California are required to attend a 52-hour course, of which 14 hours incorporates ethics. After that, a new agent is required to attend 25 hours each year of continuing education for the first four years and 30 hours each two years after that. Many states, however, may have only one day of licensing preparation before the exam, and the answers are pretty much preordained by licensing instruction that's keyed to the exams. And continuing education varies all over the board.

Now, I am not saying that, in California or any other state, valid knowledge is not presented. Of course it is. But a lot of the information is old and a lot of it is simplistic. (That said, for the true professionals seeking solid information, the courses and instruction can be found.) But rarely does any of it apply to real-life situations. This is the real problem! The instruction is so far behind current product and application, it's ludicrous. It takes a lot of time and subsequent effort to accumulate the real life knowledge and competency.

There is a separate issue that is even worse—those entities that offer insurance advice that have no background or licensing in insurance at all. This topic is addressed more fully later on. But, for now, recognize that most people who charge for insurance advice without a license generally don't have a clue to the knowledge necessary in this area. And most of these planners are illegal, never mind incompetent. Be very careful.

But first things first.

Who Should Buy Insurance?

I am single. I have a couple of stray cats. That's it. No one is financially dependent upon me and I have no interest in rewarding someone or some entity when I die. (Yes, the cats are already provided for. Actually, I know an estate attorney who practices almost exclusively in trusts for pets.) Therefore I have no life insurance. That's generally the reason to purchase a policy: when someone is financially dependent upon you. If a couple is married, the breadwinner should purchase insurance in case of his or her demise. The amount to be considered (to be discussed later) is based on the person dying now and analyzing the financial deficit left for the spouse. If the couple is not married, say, for same-sex unions, and you want to cover for the same contingencies, life insurance is an excellent method to bypass family problems and provide for a loved one with less hassle than a will or trust. (A minimum of a will is mandatory. A revocable living trust might be a better alternative.)

If you are young and contemplating marriage or another type of union in which someone will rely upon you, you may want to consider life insurance—even though you may not have yet found that other person—solely to be sure that coverage will be available. This is normally not what most advisers suggest and certainly what I have discouraged in the past. For example, I have been absolutely loath to suggest that parents buy life insurance on their children since it countermands the basics of insurance need. But the concern that I have is the poorer health of younger children—and I primarily refer to diabetes. The younger

CAVEAT INVESTOR

By definition, obesity is being 30 to 50 pounds overweight, depending on height. From 1976 to 1980, 32 percent of Americans were overweight and 15 percent were obese. In 1999, according to a *Washington Post* article, 34 percent were overweight and 27 percent were obese. It noted that about 300,000 Americans die each year from ailments "caused or worsened" by obesity, and that the problem is likely to surpass tobacco as the leading cause of preventable deaths.

It's not just the fact that about 60 percent of U.S. adults are overweight or obese, it's that so are nearly 13 percent of children. The problem with juvenile diabetes is epidemic. Obesity rose from 12 percent in 1991 to 19.8 percent in 2000. Diabetes increased from 4.9 percent to 7.3 percent. Between 1999 and 2000, obesity increased from 18.9 percent to 19.8 percent, and diabetes increased from 6.9 percent to 7.3 percent. Two decades ago, Type 2 diabetes in children was only 3 percent to 5 percent but now it is 25 percent to 30 percent. This type of diabetes causes heart attacks and strokes. About 95 percent of all diabetics have Type 2 diabetes.

Eighty percent of diabetics are obese. Part of the problem is that 27.3 percent of all Americans do not engage in any physical activity and only 25 percent consume the proper amount of fruits and vegetables per day. Only 17.5 percent of Americans get the recommended 30 minutes of exercise.

I don't think the situation will get better—in fact, chances are it will grow far worse. For example, one school in Northern California altered their high-fat lunch menus to also offer nutritional meals. They weren't just dead sprouts and obnoxious (or just plain noxious) broccoli—the special meals were under contract by a chef. The meals didn't cost more than the fatty stuff, but they also didn't sell. The school quit the offering and went back to the standard fare of high-fat foods. The kids were happy again, pounds were gained, cholesterol levels skyrocketed, feet swelled, and so on.

Because of poor diet, lack of exercise, and weight gain, many of the health problems normally seen much later in life—even dismissing diabetes—are likely to start in people when they are in their early twenties or thirties. That's earlier than the age that many people now get married. So I have tempered some of my previous comments about insurance being purchased before the actual need, meaning that it might behoove someone to purchase insurance before getting married, certainly if there is a family history of problems.

That said, I still have a problem with insurance for newborns; that seems too early. But if a parent came to me indicating that a disease has manifested itself within a family for generation to generation, I might reconsider the normal requirements.

This certainly goes against the acceptable fundamentals of proper insurance coverage, and I never want someone to spend money needlessly. But experience in life shows that not everything follows past history. Further, obesity is a major issue with long-term care as well, so my focus in that area carries over to younger clients. You'll have to use some of your own judgment when determining whether health or other issues are serious enough to warrant purchasing life insurance for children or single adults.

generation is not getting enough exercise and they are really getting chubby, as are the adults. If the parents have had a history of poor health, symptoms of diabetes may manifest themselves in the children much faster in today's sedentary society. Obviously, the cost for the extra insurance must still fit within the family budget, but having it may be beneficial in certain circumstances.

As regards families with children, obtaining insurance for the breadwinner is mandatory unless you have lots of money. Because few people do, insurance is the easiest method of protecting them or other loved ones from the early demise of one or both of the breadwinners.

Getting insurance for the breadwinners in the family comes before you use money for investments, a 401(k) plan, or just about anything else. If you look at the pyramid of investing (see Chapter 6), you will note such coverage is at the very bottom of the pyramid and needs to be done before moving upward to other, more risky, and unessential areas. There is no excuse for not buying insurance for the breadwinners.

Disability Coverage

Irrespective of my legitimate concern about younger people dying, the death rate for young people is still relatively low. But there is a much higher chance of someone young or middle aged becoming disabled because of disease or injury. For example, a 30-year-old woman has a 16 percent chance of dying before age 65. But she has a 57 percent chance of becoming disabled, and that much larger concern requires consideration.

Currently, the main reasons for long-term disability are as follows:

Cancer: 13 percent
Complications from pregnancy: 12 percent
Back problems: 11 percent
Cardiovascular problems: 9 percent
Depression: 5 percent

The following are the main causes of short-term disability:

Pregnancy (normal): 20 percent
Pregnancy (complications): 9 percent
Injuries (excluding back): 9 percent
Back injuries and problems: 8 percent
Digestive/intestinal ailments: 8 percent

Those who are seriously overweight will have more complications with pregnancies, back, and digestive/intestinal problems. According to the *Disability Management Sourcebook*, the number of people between the ages of 17 and 44 with severe disabilities has increased 400 percent over the past 25 years. I believe that while medications will keep many of the severely disabled alive, there may be an increase in younger mortality. It's a tough call, but it's better to be prepared. So, disability insurance should be something to consider, especially if your family history reveals any of the long- or short-term problems mentioned previously.

Estate Insurance

What about insurance to pay for estate taxes? Congress has changed the amount that anyone can leave at death to $1 million (2003), moving upward to an unlimited amount by 2010.[1]

Let's look at a $1 million estate. That amount can actually be deceiving in that what you own at death can be much larger than what you might think. Why's that? Because of the way the Fed looks at a net estate versus a gross estate. For example, assume a single person had assets totaling $1.4 million at death. Let's also assume there was a $300,000 mortgage, car loan, and other costs of death, for a $450,000 total. Guess what? That adds up to net estate of $950,000—and no problem with federal estate taxes.

So what about estate insurance if your net estate is larger than $1 million? Assuming it was $1.5 million net, the taxes would be $555,800. But you can leave $1 million tax free, as of 2003, and the tax offset for a $1 million estate is $345,800. Subtract that for a total tax due of $210,000.

How do you pay that kind of a tax bill? Loan? Cash? Life insurance? Steal? Actually life insurance, properly utilized, is generally great leverage and at a most acceptable price. (That's assuming you buy the right policy, not some variable product loaded with extra fees and more.) You pay a little money over time for a large payout later. So you could buy a $210,000 policy for not too much money (assuming you can pass underwriting). Nice thought, probably lousy execution. Why? Because as long as the owner (you) is the insured, the life insurance is simply added to your overall estate, making it $1.71 million ($1.5 million plus the $210,000 policy), which adds up to an even larger tax. Therefore, using life insurance as a hedge against estate taxes tends to be folly.

What can you do? You could make your son, daughter, or whomever your beneficiary is the owner of the life insurance policy. Then, when you died, the insurance would go to that other person—not to you—and they could use the full value to pay the estate tax. (Of course, you may have to give gifts to the beneficiary to pay the bills for the insurance, so be careful that you don't give it to a habitual spender who might let the policy lapse. I'd never let that happen.)

You could also initiate an irrevocable life insurance trust and make the trust the owner of the policy. These special and separate trusts keep the insurance out of the estate through compliance with certain tax codes.

Right? Fuhgetaboutit!

By the time you paid an attorney for all the forms necessary to do this, got a CPA to do the tax filings each year, and tried gifting with a Crummey power, you wouldn't have any money left to tax anyway. (As stated, the focus for this book is the "average" American consumer, not some family with a $10 million estate. If you have a large estate, there are a number of tax avenues to attempt with insurance. And as for the Crummey power—don't ask. It is not relevant to the average consumer, certainly in context with President Bush's new tax laws that increase the estate amount you can leave at death.)

Some of my clients do have an estate currently exceeding the minimum exemption to be left at death. In one situation, the client was aware of the tax consequences of dying early with the larger estate, but he was also aware that the cost of insurance and the other alternatives was far more involved. He did not want to involve his kids with various estate strategies—and he didn't want to buy some life insurance anyway at his age (72). He was healthy and active, so I asked him if he could just live a few more years. He opted to take the chance. I also told him to spend more money since he had more than necessary for his lifetime. It just does not make sense to burden yourself with extra insurance or trusts unless you have a lot of money to make it financially and emotionally worthwhile. Sure, taxes can be a burden. But the payment is not the be all and end all of your life.

The above examples referenced a single person. Can you leave more money if you are married? Yes. The amount of an estate for a married couple can be $2 million together (as of 2003, if it's allocated correctly) before taxes are applied. Therefore, the use of insurance to cover any excess taxes is relatively moot for the average consumer. We'll talk more about this topic in Chapter 14.

Amount of Insurance

You'll know when you have too much insurance when you are afraid to go to sleep before your spouse does.

Assume you need insurance. You first need to determine the amount, then the time frame, and then the type. Numerous rules of thumbs can be used to estimate the amount insurance. I don't like such simplistic methods since they are apt to omit important information or dismiss the present value of money. However, I do admit there are times where the longer, more analytical methods are not necessarily valid. For example, if I am dealing with term insurance and the price is low, I may indicate a lump-sum amount based on my experience and judgment.

If I had opted to analyze the situation using a more complete formula, I would have used the one shown in the worksheet in Table 11.1.[2] This particular worksheet does use a few rules of thumbs and should get you close to the figure you need to determine.

Simple, wasn't it?

Calculate the number using the worksheet in Table 11.1 for the situation in which the other spouse dies first. Remember, you are basing the amount on the assumption that the person died at the time of the application, not some time in the distant future.

Table 11.1 Funds to cover for breadwinner (assume that the breadwinner dies now).

1. Funeral expenses	_____	5 percent of estate
2. Estate taxes	_____	$0
3. Mortgage	_____	Optional
4. Other debts	_____	Optional
5. College funds	_____	$5,000,000 (hey, you wanted kids, you've got to pay)
6. Miscellaneous	_____	Optional
7. Subtotal	_____	

FUNDS FOR SURVIVORS LIVING EXPENSES

8. Current household expenses	_____	Demands complete budget for correct interpretation
9. Percentage of budget for survivor	_____	60 percent, 80 percent, or whatever
10. Survivor annual expense =	_____	
11. Social security benefits	− _____	Always call the Social Security Administration
12. Spouses take-home pay	− _____	
13. Annual needs	= _____	
14. Number of years needed	_____	Look at actuarial table (see a lifetime table in appendix)
15. Subtotal (13 × 14)	= _____	
16. Total assets needed (7 + 15)	_____	
17. Existing insurance	− _____	Be sure to subtract any loans against insurance.
18. Income-producing assets or assets to be used up	− _____	Such assets can include IRAs, 401(k)s, and so on—assuming after the market losses of 2000–2002 you have anything left
19. Additional insurance needed	_____	

Explanations, line by line:

1. The rule of thumb is to estimate between $5000 and $20,000 for funeral expenses. Others suggest 5 percent of the estate.

2. With an estate under $1 million for a single person or $2 million for a married person, and transfer of assets of the first to die with unlimited marital deduction or with appropriate trusts, there need be no estate tax. I think most average middle-class people can avoid estate taxes altogether since most combined assets will not be that large.

3. and 4. Some may feel that paying off these debts is optional, though most people do like to focus on the mortgage at least being paid off. But, if not, will there be sufficient income from the surviving spouse's salary to continue making the debt payments? It's generally suggested that both these be paid in most cases.

5. Okay, the costs of college will not be $5 million, but they are still going to be a lot for sending your children through school. The average college costs in 2002 for private schools was $17,123 and public schools $3754, and most recent increases at some colleges exceed 20% annually. That does not include room and board. For a newborn, the estimated cost of college 18 years from now is $268,335 for a four-year private school. But you do not necessarily need to input the whole amount for college. Why? Because if you died today and your child were just born, the current amount you need would be based upon a figure that would grow over time. For example, if you did need $268,000 (rounded) 18 years from now and the kitty would grow at 6 percent, you would need $94,000 today. If your child is already closer to college age, you have to put in more because the amount has a shorter time to grow. I definitely

suggest you review your state's 529 plan, where earnings can be totally tax free.

6. Perhaps a miscellaneous item could be a charitable gift or a lump sum for a special friend.

8, 9, and 10. Most articles suggest using a percentage of your current income. But there is a big difference between your total gross income and the net you live on or should live on. A formal budget, as identified elsewhere, is the only valid way to figure out what you are spending and whether it should be adjusted up or down (usually down). Without that budget, taking a percentage of a bogus number is mostly useless.

11. These pages will not delve into the intricacies of every level of social security for survivors. Suffice to say, if there are no children, the survivor cannot generally get social security benefits till age 60 (widows and widowers). If there are children, the survivor can get benefits for him- or herself and also for the children until they reach 18 (or 19, if the child is still in school). You can go to the Social Security Agency site for more detail (www.ssa.gov) or call the agency directly. If you are dealing with an advisor, that person should know this area cold. If not, walk away.

    Social security benefits can be a godsend to survivors. Furthermore, in my personal experience, the Social Security Agency has done a very good job in relating to a survivor's emotions and needs. The employees have been understanding and competent—a critically important element when a loved one has been lost.

12. Will the survivor work after the spouse or partner has died? If there are children, recognize that the survivor may not be able to work full time. Or, if so, that there may be extra costs for childcare and other items.

13. Simple question: You are age 65. How long do you have to live? Check government tables and you will find that

a male has about another 15 years and a woman 20. Normally you also add about another few years—say five—so that the coverage is adequate. Of course, if you are constantly eating deep-fried food and sitting on the sofa all day with the TV remote grafted into your hand, you might subtract a few years.[3] Regardless of the time period you use, this type of form simply has you multiply the annual needs by the number of years to get the amount of gross coverage needed. Actually, the correct method is done differently with a present value calculation. Nevertheless, this simplistic method should help you judge whether numbers suggested by an agent are within reason. (But if you are using an agent—actually anyone—who is not using a personal financial calculator, I'd immediately go elsewhere. Computer programs that predict lifetimes are fine, in certain cases, for developing numbers. But the adviser has to know the fundamentals in order to be sure that the ultimate figures are within reason and are justified.)

Type of Insurance

A tremendous disservice is done to consumers regarding the immutable need for cash buildup in a life insurance policy so it can be used for college, retirement, flower arrangement lessons, or whatever. I am not stating that an inherent cash buildup may not be necessary to keep a policy afloat, but let's get real. You supposedly need to buy insurance. So buy insurance. If you are going for the inside buildup of assets, you invariably are crossing two different purposes in the same contract. Using cash buildup in life insurance policies can work, but it is costly and generally there are no guarantees. That, in itself, defeats the need for insurance. Buy just what you need.

Term Insurance

Most readers are familiar with pure insurance. The cheapest is *annual renewable term,* which goes up in cost each year. It is designed for short-term use. Even the best advisors use it incorrectly. Read on.

The first year of annual renewable term insurance is very cheap, but then it escalates dramatically after that. I've seen some real charlatans have a client buy a cheap policy with one company, wait a year, and then reapply to another the second year, and so on. (Believe it or not, this was a "fee only" planner.) Sure, the client could get some really low rates year after year, but it breaches the fiduciary duty to the insurance companies because the intent violates the duty to send the company only long-term clients. On the other side, first-year commissions are the highest, so it's another obvious fiduciary violation if implemented by a regular agent.

This tactic also puts the client into an untenable position. If the client suddenly becomes sick or injured and now becomes uninsurable, new acceptable insurance would be impossible to obtain. The client would be left with increasingly higher annual charges that, undoubtedly at some point, would become financially insufferable. The unfortunate client might have to terminate the policy simply because he or she could not afford it—where the initial intent was to be sure that the client got the lowest cost. Ethics is limited in this business. So is common sense.

Level Term Insurance

Level term is really straightforward insurance. It is based on the time frame in which you will need coverage. For example, say you have a newborn and you want coverage until that child is 18 and leaves the nest. You should very well consider a 20-year level term policy. Once you are accepted by the company, you pay the same rate for the next 20 years. Then it terminates. (There also are 5-, 10-, 15-, 20-, and 30-year level policies. You might find longer periods more suitable, depending on your age or need.)

Pundits of this type of pure insurance with no cash value reference the fact that you don't get any money back when the term is completed. So what? I buy car insurance and haven't had to use it for more than 30 years. You buy fire insurance on your house and have never had a fire. Term insurance—actually *any* insurance—is to provide emotional well being in case something bad should happen to you. If nothing bad happens, what's the problem? You never wanted to die early, see your house burn down, or whatever. You simply pooled your money with a bunch of other people, and only those unfortunates who had an accident or fire were reimbursed. There's nothing wrong with that at all. Term serves a purpose in that it provides the security that you want and need for a set period of time. It is cheap, because the statistical odds of dying, particularly for a young person, are very small.[4]

Whole and Universal Life Insurance

Two types of policies provide a cash buildup: whole life insurance and universal life insurance. You can (supposedly) make all sorts of money with one of these policies. Once in a while, and for certain specific purposes, they can be viable investments. For example, if you have an individual who just won't save at all and he or she needs insurance, the internal buildup of cash—available as a loan—can be a forced method of savings for years in the future.

But I have rarely found whole and universal life insurance to be that worthwhile or productive. And it costs you a lot more to utilize this type of product. I contend that if you want an investment, buy it separately. If you want insurance coverage, buy insurance.

Whole Life Insurance.   This is a quiz: How long do you think you will have to keep paying premiums on a *whole life insurance* policy? That's right—your whole life. Is it worthwhile? Maybe, since the guaranteed coverage for your whole life is the key feature you tend to look for if you need coverage for an extended period. (But use caution: These types of policies can also be imbued with all sorts of cash value gimmicks.) There aren't too many of these whole life insurance policies now being offered, and they tend to be more expensive than the universal policies.

Universal Life Insurance.   Rather than being forced into set payments for life, the *universal life insurance* policy is designed to separate the premium payments into costs for three things:

- Insurance coverage (for mortality—these payments rise each year as you get older)
- Expenses by the company for carrying the policy
- The return that the company is offering (generally guaranteed for a year)

The major difference between whole life and universal is that you can start and stop your premiums with universal life as you may desire, depending on the cash buildup in the policy. It provides flexibility that whole life does not generally provide.

Are there any inherent problems with these policies? Yes, you have no idea how long they might last if interest rates and the economy were to change—specifically when economic rates drop, as they have in the last 20 years or so. For example, policies in the 1980s were illustrated with 10 percent and higher interest returns and showed that the cash buildup would be so enormous that there would be a time when you wouldn't have to make anymore premium payments (sometimes called *the point of vanishing premiums*). When rates continued to decline, many policyholders got notices they had to infuse their policies with a lot of cash in order to keep them afloat. For those of you who bought such a policy just a few years ago, do you have any idea what might happen now that rates have declined precipitously?

Universal Variable Life Insurance.   As mentioned earlier, if you want to buy an investment, buy it outside of a life insurance policy. Don't jam up two entirely different tools designed for two entirely different purposes. A *universal variable life insurance* policy substitutes the fixed-interest-rate position with a selection of mutual funds with the intent of increasing the potential return substantially. Say, that sure sounds good, doesn't it? The problem is, you are invariably dealing with a dual licensee that is out to lunch on both fronts. First the life license, as repeatedly identified, is woefully suspect to begin with in the offering of most products, never mind a variable element. Secondly, the agent must also be securities licensed where the fundamentals of investing have never been taught. It's a double mess. Sure, these types of policies can work. But, as Harry Calahan once said, "do you feel lucky, punk?"

CAVEAT INVESTOR

A few years ago a Principal agent extolled the illustration he had done for a 35-year-old physician. By putting in hundreds of thousands of dollars over his working years, the client was then going to be able—at a 12 percent return—to remove millions of dollars during his retirement.

There was just one little kicker in the presentation to the client. The illustration did not show any impact for taxes—and neither the client nor the agent had any clue.

I don't know whether the client did anything, but it reinforces the problem in using an agent with just a license. Additionally, the odds of getting a 12 percent average return—though allowed for presentation purposes by law—is so statistically corrupt that it will rarely come to pass.

Another example: An ING and Washington Securities representative sold a 75-year-old widow a $20,000 variable life policy when she had no need for life insurance. She had an initial $500,000 estate—hence, no estate tax problem. But he illustrated the policy at 12 percent in 2001 that, with continued payments, would grow to well over $1 million (yeah, right!). Hence, he had an attorney draw up an irrevocable life insurance trust to protect that potential windfall for her beneficiaries. But the situation was worse than this. When she became my client, I did a budget analysis as identified in the retirement section. She never had $20,000 extra to spend on anything, certainly an unnecessary variable life policy. In fact she had to reduce her current spending habits by over $15,000 annually. Anyway, after $25,000 of payments, her account had "grown" to $7000.

More on this situation? The securities representative had filed for bankruptcy just before becoming licensed. A representative for the commissioner in the state where he practiced noted that such a person has "no business advising others on money."

The situation is now in the hands of an attorney.

True, the use of mutual funds in a life insurance policy does escape ordinary income tax as well as short- and long-term capital gains, assuming you maintain the policy for life. Otherwise you end up with ordinary income on anything over that which you paid for the policy. You need to understand and remember those implications.

The average consumer can use IRAs, 401(k)s, and other standard tax-sheltered vehicles without resorting to expensive variable annuities and variable life insurance as investment vehicles. Always use the less cumbersome tax-deferred or tax-free accounts (such as a Roth IRA, for example) before utilizing a separate account like this. The costs will be much cheaper.

Guaranteed Insurance for Life

Term insurance is guaranteed for the time frame in which you buy it. You don't worry about cash value or return of premium (generally)— it's just insurance. Hence, it is the cheapest policy for the time frame.

But is rarely offered past age 80. So even though you may have bought a perfectly good 30-year level term at age 50, if you still needed insurance past age 80 and went to reapply, you'd be shocked once you saw how large the premiums would be. Even if you are healthy, the premiums for annual renewable term are expensive. *Very* expensive. And if you happen to be in the poor health (but still insurable) the premiums will be higher still. Worse still, at age 80 (or whatever), you might now be uninsurable, and your plans for having insurance to last a lifetime are sunk. While insurance pundits talk about buying term insurance and investing the difference, it just won't work when you look at long time frames.

Of course, someone could say that insurance to last a lifetime is not necessary. This thinking is unacceptable. There are needs and wants that do exist for a full lifetime—estate planning being one, insurance being another. End of discussion.

So, if term can't provide the coverage and I have already discounted the standard and expensive whole and universal life products designed with cash value buildup, what's left? Whole and universal life policies that are designed for insurance and not the cash value buildup. For example, in the 1980s and 1990s, there were whole life policies where the cash value was effectively irrelevant. Because of that, the prices were the lowest you could find. Did they sell? Generally, no. When prices are low, the marketing is limited and so are the commissions. The best company was bought out in the mid-1990s. So, are you out of luck? Nope.

There are now many no-lapse universal life policies, which simply mean that as long as you pay the premiums, you keep the insurance. It won't lapse due to lower interest rates, higher costs of insurance, higher fees, and so on. It just keeps on as long as you pay the premium. This means no loans, no caring about the internal interest rate, no nothing. You wanted insurance for your lifetime and that is what you bought.

There may be whole life policies designed the same way by the time you read this. Again, the cash value buildup is irrelevant—you don't look to take out any money at all unless you want to simply terminate it.

You will have to use a good agent since these are all commission-able products. But good agents are out there. Get them from a highly rated company and simply be satisfied.

Company Ratings

This consideration is pretty simple. Don't buy insurance (or an annu-ity) from a company with less than an A rating. Period. Sure, other com-panies might be all right, but I think the risk is just too high. Check out Chapter 7 for my commentary on bond ratings.

From Whom Do You Buy Insurance?

Chapter 3 tackles who you can trust in the financial industry. It clearly identifies the kinds of agents, brokers, planners, and the like, in the busi-ness who have various backgrounds. Let's dismiss some right off the bat.

First is an insurance agent. By that I mean, someone with just an insurance license with no additional designations, classes (outside of continuing education), and so on.

I know that that thinking will offend many. By the same token, I know exactly what is taught in licensing classes in California. A 52-hour intensive class. About 14 hours of ethics. As to the other mind-numb-ing hours of instruction, the material is necessary to know, but it's not much good for real-life application. They just don't teach how a prod-uct might work given various situations, nor, for that matter, do they offer any insight whatsoever on new products coming to market. As such, new agents have an extremely limited knowledge base about how to use insurance properly. Additionally, major companies no longer pro-vide intense continuing instruction as they did many years ago in the 1970s and 1980s. That instruction is left primarily to the product agen-cies to do.

Probably one of the most hard-hitting comments about licensees is that all the sales are through commissionable agents. A recent study noted that many people question the objectivity of commission-based advice from financial firms and advisors.

But it's not all bad news. Most states require continuing education. (California mandates 25 hours each year for the first four years after licensing and 30 hours each two years after that. And if an agent wishes to be involved in long-term care, the state mandates an 8-hour course solely in this area every two years.) These courses can provide excellent information to students. Nonetheless, the knowledge tends to be presented as theory and as not real-life application. Certainly, as time goes on, an agent may stumble upon a good instructor. Or, perhaps, experience may provide the insight needed. But that provides little comfort to the consumer who needs—and demands—solid competency in this extremely difficult and ever-changing arena.

So let's move to the higher plane of competency. A Chartered Life Underwriter (CLU) or a Chartered Financial Consultant (ChFC) has extensive education in insurance because that is the main thrust of her or his training. They certainly can do a better job deciphering an illustration—but why get that involved to begin with? You are looking for insurance, not how to design the Sistine Chapel with the cash buildup of a policy. I certainly suggest you consider such individuals, but as with everything else, you will need to keep an open mind.

How about a Certified Financial Planner? I don't recommend you use them. I am not being unreasonable. I am a CFP and know many others. I am not impressed, certainly, when it comes to many CFPs' insurance knowledge or application. I have acted as an expert against some and filed complaints against many.

Remember, I am referring to a person's understanding and practical use of insurance. The College for Financial Planning eliminated its separate course in insurance in 1995. A ChFC absolutely has more background in insurance than a CFP. And ChFCs are universally licensed as agents. This is a very important distinction: Like it or not, you had better use someone who is licensed. Why? Very simply, you need someone who stays abreast of the rapidly changing laws and applications. And

CAVEAT INVESTOR

In one of the most egregious violations of fiduciary duty, a CFP who has earned millions of dollars had an elderly couple sell all existing singular policies and purchase a separate second-to-die policy. The intent was to cover taxes on a $5 million asset base that was expected to grow, through his expertise, to more than $15 million.

Through such "expertise," the husband lost his insurance and the only insurance then available was on the wife. He flipped the policies three times and went from a whole life guaranteed policy, to a universal life, to finally a $5 million universal variable policy for a 77-year-old while the value of all assets fell below $5 million. The wife had to take money out of an IRA, incur the highest income tax rate, and then gift the lessor amount to an irrevocable trust.

You don't have to grasp all the implications and innuendos. But suffice to say that it took more than $400,000 to come out of an IRA to pay the $264,000 of annual premiums on a nonguaranteed policy for an asset base that had actually diminished below the amount of the insurance purchased. Each time the policies were switched, huge commissions were earned. That's where the CFP's millions came from.

I completed a very extensive report and submitted it to an attorney in the state where the activity took place, where an arbitration has been filed. Unfortunately, the statute of limitations will bar some elements, but at least some return should be forthcoming.

The plaintiff initially contacted the CFP Board of Standards for any assistance. They told the client that more information was needed, yet privately exonerated the agent.

licensees have to do that. They need to attend seminars. They have to wend their way through a mind-numbing amount of mail, email, faxes, and other communications that are sent out by every agency, company, or other organization that is trying to offer its products. It is not only unlikely, but generally impossible, for any unlicensed entity to gather the insight and practical knowledge without licensing.

Let's address the minimum requirements for a good insurance agent/adviser. The following is what a highly respected text in life insurance has to say:

> Despite the widespread belief in the need for life and health insurance, and its vital importance to those who purchase it, few persons attempt to become familiar with the management, business policy and practices of the insurers backing their contracts. Even assuming that a considerable portion of policy owners could be induced to take an interest in the condition of their insurers, few would be sufficiently knowledgeable about insurance matters to ascertain intelligently the true state of affairs.
>
> A competent, informed, trustworthy insurance adviser is perhaps the consumer's best insurance against making an unwise purchase decision. Regrettably, some agents and other insurance advisers, although well intentioned, simply are not well informed. Too often, a state agent's licensing examination is not sufficiently rigorous to disqualify those with the inadequate knowledge. Additionally, in most states, many persons who give advice about life insurance are not required by the state to demonstrate any level of professional competence in life insurance matters. The use of an unqualified adviser can result in any inadequate, poorly designed, or unnecessarily costly insurance program.[5]

The authors also suggest that anyone dealing in this area have a minimum five years of experience. Maybe I am going too far, but I'd suggest as much as 10 years. Insurance really is a tough area, and you want someone with as much training and expertise as possible.

So what about going to an attorney or CPA for advice? Nope, I wouldn't recommend that either. I have a law degree. It's pretty useless when it comes to insurance. Some attorneys might like to think otherwise, and some will take your money for some esoteric analysis, but I sure wouldn't go that route. Per the *National Underwriter:* "Given that the subject of life insurance is rarely taught in law schools or accounting courses, most lawyers and accountants know little more about insurance than does the general public. When asked by their clients to advise on insurance, then, it is often easier to discourage their purchase than to expose the fact that they are truly ignorant about life insurance and how it works. Even the training that is available on these subjects may be inadequate to provide a level of comfort that lawyers or accountants need in order to recommend a purchase. As things now stand, we know of no reference material that is currently available that would enable an insurance professional or lawyer or accountant to access the technical information that applies to these new insurance products."

And while a CPA might be able to run some numbers on an illustration, so what? You want advice on insurance: Is it the right policy, and is it guaranteed? If you are playing some numbers trying to figure out whether the policy will last 15 years, 23 years, 37 years, 16 minutes, and so on, and whether the cash value is going to go to so many dollars, I think you missed the reason for buying insurance coverage.

What about fee-only planners? Let's talk about them. Actually, let's talk about any planner or planning firm that offers a fee for advice that includes a current life insurance policy. Most of them are doing so illegally. In at least 33 states, there is a separate license for those wishing to offer fee advice on insurance. I know some states' fee licensing requirements are relatively little more than a rehash of the existing licensing material. That isn't worth much, but at least the person is properly licensed, legal, and, perhaps, ethical. At least the state has some control over activity.

In California, the licensing requirements to provide fee advice on insurance includes five years of insurance experience and a mandatory 115 hours of continuing education required before taking the separate, very difficult analyst's exam. There are only about 40 Life and Disability Insurance Analysts in the state (of which I am one) who have a unique background and proven competency to address convoluted and difficult insurance issues. Those that do not have such a license and offer such advice—simplistic or otherwise—are operating illegally and, hence, unethically.

CAVEAT INVESTOR

Does the illegality discussed above stretch to CFPs, CPAs, ChFCs, and the associated entities in the Financial Planning Association (FPA), National Association of Personal Financial Advisers (NAPFA), and others, beyond that of the brokerage firms? It sure does. They all know it, but they also refuse to do anything about it since they would lose too many members. The problem? None of them could pass the analyst exam.

Per California Statutes, "... a person who, for a fee or compensation of any kind, paid by or derived from any person or source other than the insurer, advises, purports to advise, or offers to advise any person insured under, named as beneficiary of, or have any interest in, a life or disability insurance contract, in any manner concerning that contract or his or her rights in respect thereto must be licensed as a life and disability insurance analyst."

The CFP Board of Standards says it will not enforce an ethical violation unless it is preceded by a legal one. NAPFA, which presents its members as having the highest fiduciary duty, stated that it hoped that California would not enforce their laws since, if they did, other states might follow. (If you are wondering what has happened since, get the list of NAPFA reps in California and find out how many are properly licensed as required by law. Want a head start? Zero.)

I have developed this topic more fully in Chapter 2. But suffice it to say that literally all the entities involved in the supposed independent fee analysis of insurance need to work much more on exercising fiduciary responsibility, ethics, and legality.

Per the CFP Code of Ethics: Preamble, third sentence: "Implicit in the acceptance of this authorization [to be a CFP] is an obligation not only to comply with the mandates and requirements of all applicable laws and regulations but also to take responsibility to act in an ethical and professionally responsible manner in all professional services and activities." This hasn't happened, since officers and directors are violating this tenet.

Consumers must get competent advice. It surely should be legal. The cases above, admittedly some of the worst, are simply examples of a wholesale breach of duty to the consumer. You are not getting assistance from the industry.

Who would I suggest you use for advice on complicated insurance areas? The licensed fee adviser element is good, but I'd demand someone with a minimum of 10 years' experience who is also actively involved in the area. If no extra license is required in your state for fee advice, I'd still opt for the minimum of 10 years of agent licensing. I'd also suggest that you use someone with a degree in planning—at least a planning designation. Be aware that this individual will be tough to find. Furthermore, using one will not be a panacea for success. However, the additional study time and experience generally leads to more critical and objective analysis. But the focus on exclusively the fee element may also be compromised, since the purchase of some of the cheapest insurance can only be done by commission.

Other Insurance Issues

The following issues address a different spin on insurance—instead of providing value at death, the policy might possibly be used or sold while the policyholder is still alive. For those uninitiated with the relatively new developments in the field, it can offer those who are seriously ill an opportunity to utilize a policy prior to death. These are known as *viatical settlements*. An even newer type of policy use allows an elderly insured person (say, over 70 years of age) the ability to sell an unneeded policy rather than let it expire or be surrendered. These may be called *life settlements*.

Viatical Settlements

The viatical settlement involves an individual who owns a policy and is terminally ill. The definition may vary somewhat, but typically it is where a physician determines that an insured person has less than 12 months to live. Some policies may allow an insured person to use at least part of the policy now, before death. In other words, assume someone has a $200,000 policy and she has just six months to live, as certified by a physician. The company may allow a certain percentage of the policy—say, 75 percent—to be paid to the insured during the last stages of her life. Of course, the beneficiaries will and may be disinherited, and that issue needs to be addressed. But for those situations that fit, the service provides a godsend.

But viatical settlements are not without risk. They earned a horrendous reputation when they first started, because they were almost totally unregulated by the states. Policies were sold to the desperate insured for next to nothing. Or the investors (consumers looking for higher investment yields) were scammed because of nonexisting policies, managers simply took the money, and so forth. Florida regulators, in particular, cleared up a lot of the mess through aggressive filings, but caution is still advised. Even where the situation has been above board, the investors have often been on the losing side anyway if the insured live longer than their perceived actuarial lifetimes. For example, when protease inhibitors were given to AIDS patients, they lived much longer than anticipated. Some of the investors lost everything, because they subsequently had to default on making more payments to a never-ending insurance policy.[6]

Life Settlements

A life settlement is the sale of an unneeded or overly expensive life insurance policy to a group of investors. The insured should be over 70 at a minimum and in poor health.

A prime example comes from a client with whom I worked. She was 77 years of age and in medium health. She had been sold a $5 million policy costing over $200,000 per year. (See the case in the sidebar above.) No cash value. She could not afford the premiums. She could, of course, have simply terminated the policy and be done with it. The agent who sold her the policy suggested that she do just that. The problem was that the surrender of a $5 million policy would have provided nothing to the owner. There was also another difficulty: the policy had not yet been owned for two years. This is called the *incontestability period*, the minimum time frame before a policy can be sold. So I had the owner take some money and pay the premiums of $13,000 monthly. (I realize that does not add up to $200,000 annually, but this was a universal life policy.) The point is that the subsequent sale of the entire policy resulted in a $677,000 check to the owner. Think about it. No money by surrendering the policy, or $677,000. You need advisers who are aware of what is going on in the industry and can properly apply such elements for the client.

This can also be done for business policies where the owner or key person retires. Any type of policy may be utilized. Some people may be asking how that is possible with a term policy. First, the actuarial lifetime of the insured may be very short—shorter than the term policy. But consider this: Some term policies can be converted to a universal policy unilaterally without a new incontestability period. So, now the policy might be sold.

I have made the above scenario short and simple, because it is impossible to list all the various subtleties and roadblocks. But keep in mind: Such policies should be shopped with various companies in order to get the best deal. Note that thousands of policies each year are being terminated outright or surrendered for limited cash value where substantial sums could be available for the owners through an independent sale. If such a policy was simply terminated by a planner or agent because of his lack or knowledge or licensing, you would have cause for a breach of duty.

Summary

I think that of all the life policies I have seen clients purchase to date, half or more were incorrect or unsuitable; a quarter were possibly acceptable but still had various contingencies; and maybe, just maybe, a quarter were proper for the client. No wonder the industry and agents can have such a bad name. The fact is that that many people do not have the background to have a true level of competency. Even for those that do, the commissionable activity distorts objectivity and shuns the cheapest coverage.

All that said, insurance is a basic asset and covers a multitude of situations for the average consumer at a most acceptable cost (assuming, of course, that the right policy has been chosen).

As regards using an agent or adviser—be very careful. Make sure that the person is licensed, commission or fee. Never use anyone without 10 years of experience.

Unfortunately, readers might have hoped that I had the Holy Grail of insight as to whom you might use and for what conditions. I don't. I can only indicate that the consumer needs to do a lot of homework, because the industry is clouded with incompetency and illegality. Caveat Investor!

Notes

1. Yes, it is supposed to revert to the old tax rate after that, but it won't. Taxes may be applied to the very rich, but the average taxpayer will not be affected. The country will need lots of tax money as times goes on, but not that much ever came from estate taxes, so I don't believe that the taxes will be applied for estates anything less than $1 million and perhaps more than $2.5 million. Also note that as I write this, President Bush effectively got a mandate when the Republicans won the 2002 elections. So, while my opinions and forecasts are not preordained, they may be close.
2. I have a more detailed form at my Web site, at www.efmoody.com, but you'd need to use a financial calculator. There are also usually one or two links to other sites offering insurance estimates.

3. Actually, there is a good site (see the section "LTC" on www.efmoody.com) where you can put in all sorts of valid data on their form–patient history, family history, weight, and so on—to determine your actuarial lifetime. Then you hold your breath and press the button to see the estimate. No cheating!

4. True. But I had a dear friend die of cancer when she was only 27. And a relative died of a heart attack at 44. You get the idea. Things happen, and you try to cover the odds appropriately.

5. From Kenneth Black Jr. and Harold D. Skipper Jr., *Life Insurance*, Prentice Hall, 1993.

6. There is a consumer advocate named Gloria Wolk who has written extensively on the subject. Check out her Web site at www.Viatical-Expert and her books for more information before proceeding on your own.

CHAPTER 12

LONG-TERM
CARE PLANNING

*M*ANY ISSUES ARE INVOLVED in the determination as to whether and what type of long-term care is appropriate for a client and when it should be initiated. Some factors that enter into the decision are age, onset of Alzheimer's disease, ability of the caregiver to give care, likelihood and preparation for death, symptoms of depression, suitability for hospice care, and the need for housing in nursing homes or assisted living facilities. The list could go on and on.

Massive amounts of literature and information have been produced about the subject—more than could be covered in adequate detail in any one chapter. This material is intended to distill the key elements that you need to recognize for the potential implications of long-term care. (*Note:* I include many links and much information about the topics on my Web site. You are encouraged to go to www.efmoody.com and investigate further.)

Real-Life Elements of Long-Term Care

Lots of real-life elements come into play when anyone is considering long-term care insurance. For instance, there is a huge emotional, physical, and financial commitment that caregivers face. My own family knows how much time, work, and emotional energy goes into caring for someone with a serious illness. My own mother has been institutionalized for Alzheimer's for more than 8 years and is in the later stages of the disease. My uncle had it for more than seven years until he died. (Actually, you don't die from Alzheimer's directly—it is a fortuitous disease that intercedes.) And my father suffered from all sorts of maladies from the time he took early retirement until he died about 15 years later; he had been in the hospital 65 times. My sister has fibromyalgia and cannot work. Long-term care is an issue that affects us all and I have seen the impacts that need to be addressed when frailties befall us or our loved ones.

Caregiving and Its Effect on Caregivers

The life-altering effects of long-term care may be even more significant than the financial considerations. First and foremost, caregiving almost always is entrusted to women. Often, in a traditional marriage, the man is several years older. Statistically, he will need care first. But some men refuse to consider their mortality: It isn't a matter of *when* they will die, it is a matter of *if* they will die. (That's actually a main reason why a lot of men do not do wills and trusts.) A man may not even consider a long-term care policy because he thinks (1) he is invincible or (2) that his wife will take care of him until, possibly, death.

The first problem is a psychological obstacle beyond the scope of this work. But it is a real concern. The male ego is unquestionably a major obstacle to objective planning in almost all facets. (Frankly, I simply do not know how you women handle it.)

As to the second comment, it is generally true that the wife will act as caregiver.[1] Women represent about 75% of all caregivers. Slight changes in that statistic may have occurred in recent history as more men take responsibility. But the real-life issue is that women have been, are today, and will almost universally be tomorrow the caregivers of our society.

The point is that it is not just the one person who needs physical care who is suffering. It is the caregiver who needs the added assistance of a long-term policy to remain physically and mentally whole. At least two people are impacted by the frailties of life, and sometimes many other people are as well. If the wife has worked that hard at providing care at home, she, almost assuredly, will have ended up in poorer physical and mental health as the effort of unceasing caregiving grows increasingly demanding. She may very well need long-term care of some sort for herself sooner than necessary or expected, and for a longer period of time. The use of a long-term care policy therefore is not only to provide care for the patient but to offset the deteriorating physical and mental health of the caregiver, who is usually female.

The Effects on Caregivers' Health

Consider this simple example of the affect of caregiving upon a caregiver: The average weight of the elderly woman is 160 pounds and an average elderly man about 180 pounds. A caregiver would have difficulties trying to move anyone at either of those weights, especially if the caregiver had to do so several times per day. The physical exertion often leads to bad backs, pulled muscles, and more, along with the emotional frustration of performing many thankless tasks, which can lead to depression and other maladies.

To illustrate, one elderly client of mine, who lost her husband several years ago, cared for him at home while he was dying. She did all she could day after day. And when he died, she was in such poor health—particularly her back—that she was hospitalized for a short time thereafter. She is back to her vibrant self but she also told me that she would never get married again because she could never handle either the emotional or the physical demands of caring for another loved one.

Further verification of the problem of caregiving poorly affecting a caregiver's psyche is found in many books, but one article in particular is especially relevant. While it specifically addresses Alzheimer's, I submit that the commentary is valid for all caregivers. According to *The California Daily Review*, "It's not just the person that has Alzheimer's that has all the health problems. Caregivers are under greater and greater stress in trying to take care of loved ones that need greater and greater care. Current estimates indicate that 4 million people have Alzheimer's and three million of these are cared for at home."

The article also noted that the hardship for caregivers is well documented in medical literature. "Alzheimer's has two victims," said Doug McConnell, resource adviser for the San Francisco Bay Association of the Alzheimer's Association. "The Alzheimer's patient can't change the course of his disease, but the caregivers must learn to take care of themselves."

Several studies document the poorer health of caregivers. Caregivers have poorer immune systems and reported more days of infectious illness, consisting of upper respiratory tract infections. At the end of a 13-month study, 32 percent of the caregivers suffered from depression compared to only 6 percent of a noncaregiver control group.

One professor noted that the stresses are a result of the demands of daily care, such as supervising a patient, restraining him or her from harmful actions, performing bodily maintenance tasks such as bathing, eating, dressing, and so on, and instrumental tasks such as paying bills. Secondary stress may result from the result of family conflicts, economic hardships, restriction on social ties and leisure activities, and the feeling of being locked in an unwanted role.

Per McConnell: "Placement in a facility can be more than ridding yourself of a burdensome relative. It should often be looked upon as a rational, reasonable decision and it shouldn't represent failure or produce guilt."

Let's look at a couple of additional points that may not be so obvious.

Caregiving at Home.   Of 4 million elderly patients, 3 million are cared for at home. In other words, 75 percent of care is being offered by friends and family at no or low cost to the government. These unpaid caregiver positions save society (read: taxpayers) millions upon millions of dollars that would normally have to be spent through professionally provided facilities and aides (assuming they were available, which they often are not). Clearly, the government will never have enough money to pay for institutionalizing the elderly. No amount of government spending will ever offset the sacrifices by caregivers. Individuals, therefore, have to plan accordingly.

The Need for Long-Term Care

Let's review some numbers from the Administration on Aging that define the necessity of long-term care. The older population—persons 65 years or older—numbered 35 million in 2000. They represented 12.4 percent of the U.S. population, about one in every eight Americans. The number of older Americans increased by 3.7 million, or 12.0 percent, since 1990, compared to an increase of 13.3 percent for the under-65 population. However, the number of Americans aged 45 to 64 who will reach 65 over the next two decades increased by 34 percent during this period.

In 2000, there were 20.6 million older women and 14.4 million older men, or a gender ratio of 143 women for every 100 men. The female-to-male ratio increases with age, ranging from 117 to 100 for the 65-to-69 age group, to a high of 245 to 100 for persons 85 and over. Since 1900, the percentage of Americans 65 and older has more than tripled (4.1 percent in 1900 to 12.4 percent in 2000), and the number has increased eleven times (from 3.1 million to 35.0 million). The older population itself is getting older. In 2000, the 65-to-74 age group (18.4 million) was eight times larger than in 1900, the 75-to-84 group (12.4 million) was 16 times larger, and the 85-and-older group (4.2 million) was 34 times larger.

In 2000, persons reaching age 65 had an average life expectancy of an additional 17.9 years (19.2 years for females and 16.3 years for males).

The longer people live, the greater the chances are that chronic conditions may develop, resulting in an increased need for assistance with activities of daily living (ADL). When you consider these statistics, the issues for long-term care should be evident. Older women outnumber older men by 20.2 million older women to 14.3 million older men. About 31 percent (9.9 million) noninstitutionalized older persons live alone (7.6 million women, 2.3 million men). Three of every five women age 85 or older live alone.

Other estimates from Heritage Foundation show that the total number of elderly in nursing homes will climb from about 2.8 million in 2000 to 5.3 million in 2030. Yet only 330,000 of those aged 65 to 74 will be cared for in nursing homes, compared with 1.46 million adults over age 85. In 2030, the 65-to-74 age group will have increased to 650,000, but the over-85 age group in nursing homes will swell to 2.69 million. Although one in five persons will need long-term care sometime this year, 65 percent of those who are older than 85 will need long-term care during this same period (2000–2030).

The New England Journal of Medicine said in an early 1990s article that about 43 percent of those people who turned age 65 in 1990 would enter a nursing home at some time during their life. Further, 24 percent of the elderly over age 65 will need nursing home care for more than one year. The same study reported that among all persons who live to age 65, only one in three will spend three months or more in a nursing home; about one in four will spend one year or more in a nursing home; and only about one in eleven (9 percent) will spend five years or more in a nursing home. In other words, two out of three people who turned 65 in 1990 will either never spend any time in a nursing home or will spend less than three months in one. The risk of needing nursing home care is greater for women than men; 13 percent of the women in this study, compared to 4 percent of the men, are projected to spend five or more years in a nursing home.

It should be noted, however, that at the time many of these statistics were calculated, assisted living facilities were not available. So instead of focusing solely on care in a nursing home, many of the elderly will be able to use the less intrusive and less intensive setting of an assisted living facility. Nonetheless, once two ADLs are impacted, some form of formalized care will be necessary, either by family members or through an institutional setting.

Recent statistics from the National Center for Health Statistics noted that the "chances of needing long term care increase with age; 17 percent of people between ages 65 to 74 need long term care; 28 percent between 75 and 84; and 49 percent for those over age 85. The average age of those buying a long-term care policy was age 63."[2]

Let's take a closer look at the statistics above because many journalists have gotten this wrong. *USA Weekend* (a publication included in many Sunday newspapers) had a blinding headline in 2000 that said, in reference to long-term care policies, "Don't pay for insurance you may never use!" I suppose that is valid on its face, but once you put it into real-life focus, you find that it borders on plain dumb. The following are the odds of bad things happening, according to the *Journal of the American Society of CLU* [*Chartered Life Underwriter*]:

- The chances of using your homeowners insurance are about 1 in 88.
- The odds of using your auto insurance are about 1 in 47.
- The chances of having a fire in your home are about 1 in 1200.
- The odds of using your LTC insurance are about *2 in 5.*

The author of the *USA Weekend* article, probably 25 years old and a part time maid, didn't have a clue to how the world works because, if she did, she would have had to suggest that you lapse your home and auto insurance first since the odds of using those policies were far, far less. But she, like most others, I submit, had failed to address what insurance—of almost any type—is about. As stated previously, while you want to have insurance, you never want to use it. Insurance, properly utilized, is nothing more than a pool of money to reimburse those that have a misfortune befall them. The others simply get the emotional protection for a loss that never occurs. In essence, therefore, you hope to never use it. But that doesn't mean you shouldn't have it.

For those who will die nicely and neatly, and who have paid for a policy they never used, I simply say, I'm so happy for you. Dying without having to actually use your LTC policy is nothing different than dying without ever seeing your house burn down. Or dying without ever getting into a major car wreck. Or never having a heart bypass. You should hope that you are one of the few who has spent money for a policy on which you never got a financial reward. However, you certainly got a true benefit of the insurance because you got some peace of mind.

Value of a Long-Term Care Policy

Consider this real-world example. A friend of mine, age 79, was going through chemotherapy. It was touch and go. She was very weak and needed someone to watch her. She had money and could pay for care, but her two children decided they would do it. Well, I knew them and I wondered if they were offering care altruistically or just because they wanted to save the inheritance. (I know that is tacky, but we were both thinking it.) However, forgetting that, assume it was done with the best of intentions. No matter, the children were not skilled in any medical functions and my friend got worse to the point where she was hospitalized twice due to complications. I called her when she was in the hospital and advised her (again) to just pay for care full time because she could not afford to have her health jeopardized by these setbacks, no matter how well intentioned the family care was. She did, but it was too late. She didn't make it. Now there is no way that anyone could prove that the caring by untrained people may have shortened her life by six or more good months—even weeks—but the thought has stayed with me.

Anyone who buys an insurance policy, of any type, is always completely aware that they own it and for what purpose. I would argue that if my friend had owned an LTC policy, once her problems were identified, she (or her children) would have immediately contacted the company and gotten professional care that could have extended her lifetime for another few good weeks or months or even longer. Would she have ever gotten back her "investment" of, say, 20 years of premiums at $3000 annually ($60,000)? Probably not if she had received only various elements of home health care till the very end. So, would it have therefore been a useless purchase? Tell me, how much would have 6 more months of an active life been worth? No matter what the costs, the value potentially received would have been invaluable.

I have not see this situation identified in seminars or articles probably because statistical evidence proving the added lifetime is not possible. But once you have paid for an LTC policy, there need be no hesitation in contacting the company for immediate assistance. That's exactly what insurance is supposed to do.

It's emotional security beyond just the financial benefit. Knowing that you have something available should a problem arise provides peace of mind that, in itself, can provide a better quality of life. Further, remember that you never actually want to use insurance. You always want the other person to have the problem. It's a tacky view perhaps, but true. Your money is simply pooled with others to provide benefits for those less fortunate enough to have encountered a problem.

Long-term care extracts not only emotional and physical costs on the caregiver and the patient's family but also significant financial costs. Conflicts ensue within families as to who should provide care for a parent, how much it will cost each person involved, where the parent will live, with whom, for how long, and so on. And the patient, if it is a mother or father, may still end up passing lifetime assets to one of the other siblings who may not have participated as much or at all in the caregiving process, which may breed resentment among family members.

All of this is not fair—it just exists. The idea is to be prepared for the eventualities that might occur. The best solution is one that everyone is familiar with: communication. However, that is the one issue that tends to be most lacking when it comes to long-term planning (and most others for that reason). Even in families with close communications, it may still not be possible to eliminate or reduce all the problems that may arise. It is unquestionably more difficult to do so with limited resources. But it's not impossible. In almost every metropolitan area of the United States, you will find an Area Agency on Aging. They offer a wealth of services and information on Medicare, nursing services, Meals on Wheels, and much, much more. I suggest everyone call their local office right away, and certainly before any of the services are needed.[3]

The fact is that the statistical odds for needing long-term care do exist and they are not in your favor. Long-term care will quite probably impact you, your spouse, partner, parents, grandparents, and other loved ones. A policy can certainly diminish the potential financial losses and will absolutely limit the emotional trauma, which is, quite probably, worse than the physical trauma. I fully admit that insurance often has a bad rap and that few truly want to think about their potential demise and the assorted cruelties that age may instill. But headlines suggesting that you ought not to pay for something you may not use belie the odds of such use.

Most articles that attempt such "strategies" of not using or even considering insurance suggest or even state outright that Medicare or Medicaid are acceptable alternatives. That notion is simply not realistic. It's even foolish. Further, that strategy can put the patient in further emotional distress and deteriorating care. This is not the way to die if you can afford otherwise. (I am assuming, of course, that the patient has the financial wherewithal to purchase private coverage.) That may appear as an obvious statement, but it is truly amazing how seldom the topic is addressed when someone attempts to obtain second-rate forms of care, which include Medicare and Medicaid.

Medicare and Medicaid Coverage

Surprisingly, surveys of the elderly show a remarkable ignorance of LTC coverage provided by the government. Statistics continue to show that about 50 percent believe that Medicare covers LTC. Unfortunately, a large percentage of the elderly get their information via a cocktail party, next-door neighbors, coworkers, and so on, but not through intelligent research. I repeat: The local Area Agency on Aging has lots of information and is an excellent guide to community resources.

A lot of bad information is out there on which the elderly believe they can rely. This is evidenced frequently, and in one particularly disturbing violation was noted in the *San Francisco Chronicle* in a 1998 article by a national writer who writes "Dummies" books (seems appropriate). The article indicated that Medicare would pay in full for up to 200 days in a nursing home. Sorry to burst everybody's bubble, but Medicare effectively offers zero days of nursing home coverage. That's because Medicare covers only the sickest of patients who are under skilled care.

The following are some facts; please pay considerable attention to these statistics. First of all, how many people go into a facility just for basic care, meaning that they are simply impacted by two of the Activities of Daily Living (see Table 12.1)? About 95 percent of all nursing home patients receive the basics of custodial care. Does Medicare cover for custodial care? Nope. How many are institutionalized for intermediate care? About 4.5 percent. Does Medicare cover that type of care? Nope. That leaves only 0.5 percent of institutionalized patients under skilled care. And they must have been in a hospital for three days and have entered a facility within 30 days of leaving the hospital. And even if that is covered, Medicare covers only 20 days at full pay. The next 80 days require a copayment by the patient of $105 daily. That's $8400 for a full 80 days. Yes, that is cheap for skilled care, but the odds of needing skilled care that long is remote. Most of the time you are already dead or have at least been upgraded to intermediate care. And Medicare does not pay for that.

You may find some statistics showing that Medicare pays around 5 percent to 7 percent of total costs for LTC, but that is because whatever skilled care was required was expensive. When you do your planning, you must not focus on or plan for any LTC coverage by Medicare.

Table 12.1 Long-term Care Needs

Type of Care	Percent Requiring Care
Skilled	0.5%
Intermediate	4.5%
Custodial	95%

Medicaid does cover for the bulk of long-term nursing home care. Per AARP, "Medicaid is the single largest public source of funding for long-term care (LTC) in the United States, accounting for more than 38 percent of total long-term care expenditures in fiscal 1996. Medicaid spending for LTC more than doubled from fiscal 1987 through fiscal 1997, rising from $21.1 billion in fiscal 1987 to $56.1 billion in fiscal 1997. The bulk of Medicaid spending has gone to nursing home care over the years, but recent expenditure reports show states allocating an increasing share of that spending to home care services." Recent California statistics indicate that Medicaid covers over 50 percent of long-term costs.

Medicaid is designed for those with limited assets—or for those who will end up with limited assets—who have to request the state to provide care. If you are single, you use your own assets to pay for care until you only have about $2000 left, and then Medicaid takes over. (You will get to keep some income, but most states will allow less than $100 monthly.) Many people using LTC become destitute very quickly, as the cost of annual care is approximately $54,000. (Of course, the costs vary considerably by state and county.) About 63 percent of people entering a nursing home exhaust their assets within 13 weeks; 90 percent exhaust their savings in 16 weeks.

If you are married and go into a nursing home, your spouse no longer has to become destitute as in years past because Congress passed the Medicare Catastrophic Coverage Act of 1988. That act allows the at-home spouse to retain some income and assets (roughly $2200 and $100,000, respectively). Assets include the house, car, and personal assets, along with a certain amount of income and some financial assets. Medicaid will attempt to put a lien on your house while you are alive in order to get reimbursement for the cost of care after you die. Your individual state rules will vary, and you need to check those laws.

Of course, the bulk of senior citizens feel this is a violation of their rights—they paid taxes and are therefore entitled to state LTC coverage regardless of income and assets. Not so. Government provides benefits to the indigent as it rightfully should do. And it struggles to assure adequate care. Yet it is being inundated by those with assets who strain the system to the breaking point.

You can divest yourself of assets—even if you have lots and lots of money—and still be able to qualify for Medicaid. But what is missing in the advice given by eldercare attorneys, insurance and annuity agents, and others is simply the fact that Medicaid does not have enough money to provide quality, professional care.

I have stated in every LTC class I have taught that you never want to die in a Medicaid ward. The reason? While it is possible to find an acceptable Medicaid facility, Medicaid pays approximately 80 percent of the cost for patient care. According to the National Committee to Preserve Social Security and Medicare, about 88 percent of U.S. Nursing homes certified for Medicaid are "drastically short" of qualified medical personnel.

Additionally, other studies show that residents in homes with more Medicaid patients are 30 percent more likely to experience health declines. That's about all that's necessary for an understanding of the quality of coverage Medicaid may potentially provide. You can have, say, six staff members overseeing you at $8 per hour in a Medicaid ward or 10 staff members at $12 an hour in a private pay facility. Additionally, the experience level of employees at a Medicaid facility generally is lower and the turnover rate is higher than at a good private pay facility.

Here is a fine indication: Medicaid covers the cost of care for 7 out of 10 Massachusetts nursing facility residents, but less than one in four facilities receives enough money to cover the cost of care, according to the Massachusetts Extended Care Federation. And, "a nursing home in Virginia noted that it had a daily $33 shortfall between the cost of care for residents and the amount of Medicaid reimbursements it receives from the state; over the course of a year, the shortfall totals $1.3 million."

While you may think that all patients are treated equally, some situations lead to differences in care that are more than subtle. For example, during my continuing education LTC class in October 2002, a student told a story; I call it the red and blue blanket problem: A son had his mother in a nursing home and was paying directly for her care. He noticed that some patients had blue blankets and some had pink. His mother had pink, but her favorite color was blue. So he asked the nurse for a blue blanket. The nurse first offered some simple excuse. But the son pursued the issue, saying he would even pay for a blue blanket. The nurse finally told him that blue blankets were only for Medicaid patients and they had to spend less time with them.

So, tell me, where do you want care? It's almost that simple. This is not a diatribe against Medicaid—most people try to do their best. But if the government has inadequate reimbursement levels, it inherently has a potential for inadequate staff, training, facilities and technology. Add on the huge budget deficit we now face and the further eroding of both Medicare and Medicaid budgets, and the following advice should be obvious: If you have sufficient money, buy an LTC policy when you are younger and healthier.

Redistribution of Assets and Medicaid Qualifying Trusts

A transfer of assets in order to qualify for Medicaid is definitely not advised. It can be done, but there are caveats.

Let's say you have $500,000 and you want to give it to your son so you don't have to pay Medicaid for your care. It is possible to give a gift this size without taxation, but you have to remember that it is now the son's money, not yours. If he gets a divorce, has a bad accident incurring liability, is on drugs, or simply does not like you anymore, you are out of luck. The money may simply be gone. Even if he does provide you with income, Medicaid has a legal look-back period of 36 months where they can say that the transfer of assets was in contemplation of the need for Medicaid. They will, therefore, deny coverage until a certain time period has elapsed where you must pay for care yourself. Either way, it is awfully easy to make some big errors.

Medicaid Qualifying Trusts follow the same format. You can transfer assets to this special trust—set up by an attorney—and still be able to qualify for Medicaid nursing home coverage. However, Medicaid has the right to look back 60 months and deny coverage if the transfer occurred within that period.

Such trusts are generally designed to leave assets to beneficiaries that would be lost to payments for private care. However, any attorney that attempts to divest the wealthy of assets for potential Medicaid coverage should clearly state to the patients that they are apt to suffer inadequate care that they could have avoided by buying a policy—even paying for the care directly personally. I state that unless the attorney discusses the element of inadequate care—possibly even taking the client down to view separate private pay and Medicaid facilities— then the transfer of assets, though legal, may have been breached by the lack of the attorney's fiduciary duty. It's the same breach by an agent or planner who suggests the same.

There are a lot of articles that try all sorts of rationalizations to justify the use of Medicaid for nursing home care, but this concise commentary concisely addresses the problem: If you have money, plan ahead. Do not plan to die in a Medicaid ward, because the odds are you may die badly. Yes, not all private pay facilities are good, but at least you generally have a larger selection to choose from. If you do your homework, you should be able to find something acceptable.

Lastly, on this issue, I offer this from *When Caring Isn't Enough: Meeting the Need for LongTerm Care with LongTerm Care Insurance*, by Samuel Larry Feldman and the National LTC Network:

Many people who become convinced that transferring wealth to become eligible for Medicaid is a good idea ultimately discover that, by protecting their assets for someone else, they have drastically limited their own options and choices for longterm care. For instance, the level of Medicaid reimbursement for Assisted Living facilities and Alzheimer's centers is so low that these types of institutions seldom accept Medicaid residents. Most skilled nursing facilities accept Medicaid recipients now, but may have a limited number of Medicaid beds and may have long waiting lists of people ready to fill them. Those facilities with large numbers of Medicaid residents find they cannot provide an optimum quality of care on Medicaid funding, which is far lower that private pay rates. This often drives privately paying patients to the better facilities where larger numbers of privately paying residents provide funding for better quality care. Sometimes the only Medicaid openings available are some distance from relatives and friends with whom the resident would like to maintain contact. Home care, which is preferred by most people when possible, is difficult to get via our overburdened welfare system. All in all, much of the freedom to choose how and where you will be cared for is lost to people on Medicaid. Medicaid was designed to be a safety net for those who lack the means to provide longterm care for themselves. It was never intended to be an entitlement for a prosperous middle class.

Per *US News and World Report*, in a September 2002 article, "Government payments are so low that homes lose seven cents on the dollar for every patient through the door; budget woes in the state tighten the screws all the more."

And the beat goes on in every valid article on LTC. So, once you recognize that private care is preferable and that you can afford it (addressed in the paragraphs that follow), then you need to determine what type of policy you should consider.

LTC Policy Analysis

The insurance industry has never been renowned for its objective information for consumers. Nor are many agents, planners, or attorneys really that knowledgeable either. Add in governmental rules and bad policies and marketing and you have a difficult purchasing decision.

The following paragraphs should help you, by providing an analysis of various policies and describing what you should look for. An extra focus is given to California requirements, since those are what I know best. Nevertheless, the bulk of the information to follow is applicable on a national basis.

No matter what LTC policy you buy, the benefits are triggered by an inactivity with two or more activities of daily living (ADLs) or with cognitive impairment. In policies based on ADLs, a physician, nurse, case manager, gerontologist, or other health care professional certifies that a policyholder needs "hands-on" help, supervisory "standby" help, or directional "reminding" help to perform everyday living activities. (Old policies may require three ADLs, and you had better check them. Coverage with these types of policies will certainly be less. In fact, some old policies are effectively worthless if the definitions for coverage match Medicare. See "Old Policies," which follows.)

ADLs are described in the list that follows and will be found in every policy that is handed to you for review. These are national definitions used for tax-qualified policies and are consistent around the country. They should also be consistent for non-tax-qualified policies, but you should check your own state's policy. (For definitions of tax-qualified and non-tax-qualified policies, see "Tax-Qualified Policies.") Slight differences can make a huge difference in potential payoff.

1. **Dressing.** The policyholder's ability to put on and take off all garments and medically necessary braces, corsets, elastic stockings or garments or artificial limbs or splints usually worn and to fasten and unfasten them.

2. **Eating.** Reaching for, picking up, and grasping a utensil and cup; getting food on a utensil and bringing food, utensil, and cup to mouth; manipulating food on plate; and cleaning face and hands as necessary following meals.[4]

3. **Continence.** The policyholder's ability to control bowel and bladder function as well as use ostomy or catheter receptacles and apply diapers and disposable barrier pads.

4. **Transferring.** Moving from one sitting or lying position to another sitting or lying position; for example from a bed to a wheelchair or sofa, coming to a standing position or repositioning to promote circulation and prevent skin breakdown.

5. **Toileting.** Getting on and off a toilet or commode and emptying a commode, managing clothing and wiping and cleaning the body after toileting, and using and emptying a bed pan or urinal.

6. **Bathing.** Cleaning the body using a tub, shower, or sponge bath, including getting a basin of water, managing faucets, getting in and out of a tub or shower, and reaching head and body parts for soaping, rinsing, and drying.

The above six ADLs are required for the tax-qualified policies. California's non-tax-qualified policies also include ambulation, for a total of seven ADLs. However, most companies have dropped non-tax-qualified coverage.

7. **Ambulation.** The ability to walk both inside and outside your residence regardless of the use of a cane, crutches, or brace. The only time the inability to ambulate would be covered under a tax-qualified policy is when the person cannot ambulate in and out of bed without assistance. Ambulating clearly makes it easier for non-tax-qualified policies to trigger coverage.

Everything else being equal, I would always opt for seven ADLs even if the policy is non-tax-qualified.

Separate and distinct from ADLs, a policy could be triggered when the patient suffers cognitive impairment or, as noted in policy language, "a loss or deterioration in mental capacity that is comparable to Alzheimer's Disease and similar forms of irreversible dementia, and is documented by clinical evidence and standardized tests of memory, orientation as to people, places, and time; and deductive or abstract reasoning." Some tax-qualified policies include severe cognitive impairment and is addressed below. Suffice to say, the use of the term "severe" could be a material obstacle to future care.

Old Policies

The previous definitions of ADLs may not be consistent with definitions in policies that are even just a few years old. For example, bathing could be tub, shower, or that requiring personal assistance, and so on. In other words, one old policy may have very liberal definitions while another one is very restrictive. Some conformed to Medicare restrictions where you had to be in a hospital for three days and enter a skilled care facility within 30 days of leaving the hospital. The odds of this happening are extremely slim, and almost all of these policyholders are paying for a contract that will never provide any benefits. Further, such older policies will not cover for custodial care unless the patient/policyholder had been covered under skilled care first—another statistical improbability. So, if you are told that your mom or dad owns an LTC policy, simply do not utter a sigh of relief. It may be so restrictive as to be useless. You will have to get it and analyze it.

Tax-Qualified Policies

Congress approved tax-qualified (TQ) policies several years ago as an incentive to increase the purchase of LTC policies. The main reason that Congress offered such benefits should be obvious. The huge cost of care is so burdensome that the government will never be able to handle it.

And the situation will only get worse with the increasing number of the elderly. Hence, they offered this tax incentive to citizens so they would purchase more private LTC policies. Currently, only about 6 percent or 7 percent of the elderly populace has purchased a private policy. However, a 2003 HIAA survey showed continued growth in LTC insurance sales, from 815,000 policies sold in 1987 to nearly 8.3 million in 2001. But that is still a drop in the bucket.

Such TQ policies offer a deduction of your premium (sort of) and no taxation of benefits (perhaps, but so what!). In many states, TQ policies may be all that are offered, so you need to recognize how they work.

Let's first take a look at premium deduction. Businesses can write off the premiums, some at 100 percent. But our primary concern here is individual use. You can deduct certain amounts of your premiums annually, and, on the surface, this appears to be a considerable benefit—and is generally marketed as such. But further review shows the deduction is essentially illusory, because the deduction only occurs when the premiums, plus other medical expenses, exceed 7.5 percent of your adjusted gross income. You've got to be pretty sick that year, as well as itemize on your 1040 Form, in order to take advantage of that so-called premium tax deduction. Articles suggest that only 5 percent of policyholders qualify. Quite frankly, I think that practically no one will truly benefit from this deductibility and they shouldn't be induced to buy because of this aspect. Great marketing, though. Deceptive in part. But nonetheless, great.

That is not only the only tax offset. The tax-qualified policies do not have any taxation of the benefits received. It is a true and valid feature. But it has to be put into perspective with a non-tax-qualified (NTQ) policy or older policies in which the benefits are supposedly taxable. I question that both as an opinion and as a fact. The opinion has to do as to whether or not the receipt of benefits from a NTQ policy can be used as a medical deduction against 7.5 percent of AGI. I submit they can.

Let's assume you went into an assisted living facility or a nursing home. First of all, neither represents a retirement home. Admittedly, both facilities have various structured activities to keep patients active, both physically and mentally. But you are only there because a physician, nurse, case manager, gerontologist, or other health care professional certified you need help with at least two ADLs or have cognitive impairment. There is a medical condition; otherwise, the policy benefits would not be issued.

So, let's assume you received $50,000 from the policy company and then took that money and paid the facility $50,000 for the care. Let's also take the position that the receipt of the $50,000 was taxable income. As stated, I submit that the payment of the $50,000 to the home or facility was, in fact, a deductible medical cost to be used as a figure against 7.5 percent of your AGI. Depending on your income, there will be some small tax on the policy proceeds, since the entire $50,000 will not be deductible. But it will be, for literally all middle-income LTC policyholders, an inconsequential sum that can be more than offset by the additional ADL of ambulating and the lack of the "severe cognitive impairment."

There are several issues to my opinion on this matter. First, there are no statistics stating that anyone, at least as of mid-2000, had actually been taxed on the receipt of LTC benefits. Second, I personally called the IRS.[5] The agent to whom I spoke indicated that there are no specific regulations indicating what is or is not taxed. She did say that the nursing home or the assisted living facility could indicate how much of the time were you seen by a nurse versus the number of hours in a day to determine taxability. On that I disagreed. The point she was alluding to was that only part of any benefits received would supposedly count as a deduction, say, for the actual 30 minutes a day the nurse or doctor saw you. And the other 23½ hours would be taxable.

Stretching that illogical position, the time spent sleeping would be a taxable time element, irrespective of the fact that you were in a facility due to impairment. Worse yet, consider this: Is an Alzheimer's patient

who watches TV for 11 hours a day and cannot remember a single word
to be taxed on such time spent "relaxing"? Get real. Any reasonable person would be hard pressed to state that the patient is receiving care only
at such time as a professional aide, nurse, or doctor is physically present.

Admittedly, there is a questionable issue of home health care and
the use of an assistant to clean your house and make your meal. Is
that a taxable event? Or is it still covered by the fact that the policy (or
you independently) would not be paying anything unless you were
impacted by the ADLs? If you are in this situation, I suggest you present the position directly to your CPA and ask him or her what the
best approach would be. I think almost all of them would concur with
the position that facility care is a deduction against 7.5 percent of
your AGI.

As for the deduction for home health care, calling the IRS is a good
start. Check IRS Publication 502, Medical Expenses. Also talk to your
CPA, and look into other sources to make your own analysis of your
individual situation. It would be good to keep a log that shows what
type of care is given and the allocation of time.

There is no question that Congress and President Bush know that
Medicare and literally every other government and state organization
are severely underfunded in their attempt to provide services to the truly
needy. It is my contention that an attempt to deny the basic medical
deduction rule would result in a wholesale cessation of policy sales and
termination of those already in place. In fact, as I write this, bills are
being introduced to Congress to allow more deductions of LTC premiums overall.

But there has to be more to the issue of a tax comparison between
a TQ and NTQ policy. And there is.

First, tax-qualified policies are more restrictive than non-tax-qualified policies. TQ policies dictate that care is required for at least 90 days.
If care is not needed for that long, benefits will not commence. This
may not be particularly onerous but, nonetheless, the rule applies a
restriction not evidenced in the NTQ policies.

Probably the most troublesome issue is the requirement of severe cognitive impairment for the TQ policy versus cognitive impairment for the NTQ policy. The point is, *severe* is not generally defined by any company's contract. Therefore, it is left to the discretion of the company to define when and how coverage will be instituted. Admittedly, many TQ policies now state that such coverage for cognitive impairment will be the same as NTQ. Fine—but that does not dismiss the issue for prior policies. It has been my experience that definitions that are either unclear or, further, not even defined, can lead to questionable coverage later on.

The issue may become particularly onerous if a loved one is impacted by Alzheimer's. At what point does the individual reach the severe stage? I obtained a consensus definition of "severe" Alzheimer's from several organizations, as follows:

- Memory loss nearly complete
- Severe disorientation and confusion
- Speech declining to a few intelligible words
- Loss of physical functions like walking and sitting up
- Loss of bladder and bowel control
- Loss of appetite
- Total dependence on caregiver

If any company were to use this "accepted" definition, coverage for severe cognitive impairment would never happen until the later stages of the disease. Since the term severe may not be defined by most companies contractually, I am extremely skeptical of proper coverage. And if it is not in the contract, a company could always change from liberal coverage to the more restrictive definitions in 10, 20, or 30 years from now. That option makes me a little uncomfortable.

What about more differences between TQ and NTQ policies that would suggest you have one over another? Well, in California at least, there is an extra ADL (for a total of seven) called *ambulating*, as men-

tioned previously. It is the least restrictive of all the ADLs—or, phrased
differently, it can provide coverage faster. Now, most companies have
eliminated the NTQ policies in California, but as of late 2003, some
are still available. So put all the comparison elements together and consider this: A NTQ policy, where available, is apt to give faster coverage,
because it is less restrictive, certainly in California. Admittedly, many
TQ policies no longer require the term *severe* in its coverage, so if
you were able to get coverage faster with a NTQ policy, would you not
feel more comfortable? And if the tax position of a NTQ were effectively the same as a TQ, wouldn't you gain more coverage faster? Yes,
with both. If I had my druthers, I would opt for a nonqualified policy with seven ADLs, whenever possible. Finally, can you buy a California policy if you live in another state? Yes. I will not go through all
the machinations of doing so in this chapter. By the same token, I did-
n't go through all the benefits of an NTQ just for the exercise. If you
live out of state, it may be worthwhile to determine the accessibility of
an NTQ policy.

LTC Companies

Before you even get to the point of analyzing the specifics of individual
policies, you need to narrow down the number of companies to consider. There are around 125 to 150 companies offering LTC policies at
any time, though not all are approved in individual states.

Some companies are new in the business. Forget them. The inex-
perience is an invitation for disaster. In the past, some screwed up the
market royally by introducing rates so low they were unsustainable. Two
in particular were Conseco and Penn Treaty. Conseco filed one of the
largest bankruptcies in history. Penn Treaty was denied the right to
sell in most states. It is now making a comeback, but I'll pass, thank you.

So what does that leave you? Perhaps 8 to 10 companies in the
United States control about 80 percent of the market. They have experience, they have financial backing, and they have the wherewithal to

potentially withstand the changes in the future. But even that is some-what muddled.

Sale of Companies

In early 2000, I conducted a study of the major LTC policy compa-nies. I felt pretty smug that I had done a good job in evaluating all the companies, only to have two of these top eight—Fortis and Travelers—sold and another major company (CNA) put on the block. And the largest firm—AMEX—had already been sold to GE Capital. I had to rethink the value of looking at an individual company, per se.

All this activity started to remind me of a *Newsweek* article in the 1980s regarding the fragmented banking system. That article suggested that there was going to be a mass consolidation of banks culminating in just a few giants. Essentially they were right. The sale of Fortis and Travelers made me think that you will see the same thing in the insur-ance industry and with LTC companies. Furthermore, during the 20- to 30-year time frame when you own a policy, the bulk of the compa-nies will undoubtedly be sold. In fact, as the final review was being done, John Hancock was being sold to a large Canadian firm.

So, in an analysis of who to use, I absolutely opt for the larger, highly rated companies (A.M. Best, for example) that have offered LTC policies for at least 10 years. That will limit the number of quality companies to no more than about 10. You should consider GE Capital, John Han-cock, Allianz, UNUM, and a few others. (Additionally, as of this review, CNA—a well respected LTC provider—ceased its offering of individual policies.) You might consider companies like Lincoln Benefit, since it is owned by Allstate and is a very highly rated company. No one can say that Allstate might not be bought in the next 30 years (and I bet it will). But, if so, the purchaser would need to be a major entity in itself.

There is nothing you can do to guarantee the longevity of the com-pany. But the policy purchased from the best of the best should provide some emotional comfort when looking forward 20 or 30 years.

Guaranteed Renewable versus
Noncancelable Structure

Virtually all the LTC companies use a *guaranteed renewable* structure. This means that as long as you make your payments, you will have coverage. The problem with this structure is that the companies may increase the premiums if they change the rate for an entire classification within the state. Some major companies have done this. (I repeat, don't bother with new, small, or untested companies.) Most companies will attempt to keep such changes to a minimum and will adjust new policies to make up for certain adjustments in profits.

Think about this: If you buy a policy from XYZ Company at age 50, you are very apt to be looking at a completely different company by the time you're 80 when you actually receive the benefits. Sure, the company may currently say that they have priced premiums to reflect probable underwriting standards. But if the rates are not guaranteed in the contract, you may have hollow words. The number of elderly people is going to double in the next 30 years, and medical health premiums are increasing at a 10 percent or higher current rate. So, there is no way that they can validate the statement to not raise rates.

Is there anything you can do to protect yourself? Yes. It is called a *noncancelable policy*. It simply means that the company cannot change any of the policy terms as long as you make the premium payments. The difference between the two contracts, however, is that noncancelable policies are paid up quickly. For example, you would make a larger one-time payment, or over periods of five or 10 years, or perhaps to age 65. But once you make the payments, you are done. Finis. The end. No more. And there is no problem with increases later in age.

Obesity and Long-Term Care

The costs for care will rise appreciably and nullify many anticipated actuarial budgets for one reason: obesity.

About 61 percent of U.S. adults are overweight or obese. That's 5 percent higher than the study conducted between 1988 and 1994, and 14 percent higher than a study conducted between 1976 and 1980. Most of the gain is to people who are obese. (Obesity is defined as being 30 or more pounds over a healthy body weight; overweight is roughly 10 to 30 pounds over a healthy weight.) Over the last 20 years, the number of people who are overweight has increased only slightly, while those who are obese have increased almost 50 percent. You can stay alive if you are overweight, but you will have far more medical complications and require a lot more care and a lot more prescriptions than those who are a healthy weight. Being obese, however, shortens your lifespan about the same as being a smoker (on average, you will live seven years less).

It is true that if an obese person applies for coverage, underwriters may simply decline coverage outright. But let's assume the person is merely overweight and can get coverage. The person may—and often does—become heavier and heavier as the years go by so that eventually the policyowner is, if not obese, than overweight to the point where additional health care would be needed. The real problem would be diabetes. There are more than 44 million obese Americans in 2001 and 16 million with diabetes.

The Nursing Shortage and Increased Long-Term Care Costs

Another major reason why long-term care costs will increase is because there is a dire shortage of nurses in the United States. Many nurses are older and retiring—or retiring early due to the demands of giving care and the associated stress. And for every nurse that retires, only one enters the profession. Frustrated with long hours, a lot of overtime, and a heavy workload, many nurses have stopped working or have changed professions. The American Medical Association projects a 20 percent shortfall of nurses by 2020.

While I have no crystal ball, it is likely that health care companies will raise rates due to the nursing shortage or obesity, or both. And it makes sense to try to insulate yourself from something that, in my opinion, is preordained. Even if the companies do not raise rates on old policies, they assuredly must raise rates on new policies in order to cut their losses due to rising costs, so it would be best to buy one soon before all this hits the fan. So what is a person to do? Once again I point to a noncancelable policy with short-term payments.

Noncancelable policies provide a couple of other benefits. One is that some elderly people might pay for 10 or 15 years under the standard policy. Let's say they are age 77 and still healthy. They figure they are going to stay healthy and drop the policy. But, they forget that it's the very last years of life where care is generally required. So they let the policy lapse—just when they need it the most. A fully paid-up policy does not lapse and will provide the coverage needed later in life.

Another benefit is that, if you are 55 or younger, you are paying for the policy while you are still working. None of the premiums will come out of your retirement budget or assets, and that makes the subsequent 30 or so years of retirement much easier both financially and emotionally.

There are caveats to the noncancelable policies. If you died, say, in the eleventh year of a 10-year pay policy and never had a chance to use the policy, you'd have paid more up front than if you had purchased the policy over time and you would have gotten no return. (But you'd be dead and you wouldn't know.) While that scenario might happen, I think that is a statistical anomaly. Another danger is that the company underwriting the policy could go under. But since you will only use an A+ Best-rated company, the odds of that happening should be remote. Further, many state insurance programs should protect you from such outright failure.

I truly believe, at this point in time, that the purchase of a policy that is fully paid up can provide the benefits you want and need while also avoiding what I perceive as difficult underwriting problems and higher costs in the future. They can provide added financial and emotional security. Is it worth it? You decide. The issue is whether you can afford the shorter but much higher premiums.

Basic Policy Coverage

Remember that the average cost of long-term care is $54,000 annually for nursing home care. Assisted living is about $26,000 annually, and most policies now cover for that. That's a much desired option. Caution is advised, however. Most older policies were written before assisted living was even a consideration. So, they may not provide for assisted living facilities at all. Nowadays, many elderly people prefer to use these facilities as much as possible, so assisted living has become a basic staple of long-term care. So, review your old policies very carefully.

A few companies may offer a subsequent rider that will include assisted living. My experience has been, however, that most will not include assisted living. If you want it, you need to reapply and your current age and current medical condition may preclude coverage or cause it to be more expensive, perhaps considerably so. (If you do apply for a new policy—actually, any insurance policy—do not let your old policy lapse before getting acceptance on the new one.)

Elimination Period

The *elimination period* is the time period in which you pay for coverage before the policy benefits start. The longer the period, the lower the premiums. Standard periods might be 0 days, 30 days, and 90 days. Some periods will be 180 days and even longer. I tend to exclude the 0-day elimination, since you might actually end up with coverage by Medicare for the first 20 days (which are free and the next 80 days are at $105 per day or higher). So, excluding this period, how do you choose between, say a 30-day period and a 180-day period? Generally, your choice depends on the money involved.

Let's say you select a policy with a 30-day elimination period. An annual premium might be $2500. With a 180-day elimination period, the premium drops to $1900. Is a $600 yearly savings worth it? Assume you would not need care for 15 years. You saved $9000 by selecting the 180-day elimination. But if you actually needed care then, you would have to pay the extra 150 days of care yourself. By using the $54,000 current cost of care and an inflation rate of 5 percent per year, the 150 days would represent an expenditure of roughly $46,000. So, what do you do? Unfortunately, there is no formula that can make that decision. You simply take this one factor and include it in all the other costs and weigh them together.

Period of Coverage

Some bad journalists suggest that a couple simply split the overall long-term care budget between the husband and wife. Wrong! Men tend to either get well and leave a facility or die. Women tend to live for a long time in a facility. So I suggest, depending on a couple's budget, that a husband gets around two or so years of coverage and the wife gets four or more years.

Daily Rate

As mentioned, the average cost of long-term health care in a facility in 2002 was about $54,000 annually. You need to check your state for more specific rates, as well as consider where you will retire.

Table 12.2 details the average daily nursing home costs per region for a private room.

Table 12.2   Average Daily Nursing Home Costs

Albany, NY	$200	Indianapolis, IN	$161
Atlanta, GA	$110	International Falls, MN	$91
Baltimore, MD	$163	Jacksonville, FL	$150
Battle Creek, MI	$195	Kansas City, KS	$117
Birmingham, AL	$105	Las Vegas, NV	$133
Boston, MA	$278	Lehigh Valley, PA	$167
Bristol County, VA	$199	Long Beach, CA	$138
Buffalo, NY	$193	Los Angeles, CA	$122
Charleston, SC	$108	Macon, GA	$98
Chattanooga, TN	$136	Maryland (suburban DC)	$173
Cherry Hill, NJ	$193	Middlesex City, NJ	$195
Chicago, IL	$120	Milwaukee, WI	$179
Chicago (south suburbs)	$138	Minneapolis, MN	$106
Chicago (north suburbs)	$165	Nashville, TN	$135
Cincinnati, OH	$127	New Brunswick, NJ	$161
Cleveland, OH	$200	New Haven, CT	$227
Columbia, SC	$120	New Orleans, LA	$97
Columbus, OH	$162	New York, NY (Manhattan)	$295
Dallas, TX	$149	Newark, DE	$139
Dayton, OH	$162	Newark, NJ	$228
Denver, CO	$141	North Metro Atlanta, GA	$131
Des Moines, IA	$102	Oakland, CA	$157
Detroit, MI	$113	Oklahoma City, OK	$134
Dover, NH	$200	Omaha, NE	$149
Fairfax County, VA	$172	Orlando, FL	$125
Flint, MI	$134	Pensacola, FL	$123
Florence & Decatur City, AL	$108	Philadelphia, PA	$163
Fort Wayne, IN	$137	Phoenix, AZ	$152
Gary, IN	$98	Pittsburgh, Napa County, CA	$127
Grand Rapids, MI	$154	Pittsburgh, PA	$181
Greensboro, NC	$132	Portland, ME	$192
Hartford, CT	$210	Portland, OR	$144
Hibbing, MN	$90	Providence, RI	$160
Houston, TX	$111	Provo, UT	$135
Huntsville, AL	$113	*(continued on next page)*	

Table 12.2   Average Daily Nursing Home Costs (continued)

Raleigh, NC	$120	Stamford, CT	$286
Richmond, VA	$147	St. Louis, MO	$138
Rochester, NY	$187	Summit, NJ	$242
Salt Lake City, UT	$135	Syracuse, NY	$196
San Antonio, TX	$114	Tampa, FL	$128
San Diego, CA	$149	Toledo, OH	$128
San Francisco, CA	$169	Trenton, NJ	$195
Savannah, GA	$103	Tucson, AZ	$149
Seattle, WA	$174	Washington, DC	$165
Springfield, MA	$181	Winston-Salem, NC	$137

Depending on the budget, you can review a policy starting at $150-per-day for full coverage. You may purchase additional amounts in $10-per-day increments up to around $300 per day. (Companies vary tremendously on the rates allowed.)

Let's say you picked a three-year policy at $150 per day. What do you get for coverage? The answer is not quite that obvious. You might simply get three years of coverage even though the daily payment was less than $150 per day. In other words, if your bill was $125 per day and it lasted three years, that would end your coverage. However, many states require a pooled account wherein you have a pool of money to use. If the policy you bought was for $150 per day and it was for three years, your pool of money would be 150 × 365 × 3, or $164,250. If your bill was $125 per day for three years, the total amount paid would be $135,000. But you'd still have $29,250 left for continuing coverage.[6]

I just presented the standard coverage dialogue you would tend to get with an agent. However, it isn't necessarily real life. The numbers above are correct and the pooling element is a critical element in policy evaluation. But literally all numbers are developed on the use and cost of nursing home care. That simply "does not compute" since you will not be spending the bulk of your care in a formalized and intensive nursing home environment. Most policy owners will be utilizing assisted living—which costs about 50% of nursing home care. If we assume that roughly two-thirds of the care is in assisted living, then we can potentially try this: $150/day for two years or a pool of $109,000. Assume care in an assisted living facility at $75 day for 1.5 years. That's $41,000. That still leaves $68,000 for one year of nursing home care. By using some real life elements, we have essentially "dropped" the highest of coverage—which you may not have been able to afford anyway—and yet retained an acceptable level of care due to the recent introduction of assisted living. Admittedly, everyone tends to want full coverage but our pocketbooks simply won't allow it. This may be a valid alternative in the real world.

Compounding

In my mind, the option of *compounding* is not an option when it comes to long-term care policies. It is mandatory. If you are at least 10 years away from a potential need (say, age 65, where the average age for use is 80), it is preferable to use a compounding factor than no increase at all.

Here is how it works: Assume you purchased $150 per day in benefits. We know that medical costs are increasing at an alarming rate, and long-term care costs are no different. If rates increased at 5 percent annually over a period of 15 years, the daily cost would then be $312 per day. It is mandatory to use the compounding factor to cover for this expensive contingency. However, compounding takes a while to really increase—that's the point of having over 10 years to compound. If the time period before anticipated use is 10 years or less—say you were age 70 when you bought a policy—it is preferable to use a higher daily rate to begin with, perhaps $200 per day. The compounding rider is one of the two most expensive options, but you should recognize, from my point at least, it is one that most people should budget for immediately.

Home Health Care

Just about everyone wants to stay in his or her home for as long as possible. The expensive option of *home health care (HHC)* is not a substitute for assisted living or, certainly, nursing home care. However, if you have the support from a spouse or others in the community, a move into one of these facilities can be forestalled for some time. That said, if you do not have support from a spouse or other loved one, this expensive option might not be viable. It might not be workable because, according to one statistic, about six to nine months of home care would be needed before a patient is transferred out of the home for more extensive care in a facility. But if you can afford it, home health care has significant benefits you may find worthwhile.

Home health care is the second-highest-cost rider for a policy. In California, the home health care (HHC) rider is at least 50 percent of the rate you select for care in a facility. Companies generally give you an option of 25 percent, 50 percent, 75 percent, and 100 percent of the daily cost you have purchased for regular facility care. Home health care is generally less expensive than care in a facility, because you do not require extensive care by nurses nor is the care full time. However, if you need extensive care, home health care can become very, very expensive. It can even exceed that of a nursing home, so gauge your percentage of purchase accordingly.

Table 12.3 illustrates the average hourly home health care aide costs from a licensed agency in selected areas.

Figuring the cost of coverage for home health care is not simply using the 25 percent, 75 percent, or whatever formula that you might be familiar with. Companies have found innumerable ways to confuse such coverage, and policies are especially cumbersome to understand from company to company. For example, let's assume you had a $100-per-day HHC. If you had care that amounted to $75 for one day, you can see from Table 12.3 that you would be covered in full. On the other hand, assume you had care for one day that amounted to $500.

Table 12.3 Average Hourly Home Health Care Costs

Alameda, CA	$19	Mercer County, NJ	$16
Allegheny, PA	$16	Miami, FL	$14
Atlanta, GA	$15	Milwaukee, WI	$17
Baltimore, MD	$15	Minneapolis, MN	$19
Battle Creek, MI	$15	Monroe County, NY	$17
Birmingham, AL	$14	Nashville, TN	$14
Boston, MA	$19	New Castle, DE	$20
Chattanooga, TN	$15	New Orleans, LA	$13
Chicago, IL	$17	New York, NY	$14
Cleveland, OH	$17	Oklahoma City, OK	$14
Columbia, SC	$13	Omaha, NE	$16
Columbus, OH	$16	Onandaga, NY	$15
Dallas, TX	$15	Orlando, FL	$15
Danbury, CT	$15	Pensacola, FL	$14
Dayton, OH	$16	Philadelphia, PA	$14
Denver, CO	$22	Phoenix, AZ	$17
Des Moines, IA	$18	Providence, RI	$15
Detroit, MI	$17	Raleigh, NC	$15
Essex, NJ	$16	Richmond, VA	$13
Ft. Wayne, IN	$17	San Antonio, TX	$12
Gary, IN	$16	San Francisco, CA	$17
Hartford, CT	$24	Savannah, GA	$12
Hibbing, MN	$14	Seattle, WA	$19
Houston, TX	$16	St. Louis, MO	$19
Indianapolis, IN	$17	Stamford, CT	$19
Jacksonville, FL	$14	Tampa, FL	$16
Kansas City, KS	$16	Toledo, OH	$15
Lansing, MI	$16	Tucson, AZ	$15
Las Vegas, NV	$18	Washington, DC	$16
Los Angeles, CA	$17	Winston-Salem, NC	$14

In such an instance, you would pay $400 of the bill yourself. But if you had selected a higher-priced rider, the company would pay $700 for a week, even if you spent it all in one day. Another type rider would pay $3300 for the month even though you spent the equivalent amount of money in, say, 11 days. Do you see how involved this can get? For this reason, you cannot compare one policy to another just by price.

And there's more. Some policies do not pay relatives to provide care. Yet others, with more advanced riders, do allow payments. Some will even pay for training of the relatives.

Most policies will provide payments to adapt your house to accommodate disabilities—ramps and tub bars, for example. Statistics have shown that the construction of such adaptations leads to a much longer home stay for the elderly and is well worth the extra cost. Recognize that the company is not being charitable per se. It is simply a matter of good economics. If the company pays for these changes to your home, you are almost assured of staying there for a much longer time and at a much lower cost to the company than if you were in either an assisted living facility or nursing home. It's pure economics, but it is most beneficial to the policyowner. Just make sure that your policy covers the changes. Most current HHC riders will do so. If you are reviewing a new policy and intend on buying the HHC rider, do consider this aspect very carefully.

Nursing Home Care

Nursing home care is the most intensive care of a long-term care policy. But just about all the new policies I am familiar with are also offering alternative living facilities that do not require the same intensive care as a nursing home. Patients prefer it. It is not being offered altruistically: Assisted living facilities are cheaper than a nursing home and are being built around the country in far greater numbers than nursing homes.

Policy Costs

Policies can now be purchased starting as early as age 18, and some companies will offer them to customers who are even past age 85. The average age for the purchase of a long-term care policy is a little over 65 and the average age for taking advantage of policy benefits is 80. Surprisingly, as the elderly are becoming healthier, they actually need more care. Why's that? Because healthy people just won't die. They may not require care as early, but they will require even more care overall. That's another reason to consider a short pay, fully paid up policy rather than annual payments: You won't be tempted to lapse a policy in your late seventies because you are still healthy.

So how widely do rates vary? Table 12.4 might give you an idea why you can't compare by prices alone.

Table 12.4   Standard Policy Rates for a Single Person (2002)

Company	Age 55	Age 65	Age 75
A	$912	$1421	$2940
B	$664	$1260	$2926
C	$822	$1456	$3547
D	$846	$1556	$3522
E	$909	$1557	$3707
F	$965	$1756	$4068
G	$990	$1650	$3840
H	$1040	$1910	$4410

The problem with using this method to figure or compare rates—which is used a lot on the Internet—is that it supposedly indicates what product you should consider based solely on price. It's useless. Consider this. Penn Treaty offered LTC policies at about the cheapest prices possible. In fact, some agents offered a "reward" if consumers could find a cheaper policy. It ended up that the contracts were underfunded. The company ended up ruining some people's lives, as it had to increase rates so severely that many consumers had to drop their policies because rates went up as high as 600 percent. Some states blackballed the company, though it is now making a comeback. (Conseco did the same thing. It is now in one of the largest bankruptcies ever.)

CAVEAT INVESTOR

The following are a few remaining thoughts on long-term care policies.

Federal LTC Policies

Most consumers only are aware of the opportunity to use private policies. However, state and federal LTC policies are offered to their employees. Are they any good? Yes. They normally do not have as many riders in as many configurations as a private policy, but they universally cost less money. If you have access to these types of policies, give them due consideration.

Agent Training

Many of the agents I have taught as part of LTC training had little understanding of death, dying, and long-term care. The ones that had knowledge of the subject were those who had a loved one that needed care, and they were generally over age 50. While I am not stating that you need to consider an older agent with similar life experiences, with them you might be able to get more insight into both the financial and emotional considerations of long-term care. Finding the life experience and knowledge base in the same agent will be difficult to do. But those who have both will have less of a "canned" sales approach. (It really is pervasive in the industry.) Nobody said it was going to be easy.

Quality Care

The Health Insurance Counseling and Advocacy Program in Alameda County, California, notes that "people with few or no visitors are more likely to receive poor treatment because they have no advocate to complain about shoddy care." No matter the location or type of facility, the one factor that can literally guarantee your loved one better care is to VISIT. The saying, the squeaky wheel gets the grease, has perfect application to care in a nursing home.

Will people still buy policies like these now, based on price alone? Sure. Agents with nice commissions will sway the unsuspecting elderly public to purchase these once again. It's sad but true: Price will always be one of the greatest marketing tools.

Alternate LTC Coverage

Consumers can self-insure against the costs of long-term care, but recognize that substantial sums will need to be invested. Assume current annual costs of $54,000, a 5 percent CPI increase, 15 years till needed, and a 2.5-year coverage; the costs would equal roughly $275,000. That's not chickenfeed. Admittedly, there is no certainty that you personally will require care, but that's the reason insurance was invented—just in case you are the one who has the problem.

You can also consider a unique life insurance policy. Its design is not so much for the coverage upon death but to provide LTC payments while alive.

Here is how it works. Assume you have money, say in a CD or similar investment vehicle, that you really do not need except for an emergency. Let's say it is $50,000 earning 3 percent. You are a female age 65 in good health. You could purchase a policy that would earn a current 5.75 percent with a $109,000 death benefit. Note that the death benefit is relatively low for a $50,000 premium. However, if you were impacted by two ADLs, the policy would pay a monthly benefit of $4565 for four years. That's the reason you bought it: the leveraged coverage, just in case.

This type of policy looks like a way of having your cake and eating it too, since, if you never need care, a death benefit will be paid. Further, if you do need care, the first monies used will be your $50,000 (plus interest). You don't use any of the insurance funds until you use all your own money up. It's not a free lunch per se, but it can cover some useful contingencies in planning.

Summary

Long-term care is an absolute statistical risk that you should insure against, if you can afford it. And, in a lot of ways, you can't afford not to. Don't pay attention to the advertisements, agents, attorneys, and so on, that suggest you divest of your assets solely for the benefit of using Medicaid. The government will never be able to offer adequate coverage simply because it will never have enough money. Period.

As for a policy that I would suggest: A short pay, noncancelable policy, paying $150 per day with a mandatory 5 percent compounding rider. I also would add a home health care rider with the budget controlling how extensive the coverage could be. And, I would look for a 60- to 90-day elimination period and a minimum two-year period for a man and four years for a woman.

Notes

1. One reason, I believe, why fewer men end up in a facility or die shortly after falling ill is because the wife will take personal care of the husband far beyond her personal and physical capabilities. (The Family Caregiver Alliance notes that the average unpaid caregiver spends 87 hours a week taking care of a family member.) So, by the time the husband is sent to a nursing home, he may be in the last stages of life. Or perhaps he has been improperly cared for. (Simply because you want to care for someone does not mean you know what you are doing.) If so, he may be in such bad shape that he will die shortly anyway. This is not meant as a derogatory comment against nonpaid family caregivers. It's just how life works.
2. Actually, knowledge of the local Agency on Aging is good way to tell if an agent, planner, or other person from whom you might by an LTC policy really has true insight to long-term care issues. In my experience in teaching many agents, most don't have a clue. *Caveat emptor.*
3. Did you read that carefully? Sure, you might avoid institutionalization by simple being one of the lucky ones that plop over playing your last game of golf. One gentleman, age 70, shot his first hole-in-one of his life. He went up to the next tee, said, "Oh, my," and then died of a heart attack. Actually, the "best" death happened to a sports doctor who went out running, had a massive heart attack, and died. But he was 94. As for those of you who think

you will be so lucky, wrong! Dr. Sherwin Nuland wrote a bestseller years ago called *How We Die* wherein he noted that perhaps 20 percent of us will die "nicely." The rest of us will suffer a degree of pain and mess. That's the real life of dying. Raymond Burr (of *Perry Mason* fame) was asked about death when he was dying. He said there was nothing romantic about it at all. (I think he sued God. Split verdict.) Nonetheless, death and dying are inevitable, and you should plan for it accordingly.

4. You might be able to understand the difficulty with Alzheimer's patients; they will not be able to do this ADL when they are in the latter stages of the disease. The cost to help such people is greater than with others, because a separate attendant must do it all—feeding them at each meal, for example. As such, the annual current cost of care is far greater than $54,000.

5. Never be afraid to contact the IRS. If you know what you are talking about and are objective and unemotional in the dialogue, you can find some very astute agents who will engage in a qualified discussion. If you act like a jerk, are angry, or simply don't know what you are talking about to begin with, don't expect much since they will be extremely guarded in the conversation. But that is not necessarily different in acting with people overall.

6. This is a difficult suggestion due to various state laws, but it may actually be worthwhile for a nonpool, six-ADL state resident to travel to a pool state having the seven ADLs NTQ to get the better coverage. The policy premium will be more expensive, the resident will probably lose state insurance guarantees, and there is also the issue of agent reciprocity (ability to sell to a resident of another state), but it bears scrutiny by the buyer since the contract in one state will be valid in another state.

CHAPTER 13

BUDGETING FOR NOW—AND FOR YOUR RETIREMENT

O F ALL THE ISSUES IMPACTING RETIREMENT, the amount of money you project to spend during retirement has a significantly greater impact on the amount of funds needed than the projected inflation rate, return on investment, or anything else. Further, budgeting using a rule of thumb—say 60 percent to 80 percent of current budget—is invariably a simplistic method designed for very superficial analysis; it should never be used for any long-term planning. If you are off "just a bit" using such rules of thumb, the amount of funds you believe you will need may not remotely match the funds you will spend during retirement. You don't want to find out at 70 years of age that you are going to run out of money in the next five years because you did-n't do the numbers properly when you were 50. It's too late at that point to make adequate adjustments.[1]

The worksheet shown in Figure 13.1 outlines the most detailed budget currently in use. It may take quite a bit of time to get all the fig-ures. (Remember, some of your payments may be made only annually, and therefore you must track down payments made many months pre-viously.) Now, this is how you do retirement budgeting. Look at each one of the line items. See how they might change when you retired. One example is clothes purchases. You obviously are not going to be buying lots of new clothes—certainly not expensive business suits—and you should reduce the amount accordingly. Maybe you are going to retire to Florida where you can forget snow removal, but by the same token your utilities will be higher in the summer due to air conditioning.

The point is that you simply don't just take 65 percent or 75 percent of current costs, because there are too many factors impacting the decision. So take your time before putting just "any" number in the retirement column. Add up the numbers when you are through, and you should have a pretty good budget on which a good plan may be developed. I also know that the younger you are—certainly age 45 and under—the more difficult to determine valid retirement numbers. But you have to start someplace. For those 45 and older, the need to focus on retirement numbers is mandatory, and you have no choice but to complete the worksheet carefully.

Figure 13.1   Budget Worksheet

Expense Item (annualized)	Currently Spending	Spending During Retirement
Food		
Groceries		
Alcohol/tobacco		
Restaurants		
Personal		
Work related		
Appliances and cookware/kitchen		
Entertainment and Recreation		
Vacations		
Travel		
Recreational equipment/activities		

(continued on next page)

Figure 13.1   Budget Worksheet (continued)

Expense Item (annualized)	Currently Spending	Spending During Retirement
Biking/kayaking/fishing/hunting/hiking		
Sporting events		
Movies/theater		
Parties hosted in the home		
CDs/tapes		
Fitness club		
Cable TV		
Country club		
Computer		
New computer		
Upgrades		
Software		
Repairs		
Supplies		
Online services		
Miscellaneous supplies		
Gifts and Contributions		
Religious and charities		
Political causes		
Family gifts/birthdays		
Non-family gifts		
Christmas gifts		
Transportation		
Car payments		
Auto maintenance		
Auto insurance		
Parking		
Parking tickets		

(continued on next page)

Figure 13.1   Budget Worksheet (continued)

Expense Item (annualized)	Currently Spending	Spending During Retirement
Parking permits		
Public transportation		
Carpool costs		
Taxes and fees		
Tolls		
Gas		
Oil		
Registration		
Clothing		
Mending/repair		
Dry cleaning/laundry		
New purchases		
Shoes		
Work clothes		
Childcare/Dependent Care		
Daycare		
Cleaning		
Medical care		
Babysitting		
Personal Care		
Hair care		
Toiletries		
Personal care appliances		
Pocket money allowances		
Massages		
Education		
Newspapers		
Education/training expenses		

(continued on next page)

Figure 13.1   Budget Worksheet (continued)

Expense Item (annualized)	Currently Spending	Spending During Retirement
Continued/adult education		
Books		
Magazines		
Professional dues		
Personal tuition		
Personal room and board		
Child tuition and room & board (current)		
Child tuition and room & board (future)		
Miscellaneous supplies		
Obligations		
Income tax		
Medicare		
Social Security		
State tax		
Consulting fees		
Tax preparation		
Other taxes		
Life insurance		
Term		
Whole life		
Universal life		
Variable		
Disability insurance		
Umbrella insurance		
Credit card fees		
Credit card payments		
Interest		
Principal		

(continued on next page)

Figure 13.1   Budget Worksheet (continued)

Expense Item (annualized)	Currently Spending	Spending During Retirement
Finance fees		
Cash fees		
Alimony/support		
Child support		
Child care		
Child allowances		
Business expenses		
Attorney fees		
Accountant fees		
Other debts/loans		
Union dues		
Storage fees		
Postage		
Savings		
Personal savings		
Retirement savings		
Company stock/options		
401(k)		
TSAs: 401(b) or 501(c)3		
IRAs		
KEOGH		
SEP		
Investments		
Individual securities		
Mutual funds		
Real estate		
Annuities		
Fixed		
Variable		

(continued on next page)

Figure 13.1 Budget Worksheet (continued)

Expense Item (annualized)	Currently Spending	Spending During Retirement
Home		
Home mortgage/rent		
Interest		
Principal		
Maintenance		
Furnishings		
Gas		
Oil		
Electricity		
Telephone		
Property insurance		
Fire insurance		
Earthquake insurance		
Flood insurance		
Umbrella/liability insurance		
Contents/personal property insurance		
Property tax		
Condominium fees		
Water		
Sewer		
Well maintenance		
Septic tank cleaning		
Mowing service		
Landscaping service		
Snow removal		
Second home (repeat above)		
Medical		
Hospital		

(continued on next page)

Figure 13.1   Budget Worksheet (continued)

Expense Item (annualized)	Currently Spending	Spending During Retirement
Physician		
Dentist		
Prescriptions/vitamins		
Health insurance		
Medigap insurance		
Pets		
Veterinarian		
Food		
Board and care		
SUBTOTAL		
Add Miscellaneous 5% to 10%*		
TOTAL YEARLY EXPENSES		
Current Yearly Expenses – Federal and State Tax = After Tax Budget		

*This addition may seem excessive, and will need to be addressed with an adviser. However, I think that medical costs and the like might fit in here because they have been escalating beyond all reason.

Will You Have Enough for Retirement?

Probably not.

There has been a big change in retirement wealth and retiree attitudes during the 1990s and the first years of this new decade. First, there was an overexuberance concerning the stock market based on unsubstantiated euphoria via egotistical incompetency. Regardless of their age or experience, many investors felt it was preordained that returns would approximate 15 percent per year for the rest of their lifetime. And they were convinced that they could figure out which stocks would actually do it—certainly which ones would beat the indexes like the S&P 500.

Finally, there was a sobering realignment to the reality of life via the cruel fundamentals of diversification and Monte Carlo simulations. The losses sustained in retirement accounts were enormous. The University of Michigan's Health and Retirement Study has indicated that the market losses during the 2000–2002 period have erased at least $678 billion in U.S. retirees' savings. The portion of Americans ages 55 to 64 working or looking for work has increased 3 percent since January 2001, to 62.6 percent.

The Economic Policy Institute reported that "when the stock bubble burst, it left the average family facing the prospect of having only 43 percent of the income they need for an adequate retirement."

Other comments included:

Most households used the new wealth gained from the stock market to increase debt and consumption.

Between 1992 and 2000, while the stock market grew by 13.9 percent per year, households increased their debt more than they raised their assets. The ratio of total household debt to income grew from 72 percent at the end of 1992 to 83 percent by March 2001.

It will take the average household over 30 years to recover the wealth lost in 2000 and 2001.

Phrased differently, nobody had much of a clue when the market went up and many are now getting hammered due to the same irresponsibility and lack of knowledge on the way down.

Whatever made you think that you, who cannot operate a VCR, would be able to analyze stocks?

—HOEST & REINER

That paraphrased quote, tacky as it may be, is probably closer to the truth than many of us would like to admit. As we have discussed, there are a thousand more elements in deciphering the information about a singular company than in the instructions on a VCR. Hundreds of issues are involved in analyzing the outcomes for retirement. The critical lack of education by the public has led to horrendous decisions and some retirement plans that are now more than 50 percent underwater.

Many investors clearly dismissed the fundamentals of investing. But as stated repeatedly, the entire industry has to bear the major bulk of the blame by continuing the extensive marketing of how easy it was to invest; how much better retirement was going to be with thousands and hundreds of thousands of extra dollars in a their 401(k) plans; how the economy no longer would face dips, and so on. But, as has been stated repeatedly, the fundamentals of investing have never been taught to brokers, arbitrators, consumers, and more. The difficulty in retirement planning, therefore, is that it has been presented in various idiosyncratic formats with motley (fool?) software programs and asset allocation scenarios destined to abject failure or, at a minimum, limited success.

That statement would have been anathema prior to 2000. In fact, it was. When I taught a course in financial planning in the late 1990s, students simply refused to believe or accept that a bear market like the 1973–1974 one could happen again, that the use of individual stock issues was fraught with excessive risk, or that many of the other basic fundamentals of risk and reward were valid any more. Basically, those old Beardstown broads who were supposedly beating the market handily had everyone buffaloed. Making money was so easy!

The current failure with retirement planning is the refusal to recognize that the market will change and the almost absolute inability to properly address a market, actually the economy, if and when the economy keeps tanking. The key element to a successful investing strategy and a successful retirement is this: Use the fundamentals for your benefit in most economic conditions but have more active management of your assets during periods of horrid retrenchment.

What Should You Have Done?

What you should have done with asset allocation and what the industry, educators, journalists, and others might have told you are two different things. The essential elements of asset allocation might be viable for the bulk of time and I have addressed that topic in its own section. But hoping that some book or software covering allocation will work over all periods is foolish at best. All of these "financial advisers" express "stay the course" as their song and dance. But 2000–2002 has clearly shown that retention of equities in a down-trending market is fraught with added risk and increasing losses.

Bill Jahnke, Chairman of Comprehensive Wealth Management, noted that "statistical extrapolations based on historical returns cannot be relied upon to provide valid assessments of future investment prospects" and that "static asset allocation, passive asset allocation, and market weighted asset allocation are not defensible approaches where markets are not efficient and the process that generates the distribution of returns is not stable. The financial planning community has largely been taken in by dogma when it comes to asset allocation. The doctrinaire view that all forms of active asset allocation are not theoretically or empirically supportable is false. The studies that have been selectively used to support the asset allocation doctrine are flawed and misapplied. The fact that much of what operates in the realm of market timing is bad practice does not invalidate the benefits to clients of engaging in certain forms of active asset allocation."

I have personally utilized *active* or *dynamic allocation* for well over a decade. It is not market timing in the pure sense—that is, the following of 30- or 100-day moving averages or the like and spotting market highs and lows. It is far more intensive study of all market and economic issues. It does not attempt to beat the market. Instead, active allocation is an attempt to gauge the economy and risk and adjust the portfolio to reap the major benefits of a solid market while, particularly and most importantly, reducing exposure in the turbulent times. For example, a review of the yield curve reveals how you should allocate your investments. When the curve gets inverted, you had better anticipate some major economic changes and reallocate accordingly.

The point of this activity is not just to sit there and watch your money dissipate. Addressed in Chapter 4 is a simple method of reducing your exposure to a market that keeps dropping. It's called dollar-cost averaging down, or DCAD. In effect, if the market drops beyond a correction (10 percent to 15 percent), and the economics are horrid, you simply divest yourself of your more risky investments first and keep on doing so till, somewhere around a 20 percent to 25 percent loss in the market, you are almost totally out of equities. (There is always room for some minor exposure, but a wholesale reliance is unjustified.)

Admittedly, the statistics of the market do not indicate that such a period of complete tanking happens often. But the wholesale reliance on "stay the course" and the "market always comes back" is not reflective of all periods either. It may be a truism that the market has always returned to prominence, but the problem is, you might be dead by then. Theory and reality don't necessarily jive at the same time. Yet that's where all the focus has lain and, unfortunately, retirees—actually, almost everyone—have maintained an excessive exposure to equities. DCAD is relatively simple and unemotional.

But therein is the rub. People are emotional and hate to take a loss. Professor Robert Shiller, Nobel Laureate Daniels Kahneman, and many others addressing behavioral finance note that people are very averse to admitting to a loss. So they stick with stuff that they shouldn't hold while selling their winners. John Nofsinger, author of *Investment Madness*, said it most succinctly in an article when he wrote that "emotions get in the way of making good investment decisions. For example, your desire to feel good about yourself—seeking pride—causes you to sell your winners too soon. Trying to avoid regret causes you to hold your losers too long. These emotions have the consequence that you sell stocks that are performing well and keep those that are performing poorly."

Nofsinger further noted that "to avoid feeling bad about previous decisions that didn't turn out well, your brain filters the information you receive. This process, called cognitive dissonance, adjusts your memory about the information and changes your recollection about your previous decision. Obviously, remembering inaccurately will reduce your ability to evaluate and monitor your investment choices properly."

This inconsistency in thinking causes a good portion of the mess that people—certainly retirees—are in now. In theory, and the manner in which I actually practice, there is no emotion to investing. It is just reading, research, and independent critical thinking. Obviously, consumers need to pay more attention to their investments, if they expect to keep them in proper order for retirement. Yet that is not happening at an earlier age. Research by Deschutes Investment Advisors noted that employees in 401(k) plans make an initial allocation and then don't pay any more attention to their money.

The point should be obvious to any investor. If you are not going to pay attention, you are putting your future at risk. If you listen to the claptrap of the press and the marketing of the industry, you are putting your future at risk.

What to Do?

To start, you should base your initial allocation on index funds. Paul Samuelson, another Noble Laureate and Professor Emeritus of Economics at MIT, noted that " without much hope that Wall Street is paid with overlooked gold nuggets for eagle eyed portfolio managers to scoop up, most investors, unless they possess intimate knowledge of a company's prospects, are better off placing their bets with a market index."

Well, I'll tell you, folks, you are not going to get that intimate knowledge, no matter what you think. Instead, just buy some index funds, as I've advised in Chapter 4, pertaining to asset allocation. But all that said, do not allow your investments and your financial and emotional life to be swallowed up whenever the market might take a horrendous turn. It's true that the statistical odds of such a downturn are small. Yet, if it happens, as we have seen since 2000, the financial calamity can be devastating. Pay attention to DCAD. Don't be emotional. Read, Read, Read.

How to Plan for Retirement

Now that you intend to use the fundamentals to maintain a proper portfolio, ask yourself: How much do I need for a successful retirement? First and foremost almost all elements of planning require an estimation of actuarial lifetime. (For more on actuarial lifetimes, see Chapter 10.) Lifetime estimates are now around 75+ for men and 80+ for women. But that does not mean that if you are a male, age 65, you will only live another 10 years. (We're not supposing you are smoking cigarettes like a steam engine while eating a delicious, deep-fried Twinkie.)

As noted previously, the longer you live, the longer you have to live. A 65-year old male should plan for 15 more years, a woman for 20 years. Then you add a fudge factor of perhaps five years. That estimate depends on a number of factors, including family history, exercise, and diet. But we will use 25 years for our examples.

> When estimating life expectancy, recognize that if you are 65 and the actuarial expectancy is 80 years of age, it means that 50% will die before 80 and 50% after 80. A 65-year-old man, for example, has about a 30 percent chance of living to 90 and a 4 percent to reach 100. Don't underestimate a potential life expectancy.

What about historical market returns and the projections for those 25 years? In 1984, the average compounded rate return of the market over the course of 50 years was about 9.4 percent. Sure, the market was going gangbusters in the 1990s, but I don't think there is any reader who would now realistically use a figure of more than 10 percent—even with the recent surge in market returns. (Actually, I have never used more than 10 percent for any projection at any time in my career.)

So is 10 percent now okay? No. There are countless studies and comments from the likes of William Bernstein, Warren Buffett, Paul Samuelson, and other investing luminaries that reduce the projected returns to as low as 6 percent. Will they be right? I have no idea, but I am certainly inclined to use nothing higher than 9 percent overall when looking at an extended time frame. For the lower end of the returns, I opt for 7 percent (both before-tax returns). So let's see how you figure this all out.

Let's try an example. Assume you were going to retire at age 65, planned for 25 years of retirement, and were projecting a budget of $50,000 annually. (You must do a formal budget with a worksheet, as shown in Figure 13.1. But remember, if you do some sloppy estimate or use some lame number of 60 percent, 70 percent, or 80 percent of your current spending, you are doing the whole retirement planning process a disservice.) At a 9 percent return, a 3 percent rate of inflation, the kitty you would need at age 65 would be $688,000, rounded. (The process is described directly below. You will need a financial calculator.) That simply means that you could spend $50,000 annually, adjusted up for inflation each year, and at the end of 25 years, there would be nothing left.

But what would happen if the projected return were lower, at 7 percent? The kitty required would grow to $821,500, rounded. (You need more money initially to pay for something in the future if you earn 2 percent less over the 25-year period.) That's another $133,000, or almost 20 percent more assets required. It is absolutely mandatory that you recognize, via a financial calculator, just what your exposure is given various projections and, actually, given the various economics.

Here is how the calculation works[2]

1. Assume a retirement age of 65, with 25 years to live. The number 25 is entered into your financial calculator as N (number of periods).
2. Figure on a required budget of $50,000. That's goes into the payment (PMT) section of the calculator.

3. Input the rate of inflation. The inflation rates I tend to use are 3 percent, which I think is very valid, and 5 percent, as an upward hedge. The historic rates of inflation for the last decade are shown in Table 13.1. It is my opinion that you should feel comfortable with nothing greater than a 5 percent inflation rate during the next 20 years or so—perhaps even 3 percent. I certainly recognize what happened during the 1980s, when inflation rates exceeded 13 percent. But since Paul Volcker and Alan Greenspan have been at the helm of the Federal Reserve, the entire world now knows that if they let inflation go rampant, the effects would be far worse than any terrorism act.

Table 13.1   Historical Inflation Rates

Year	Rate
1990	5.4
1991	3.7
1992	3.0
1993	2.6
1994	2.8
1995	2.6
1996	2.9
1997	2.3
1998	1.6
1999	2.2
2000	3.4
2001	2.8
2002	1.6

4. Calculate the return on whatever investable assets there are. Assume 7 percent for this example. To combine investment returns and inflation rates at the same time, do the following:
   a. Put the returns and inflation into decimals—that is, .07 and .03.
   b. Take 1 + rate of return (1.07) and divide by 1 + rate of inflation (1.03). That equals 1.038835.

c. Subtract 1.0 and multiply by 100. That equals 3.8835.

d. Enter that into your calculator under i (interest rate).

5. You now have three entries: how much you need, for how long, and how the return will increase all the while being offset by the rate of inflation. So then ask for the present value (PV). It will be $821,500, rounded.

So what does that $821,500 figure mean? Under the conditions presented, you would need that much in assets (or effective assets) at the time of retirement in order to live the time frame presented and, upon death, there would be nothing left.

Table 13.2 illustrates how much you would need to sustain a 25-year retirement at various inflation and return rates. Pay attention to the figures when using a 5 percent inflation factor. You will note you need more money in order to offset the greater erosion of higher inflation over time.

Table 13.2 Retirement Needs

	3% Inflation	9% Average Return	Amount Needed for Retirement (Rounded)
$35,000 annual budget			$481,500
$50,000			688,000
$75,000			1,000,000
$100,000			1,375,000
$125,000			1,700,000
$150,000			2,000,000
$200,000			2,750,000

	5% inflation	9% return	Amount Needed for Retirement (Rounded)
$35,000 annual budget			$579,000
$50,000			827,000
$75,000			1,250,000
$100,000			1,650,000
$125,000			2,000,000

(continued on next page)

Table 13.2   Retirement Needs (continued)

	5% inflation	9% return	Amount Needed for Retirement (Rounded)
$150,000			2,500,000
$200,000			3,300,000
	3% inflation	7% return	Amount Needed for Retirement (Rounded)
$35,000 annual budget			$575,000
$50,000			821,500
$75,000			1,225,000
$100,000			1,650,000
$125,000			2,000,000
$150,000			2,500,000
$200,000			3,300,000
	5% inflation	7% return	Amount Needed for Retirement (Rounded)
$35,000 annual budget			$700,000
$50,000			1,000,000
$75,000			1,500,000
$100,000			2,000,000
$125,000			2,500,000
$150,000			3,000,000
$200,000			4,000,000

What, exactly, are *effective assets?* An effective asset does not have to be cold, hard cash sitting in an account at age 65. It could be a pension available as an income per year, not as a lump sum. If you had a $15,000 annual pension that was indexed for inflation, the income stream would be the same as a $375,000 effective lump sum (15,000 × 25 years). You can do the same thing with social security and other annual incomes. (I am taking some liberty with numbers, but as long as the budget is detailed, at least I know my limits.)

So that is how you do the basic estimate of retirement needs. Therefore, given the budget of $50,000, 3 percent inflation, and a 7 percent return in our example above, you'd need $821,500 to (supposedly) live comfortably for your life.

Making Changes

Let's look at a situation in which you did the previous numbers and ended up with only $750,000 worth of assets when you retired—about $75,000 short of your goal. How do you readjust? Pretty simple, actually. There are only certain items that you can do anything with. You are not going to change your actuarial lifetime to anything shorter because saying you are going to die earlier does not make sense. Reducing the inflation rate below 3 percent would reduce the amount needed, but I cannot justify that. Three percent is as low as I am willing to go. You could increase the return from the projected 7 percent back to 9 percent or so, but the projected economics, national budget deficit, and all the other assorted international problems do not provide a comfort zone to boost such returns. Which brings us back to the budget.

If you have done a very detailed analysis, you can review your expenses to see where some fat could be cut. Maybe there are extra or expensive vacations that could be pared—perhaps forgoing a new car, using lard instead of butter, whatever. Let's say that the estimated retirement budget drops to $45,000 annually. By going through the format in a financial calculator, you will see that the figure for the assets needed has dropped to $739,500. You made it!

Of course, you could take part-time work, delay retirement for another year, or find other ways to adjust the spending over the 25-year period and the assets needed. You do not need some fancy software to do this. However, you do need to understand the implications of the adjustments so you know what to expect throughout your remaining life. And it will work just as designed, right?

No, it won't. Not a chance—or, at least, only an improbable one.

Why's that? Because the assumption of a 9 percent return, or 7 percent, or whatever you input is predicated on an average linear return throughout the 25-year period. But that is not what happens with the stock market. There is no way that you will ever see an average annual return each year no matter what figure you use. The market bounces all over the place, and if you start at the wrong time (2000 for example), your asset base is too low to begin with. Per Professor Zvi Bodie, of Boston University: "Even if the average rate of return is high, one can run out of money long before one expires."

Now, I suppose you could be very lucky and see a period from 1975 to 2000 and do very well. You'd be able to pull out 7 percent annually because you were investing in a great time. For example, the S&P 500 in January 1975 was 92.023. In 2000, it was 4153.979. That's more than a 16 percent annual return. It looks so good because I eliminated the horrendous 1973 and 1974 as well as the most current mess in 2000 forward. But the real-life fact is that people do not start and stop at exactly the right times and you have to statistically use an average. Actually, if by including the earlier time of 1972 through 2002, the return drops about 5 percent, to under 11 percent.

Here's another scenario: Assume a portfolio in existence for 30 years ending in 1998. Over that period, if the average return of 11.7 percent had been earned each year, an individual who retired in 1968 with $250,000 could have withdrawn 8.5 percent or $21,250 annually pretax. That amount could even have been increased by 3 percent each year with the resulting income being maintained through 1998, at which point the assets would have been depleted. (Note that the return exceeded the maximum that anyone should utilize: 10 percent).

However, there still was the market debacle of 1973–1974. Those losses of over 45 percent were not factored into the planning process. As a result, from 1968 for the next 13 years, the actual portfolio performance averaged only a 6.9 percent return. Admittedly, the return was buffered by a 15.3 percent average annual return during the 1982–1998 stage. But the earlier years had already done their damage. Had the original 8.5 percent withdrawal rate been maintained, the portfolio would have been drained of all assets by the thirteenth year. The thirteenth year!

To continue the message about starting retirement at the wrong time, think about this: Assume you started retirement at the beginning of 2000 with $821,500 and figured you were going to earn 7 percent annually. But you got caught in all the marketing hype of the go-go 1990s and, even when the market started taking a dive, you accepted the stay-the-course mantra of the industry and almost all the professional money advisers. It's now more than three years later, and you have lost, say, 45 percent of your assets and are down to $452,000. There is now no way in Hades that you have a chance of taking out $50,000 annually. You are so far down that, even assuming a 7 percent return thereafter, you'd be able to take out less than $30,000 annually. A $20,000 income shortfall cannot be made up unless there was an 82 percent gain in the portfolio. Ain't gonna happen.

In this short economic period of three-plus years, which as of this writing is looking better (but with no guarantees), the inattention to economics—or more likely an attention to the marketing hype of inexperienced and unknowledgeable advisers—has led to a decimation of retirement, both financially and emotionally. (I am not sure which would be worse.) I wish there were something I could say that could turn around the problem and make a person whole again. But there isn't. You need to make hard choices: have a much lower standard of living, go back to work, live with your children, and so on.

What Retirees Should Have Done, Part 1

It's obvious that the last few years of market losses—though extreme in the odds of occurrence—required an insight by advisers that was exceptional by its absence. Almost the entire industry is predicated on an element of asset allocation as a static picture that very seldom changes.

As stated in Chapter 1, asset allocation is a required element of planning. It represents an effort to determine which investments to use, in what percentages, and at a given point in time. Few dispute its basic viability in providing good returns at an acceptable risk. But that's where I stop with the standard rhetoric. While it may be possible to find an allocation at a specific point, all investment criteria—be it alpha, beta, correlation, and, most certainly, the economics impacting all—are moving targets. What was viable at a given point may not be, and is not, valid later on. The fact of that statement needs no further factual verification than the three-plus years of continuing losses, which have destroyed retirement lives.

Per Bill Jahnke: "When it comes to asset allocation, two assumptions are commonly but not necessarily consciously employed: markets are efficient and the process that generates returns is stable. These assumptions are fundamental to the common practice of extrapolating historical returns, risk premiums, standard deviations and correlations. These assumptions are false. Statistical extrapolations based on historical returns cannot be relied upon to provide valid assessments of future investment prospects."

As stated previously, a simple method known as DCAD could have avoided a large amount of those losses (it cannot avoid all losses) and kept risk at an acceptable level. Certainly, advisers had a duty to respond to such statistical devastation by adjusting portfolios as such losses were sustained. That few have done so is a reflection of the limited expertise of many financial advisers everywhere. Advisers continue to use stay the course in a game of rhetoric drivel in order to placate the consumer. But per Jahnke: "It is also a convenient solution for financial advisors because it does not require much work aside from initially getting the client to sign off on the asset allocation policy and some occasional hand holding when an asset class is performing badly. It also sidesteps the requirement for investment acumen in the investment decision process."

The issue is this: If you confront a market and economic debacle, staying put can cause a meltdown of your financial life. On the other hand, if you are well read, the use of DCAD might be of significant assistance in allowing you an adequate retirement.

What Retirees Should Have Done, Part 2

Let's assume that you did not start your retirement in 2000, but will do so, perhaps in a few years from now, in a more "normalized" market. Can the example provided above—$50,000 annual budget and $821,500 of assets—actually work in the real world?

Not really. Why's that? Because, as stated, the assumption for a 7 percent average annual return is illogical. With all the ups and downs, statistics have shown that if you were to take out the 7 percent, you would run about an 80 percent chance of running out of money before your actuarial lifetime was completed (meaning you're dead). Of course, you can be just as lucky on the other side and have a whole mess of money left to give to your wayward cat. But the point of this exercise is to determine what statistical rate of annual distribution from your asset base would probably leave you with enough money for your lifetime.

What is that amount? A little over 4 percent. It is generally conceded that if you take all the highs and lows of the market, you probably would not run out of money if you did not take out more than slightly over 4 percent of your assets annually. You'd, obviously, take out less in the great years and more in the poor years. That way, you could be pretty confident that you would have enough money to last the 25 years of lifetime. But just as obviously, you'd need more money in your kitty to start with at age 65 in order to live comfortably. A lot more. If $50,000 was to reflect no more than 4 percent of an asset base, it would have to be $1,250,000, or a 52 percent increase in assets above the $821,500, needed at retirement.

Can such an increase be accomplished if you are already retired? Well, it depends on how much money you had to begin with and whether the budget can be adjusted to reflect these new numbers. But if we assume that you were just retired with the $821,500 and the budget was set, you simply are going to have one heck of a time to pull out $50,000 annually adjusted by inflation without running out of money prematurely. Further, if you use static allocation (no adjustments when things go wrong), you probably won't make it.

Admittedly, it is impossible to know if yet another market or economic scenario such as we were just in will impact a retiree before death. By the same token, why not? Readers were undoubtedly hoping that this material could provide an easy method to set their retirement on auto pilot. I certainly would have liked to provide that guidance—certainly since many other books show that it is so simple. Otherwise the best solution is to do the numbers as I indicated above but to stay cognizant of changing economics.

What about financial software?

It stinks. Okay, I suppose I must elaborate.

Most consumers and brokers tend to use various commercial programs to do retirement planning. In the alternative, they use the free online programs offered by many fund families. Unfortunately, study after study has shown that they all come up with different numbers—sometimes wildly varying numbers. Each program can make different interpretations and assumptions of historical returns, time frames, taxes, inflation, and much more.

Here is an actual response from a consumer: "I have used half a dozen online retirement calculators. They all have the same problem—the assumptions (average return, life span, inflation rate, monthly cash flow, and so on) are unknowable. One set of assumptions say I'll die rich while another (just as reasonable) set of assumptions say I'll be living on dogfood for the last 10 years of my life. Everyone says the ideal scenario is 'the last check should bounce.' But, realistically, I don't know if I'll have the 'financial confidence' to watch my investments decline as I get older. I don't want to leave millions to charities or children, but neither do I want to run out of money during retirement."

Most of the plans upon which financial software is based use static allocation, and I absolutely refuse to accept something that sophomoric.

They also tend to use a linear average return (such as the flat 7 percent). It sure looks good on paper, but the reality is, it probably won't work. The following quote from a Nobel Laureate says it all:

> I have been studying software provided by major mutual fund and software companies and have found that it reflects remarkably few of the lessons learned after decades of the development of financial theory and its implementation by and for large institutional investors.
>
> —BILL SHARPE

As validation of the fallacy of depending on software per se, I point you once again to debacle of the Long Term Capital Management partnership. This company had two Nobel Laureates and 27 PhDs identifying "no-lose" software scenarios for banks and institutions. In 1998, it blew up, causing an effective bailout of the U.S. banking system by the Federal Reserve to the tune of $3.6 billion. While Sharpe's point is focusing on institutional software, the use and validity of consumer software for the average middle-income class investor is even more suspect, primarily because little evidence exists that such software has what is truly needed. Software simply cannot provide the algorithms to cover the myriad of contingencies. Further, no one would have the capability to run such software. Nor would that person's computer.

In my own work, I obviously use various software programs. But I have felt that, as one becomes more engrossed with the computer and its programs, the process becomes inherently flawed. It fails to address the actual client, who has many issues that cannot be programmed (health, kids, long-term care, and more).

I have found that wholesale reliance on such programs results in too many errors or inconsistencies. So, instead, I prefer to do a lot of retirement scenarios by hand, so that I know the various implications. The resulting reports are not as pretty as those from a program. They don't have colorful charts and graphs or all sorts of mental gyrations that neither you nor the adviser understands. But they do include commentary about long-term care, Medicaid, 529 plans, and more that, more often than not, are not even addressed in software programs.

You have to remember that retirement covers far more issues than just the investments, and you will need guidance on all such areas. As such, if you want to try a software program to design your life, buy the thing yourself—don't pay an adviser to input the data for you. If you want someone who knows what they are doing, then you will have to do a lot more homework.

When to Start and What to Do

Proper planning for your retirement should start at least 10 to 15 years before the actual retirement. Throughout the 1990s, this advice sounded bogus, since all anyone had to do was put money into the market, retire early, and then have a risk- and emotion-free retirement. Unfortunately, for many people, as I have already identified repeatedly, the scenario was unsustainable, emotionally charged, and totally unrealistic.

To start the process of retirement planning correctly, with almost any given planning scenario, the one absolutely critical item to prepare is the budget. The worksheet shown in Figure 13.1 is the most mind numbing example of a budget I have seen to date—and far more than the simplistic budget plans identified in most books and magazine articles.[3]

Why am I so adamant about making an accurate budget? Because I'm the guy who works the trenches. I've seen what happens in the real world when people take the easy way out and simply guess how much they are going to spend—a ballpark guess, a flaccid estimation. Experience has clearly shown that guessing on this critical area generally leads to retirement failure. Even with people who have a pretty good handle on their expenses, unless a a formal analysis is done of how their money is spent, no ballpark estimate will suffice.

But why isn't a guess close enough? After all, when dealing with retirement of 25 years or more, you are guesstimating how long you will live. You are also guesstimating how much inflation will be and how much the investments will return. Why not guesstimate the budget? Because the returns, inflation rate, and investment returns are all finite numbers—10 percent, 7 percent, 22 years, 35 years, and so on—based on valid statistics. But a personal budget cannot be estimated since it is personal, specific to that family. Attempting to determine the asset base needed for retirement is practically worthless if the major determinant—how much is being spent—is effectively inaccurate.

Furthermore, the real world often finds retirees actually spending more money than they did while working simply because they have more time to travel, see relatives, give gifts, or just enjoy themselves. But how do people know that if they have never focused on a budget during their lifetime? A formal budget is mandatory.

Doing a budget before retirement is also valuable since it can unmask bad habits that are being covered up by the income stream from working full time. Credit card debt, restaurant meals, excessive vacation costs, and much more can be hidden when money is coming in. It is necessary to ferret (mole, albatross?) out these extra items and put the savings into a retirement account. This extra money will be needed if you can't take more than roughly 4 percent out of your assets in order to live through retirement.

Look at the budget shown in Figure 13.1. See how detailed it is. As an example, look at the line item for pets. They are expensive, and the costs for keeping pets increase as they get older as well.[4] A student of mine suggested the item for parking tickets, since it was an ongoing expense in San Francisco. Or septic tanks in rural areas. Snow removal in the north. If you don't go through this in detail, too much that adds up to real money is apt to be left out.

If a professional adviser suggests estimating a percentage of your current budget as your retirement budget, walk away. I had hoped that the simplistic 60 percent to 80 percent of current spending still presented in a lot of "financial" magazines had met their demise, but you still see it preached on an ongoing basis. It is not valid. If you see a simple budget form, I take the same position—walk away. You absolutely need to do your homework up front because you are looking at 25 or so years and you must have a good handle on expenditures before you start.

Assets before Retirement

We've discussed the analysis you need to conduct at the time of retirement. But let's assume you are 55 and plan to retire in 10 years. I'll assume you need a "nest egg" of $900,000 at age 65 and have only $700,000 in assets currently. How do you figure out what you have to do during the next 10 years to accumulate $200,000 more? Assume an 8 percent return (i), 10 years (N) and a need for $200,000 (FV, future value). In your financial calculator, ask for the present value and it will show that you would need $92,600 now. In the alternative, the PMT (payments) for 10 years could be about $12,800 per year. And you could use many combinations of both a lump sum and payments.

It is my contention that the numbers are fairly easy to do with a financial calculator. You can feel what is going on and why. On the other hand, the problem is trying to figure out what numbers to actually use pursuant to potential economics. Using preprogrammed software without a critical insight to what should or should not be used will not provide the proper or secure retirement that many thought they were going to get. These numbers and the insight must be done and redone at least every two years, or else you could end up with another mess like 2000–2002. I repeat, either you or your adviser had better understand the inverted yield curve and other such factors or you are going to put your financial life at risk. It's your call. Table 13.3 illustrates the numbers for someone who plans to retire in 10 years.

Other Retirement Issues

Factors other than budget need to be considered in retirement planning. The paragraphs that follow explore the major ones.

Table 13.3   Needed Assets; 10 years to retirement ; 6% before tax return

Amount needed		Lump Sum	Annual contributions
$100,000		$55,800	$7,157
$200,000		$111,700	$14,300
$300,000		$167,500	$21500
Amount needed	8% return	Lump Sum	Annual contributions
$100,000		$46,300	$6,400
$200,000		$92,600	$12,800
$300,000		$139,000	$19,000

Health Care—Or, No Way Out

Most of you are no doubt aware of the concern about how medical premiums have increased, and the situation is not going to get any better. For those company retirees who thought they had guaranteed medical coverage at a set price for them and their spouses through retirement, many have already been rudely notified that the company has the absolute right—under contract—to increase such premiums. At present, only about 20 percent of company retirees are still covered 100 percent for health care. That number will go down. (Consider some of the companies that went into bankruptcy and terminated coverage en masse.) Medical costs have been increasing by double digits the last few years, and I do not see a change for the near future. Therefore, of all the various issues that will impact a budget detrimentally, this is probably the major one. It is also the reason why the higher use of a 5 percent inflation factor over time may be valid.

Medicare Coverage.   Medicare HMOs have been dropping like flies. Why? Simply go back to the 1990s (and well before, if you want) and you will find that the Medicare and Medicaid budgets were exploding. There was lots more fraud, lots more retirees, lots more people living longer, and lots more people looking for increased care and more prescriptions to do it with. The excessive costs forced Congress to reduce the payments to the HMOs. The HMOs then stated that they were not making any money off the patients and opted out altogether.

While anyone losing HMO coverage under these circumstances would automatically go back on Medicare, they might not find the physicians to accept them. For those people who remember articles on the subject as far back as 20 years ago, physicians often indicated they would not accept Medicare patients because the reimbursement rate was so low. Now you are hearing the same thing because of the same issue: Physicians took a 5.4 percent rate cut in 2002 and expected another 4.4 percent in 2003. It's supposed to hit 17 percent in total by 2005. The American Medical Association's headline for an article simply said this: "Doctors May Not Treat Medicare Patients Unless Payment Cuts Are Reversed."

Unless the payment formula is fixed, Medicare rates by 2005 will return to what they were in 1991 and overhead costs have already risen about 40 percent.

Another survey by the independent Medicare Payment Advisory Commission showed "a seven percentage point drop in the number of doctors taking all new Medicare patients from 1999 to 2002." Table 13.4 illustrates the differences in medical coverage.

In short, there is no magic bullet for health care coverage, whether before or after retirement. This one element may continue to increase for many years at a double-digit rate, and the budget must reflect such increasing costs.

Medigap Policies.   But the difficulty does not stop there. If you want to cover some of the extra costs that Medicare does not pay for— deductibles, copayments, and so on—you can purchase various Medicare supplemental policies, also known as a Medigap policies, once you are eligible for Medicare. At such a time, you do not need to be medically accepted; the coverage is automatic if you sign up for one of their plans at that time. However, if you want one later on, or if

Table 13.4 Medigap Policies

Medigap Benefits	Policy A	B	C	D	E	F	G	H	I	J
Basic	x					x		x		
Part A Hospital Deductible						x		x		
Part A Skilled Nursing Home Co-Insurance						x		x		
Part B Deductible						x				
Foreign Travel At home recovery						x		x		
Part B: Excess Doctor Charges						100%	80%		100%	100%
Preventative Care										x
Outpatient Prescription Drugs								Basic $1,250 limit	Basic Same	Extended $3,000 limit

you want to change to another policy type, you will need to go through complete medical underwriting. Therefore, you need to make sure you pick the right one initially.

One blessing is that you have to pick from only 10 plans overall. That was a government decree, initiated because insurance agents in the past would sell the elderly first one Medigap policy, then another, then another, and so on (just one reason why insurance got such a bad name). So the government instituted 10 policies, which are effectively the same for all states.

Keep in mind the following important *difference* between the policies: Company 1 is required to cover Policy A, for example, in the same manner as Company 2 and Policy B, which in turn has to cover in the same manner as Company 3 and Policy J, and so forth. However, the premiums do not have to be the same at all. In fact, the various companies and premiums can vary widely, so it really pays to shop around. Also, the policy premiums vary tremendously from state to state. But the major point for budget purposes is that all company premiums have been rising at least 15 percent or more annually for the past several years—at about the same rate as general health premiums. If you are forced over to Medicare because an HMO shut down, and you purchased a Medigap policy to pay for the extra costs that the HMO covered, the costs will have a direct and detrimental effect on the formal budget and the amount of income needed to attain your desires.

The American Association of Retired Persons (AARP) sent me its premium schedule for 2003. Plan A costs $112 (rounded); Plan B costs $147; Plan C is $161; D is $149; E is $150; F is $164; G is $160; H is $188; I is $190; and Plan J costs $230.

Everyone would love to sign up for Plan J because it covers the most for prescriptions. But here is the impact. A monthly payment of $230 equals $2760 annually. The assets needed to take care of that inconvenient budget item are expensive since, instead of using a 3 percent or 5 percent inflation rate in the calculations above, you'd have to use at least a 10 percent increase to reflect in the increase in the rise of such policies. With a 7 percent return, 10 percent inflation, the asset base would need to be $98,000. If you assume a 15 percent increase each and every year, the asset base would need to be $187,000 to reflect the increases for a lifetime. That is a huge exposure just for extra coverage. Think about that. Just a few years ago, many retirees had been using $0 since they were, or were expecting to use, a Medicare HMO that would have effectively cost them nothing out of pocket. Now there is a possible $100,000 exposure. (This material does not cover the new medicare bill.)

Many retirees are seeing such budgetary ramifications that were not even on the radar scope a few years ago. Nor may this be all there is. No one can imagine what other situations may befall retirees during the 25 or so years of retirement (vaccines due to terrorist acts?), and so it is necessary to build in a conservative estimate in the budget to begin with to try and take care of some of these contingencies. Nonetheless, another $100,000 or $200,000 mandatory asset base just for health care is a mind-numbing increase that can shatter a retirement. It's one thing when you hear comments about such costs. It's another thing to see what it actually means in necessary dollars.

Long-Term Care.   We discussed long-term care in Chapter 12, but it is yet another budgetary health item that rears its ugly head as we get older. True, not all the elderly will need long-term care. But if they do, they will find that nursing home costs are now running about $55,000 annually. Very few people can pay for that type of coverage out of a retirement budget without materially impacting the lifestyle of their spouse and other loved ones. Even if someone is single and no one else is involved, $145,000 annually can devastate any existing kitty. What did I just say? How did I get from talking about $55,000 annually and then addressing $145,000 a year? Inflation, that's how. If you took a current $55,000 current cost and inflated it by 5 percent for 20 years (say, you were age 65 and did not need care till age 85), then it would cost about $145,000 a year. And remember, your retirement kitty would be severely depleted by then and it wouldn't take very long before all your money would be gone.

Medicaid.   This issue is covered extensively in Chapter 12, but suffice to say that many feel that planning for Medicaid nursing home coverage is the way to go. Spend down your assets, give them away to others, play the games by elder care attorneys, special annuities, and so on, so you can utilize the state coverage. Using Medicaid is fine—if you never had much money to begin with. Medicaid is designed for the indigent. And you can become indigent by playing the games. But here is the crux of the issue: How good is the care you want for a loved one? I repeat in a slightly revised format: How good is the care you would want your mother to get?

This is the point. The money Medicaid receives has always been woefully inadequate to provide quality coverage to its patients. As one article said: "Many people who become convinced that transferring wealth to become eligible for Medicaid is a good idea ultimately discover that, by protecting their assets for someone else, they have drastically limited their own options and choices for long-term care. For instance, the level of Medicaid reimbursement for Assisted Living facilities and Alzheimer's centers is so low that these types of institutions seldom accept Medicaid residents. Those facilities with large numbers of Medicaid residents find they cannot provide an optimum quality of care on Medicaid funding, which is far lower that private pay rates."[5]

Yes, some nursing homes can provide good care, but perhaps they are capable of doing so primarily because of the subsidy the private pay patients are providing to the Medicaid patients. Secondly, there is effectively no coverage for assisted living facilities—and this has become the major focus of retirees now and will continue into the future. Nursing homes will provide care for those that are very sick while the rest will use an assisted living facility, possibly until their deaths. If you want the best of care, in the best type of facility, and with more latitude of the types of facilities, consider an LTC policy.

Now to address a sticky issue that has not gotten the proper commentary. One study reveals that only about 43 percent of those people who turned age 65 in 1990 will enter a nursing home at some time during their life. Twenty-four percent of the elderly over age 65 will need nursing home care for more than one year. The same study reported that among all persons who live to age 65, only one in three will spend three months or more in a nursing home; about one in four will spend one year or more in a nursing home; and only about 1 in 11 (9 percent) will spend five years or more in a nursing home. In other words, two out of three people who turned 65 in 1990 will either never spend any time in a nursing home or will spend less than three months in one. The point being, why not just take the chance that you will never need LTC anyway? It seems like a good risk.

But if you attempt that, you are almost assuredly being hypocritical. How's that? Well, you bought fire insurance didn't you? You bought medical insurance, life insurance, car insurance, and many others. The odds of using some of these are far, far greater than that of long-term care. Further, the hope of any insured is not to use the policy at all. An insurance policy is as much for emotional security as it is for financial liability. Put that into perspective and the use of a good insurance policy makes perfect sense.

Homeowners Insurance

Yet another expense that can smash a budget when you use a 3 percent inflation factor is homeowners insurance. According to the Insurance Information Institute, as of 2002, an "extraordinary" number of catastrophes (think of the fires most recently in Southern California), the high cost of home repairs, and excessive jury awards for toxic mold claims would raise home insurance premiums an estimated 9 percent in 2003. And that's on top of the 8 percent increase you probably paid in 2002.

Insurers have paid out more than $100 billion in catastrophe-related losses over the past 12 years. In 2001 alone, home insurers paid out $8.9 billion more in losses and expenses than they received in premiums, the second worst year on record since 1992, when Hurricane Andrew cost insurers $11.5 billion. Don't get me wrong. I do not necessarily have a problem of using a 3 percent inflation rate for a lot of items—clothing, food, and so on—and the Consumer Price Index (CPI) has stayed very low for years. But the elderly may be materially impacted by certain items more than others, and this is one of them.

Social Security

I won't bore you with all the elements of what is going on with the polit-
ical elements of social security, but this is a nice way to get the subject
started: Why wasn't there a problem with the funding of social security
when it started? How about in 1945? 1955? You all know the answer:
No one was expected to live that long past age 65, man or woman.
Hence the use of social security as a retirement funding vehicle didn't
come into prominence until, say the 1960s, and then it didn't become
a controversy until, say, the 1980s, when actuarial lifetimes because so
much longer and the number of young workers funding social security
became so many fewer. And you know what? It will just get worse. We
will all have a longer actuarial lifetime as medical advances keep flour-
ishing. And we will not increase the birth rate; in fact, it might go lower.

As a result, changes will be forthcoming in the structure of social
security, but they will happen like this: People who do not have that
much money (though I am not sure what that number might be—
maybe $50,000 income for a married couple) will continue to receive
benefits as always. But what will happen for those who still bring home
too much bacon during retirement? If the taxpayer's income is between,
say, $50,000 to $100,000, the social security element will be taxed at a
greater amount than it is currently. (For those who are unfamiliar with
the concept, if you make, MFJ—married filing joint—over $32,000
or $44,000, respectively, then the social security is taxed at rates of 50
percent and 85 percent, respectively.) The subject is too detailed and
cumbersome for more involvement here, and I am simply giving my
opinions of the future tax ramifications. Anyway, maybe everything over
$50,000 requires that 75 percent of social security is taxed; everything
over $75,000 is 100 percent, and anything over $100,000 income, perhaps there is a reduction of social security benefits. (In fact, in late 2003,
you are already finding congressional action that may require high
income Medicare beneficiaries to pay more in premiums. You may
not like it, but such elements must transpire.)

060804 $12.05 C

0160022287-2714

0

**— EWR **

0

CANCEL

ONE WAY

NJ TRANSIT

PR JCT

0

25063-0584-05259

FARES PAID IN THE ABSENCE OF A TICKET WILL NOT BE REFUNDED, NOR WILL REFUNDS OR REPLACEMENTS BE MADE FOR LOST, STOLEN OR DESTROYED TICKETS. REFUNDS ARE NOT CALCULATED ON A PRO-RATA BASIS. SEATING ABOARD NJ TRANSIT VEHICLES IS WITHOUT REGARD TO RACE, CREED, COLOR OR NATIONAL ORIGIN.

This side up

INSERT

So, I think many people will continue to get social security in the future, save for those that have a substantial income anyway. When the adjustments will be made is unknown—maybe by 2010. But something will need to be done because of the huge budget deficits.

For those people who will apply shortly, the following is a question that is normally asked. Assume you could get full benefits at age 65 and you are now 62, when you could get reduced benefits. Do you take the lower benefits now, or do you wait? Here is the answer: How long are you going to live? Wasn't that simple?

The point is that if you are sure that you are going to live for a very long time, you are better off waiting for the higher benefits—even waiting until after age 65, if you want to work some more. If, however, you don't expect to live that long, you would be better off to take a smaller monthly amount at age 62. Just assume that the extra three years of payment before age 65 will make up for the higher amount later that you could have gotten by waiting till age 65.

That's generally all there is to it. But you will have to make the decision based on your actuarial lifetime. If you are going to live forever, hold off taking social security as long as you can. There is a link at my Web site where you can put in the various amounts and it will tell you the breakeven point in years. It would be well worth your while for this analysis.

Social Security Offset

Having some offset for social security is standard practice in many, if not most, companies that offer pension plans. And if the practice is not understood properly, it can have a major detrimental affect on your retirement.

Note that there is nothing wrong or unethical about the practice, except for the fact that it may not be effectively communicated to employees. As an employer, the company is responsible for paying half of your social security benefits. As such, they are "responsible" for half of the social security benefits you get when you retire. (Obviously you must take into account how many years you worked for a particular company, and so on, but for the sake of this example, I'll simply assume it was your entire working career.) We shall also assume that the company will pay you a pension. They therefore will subtract part of your social security payments from your pension plan and give you the difference.

Assume you were to get $1000 in a monthly pension plan and $600 in social security. Your first thought is that you will receive $1600 in retirement benefits. But the company has the right to subtract $300 from the pension half of the social security and now you get only $1300. Unfortunately, many employees—as well as many planners—will miss this computation, and it can make a dramatic difference in your retirement.

Here are some more numbers to make my point.

The $1000 per month of anticipated pension ($12,000 annually) over a 25-year period (age 65 to 90) and a 3.0 percent inflation factor is effectively equivalent to a lump sum of $215,000. (The figure is relatively small, since the pension is not increased by inflation.)

On the other hand, $700 per month ($1000 anticipated pension minus $300 of social security) with the same formula is equivalent to a lump sum of $150,000. That reflects a $65,000 equivalent lump-sum loss that you probably did not account for in your retirement calculations. For planning purposes, the difference can mean big changes in your proposed retirement budget. (Notice how the budget always impacts planning at every level?) It might mean you retire in a different location, buy a smaller house, not have the amenities you had hoped for, and so on.

If you are unfamiliar with what your company is doing, contact your human resource department and request a copy of your plan benefits. Then adjust your retirement accordingly.

Summary

The "simplicity" of retirement planning in the 1990s has been preempted by the cold reality of the 2000s. Of course, planning never was that simple. Consumers will need to recognize that they need to do a lot more reading in order to save and grow the retirement funds they now have. That attempt will not be easy, because most projections for the next decade show lower returns overall. The way to get a reasonable focus on retirement starts with a budget.

Without a solid effort in this area, the rest of the numbers may not provide a good direction for the future. You certainly will have no idea of the risk that you must take in order to meet your goals. Nor will you know the amount of review of economics necessary so a precarious financial situation like the 2000–2002 market slide will not eat up more of your dwindling retirement reserves. The calculations must address the fact that the market always goes up and down and that an attempt to take out equal amounts each year of retirement may not work. Studies have shown that no more than about 4 percent of your retirement assets can be distributed annually upon retirement if you desire reasonable assurance that you will have money to last a lifetime.

Notes

1. For the purists, I understand that there is a lot of compromise and guesstimates with some figures and that the projections of inflation and returns in the future are also based on unknown rates. That said, if the budget, which can be determined with some exactness, has no correlation to some real-life element, the whole process can be wasted. Further, if the retiree/investor refuses to do the necessary homework, the analysis will tend to be valued accordingly.

2. I am assuming that either you or your adviser has the capability to use a financial calculator and can and will be able to do the numbers yourself. You must be able to see how the numbers work. Software is fine, though limited in many aspects, but you have to know how the calculations are personally derived so you can see the implications of any variations. Per an instructor at the College for Financial Planning: "The process of using the calculator helps you learn what result to expect."

3. Charles Schwab's book, *You're Fifty—Now What?* is, in my opinion, a prime example of an oversimplification of the budgeting process. But before you think I am on a tear on Mr. Schwab or anyone in the business, let me say that

it's not so. However, just turn to page 81 in the Schwab book, *Words to the Wise on Estimating How Much You'll Need for the Second Half*, paragraph 3, wherein he notes, "When you need an estimate of living expenses or income, the key word is estimate—a ballpark figure will do. You don't have to count every dollar, every dime. Simply start with what you believe are realistic numbers."

No! That won't do at all. You do not guess!

4. Assume your mother lives in another state. She is still lucid and relatively healthy. But she is slightly depressed. You'd like to get her a pet. What do you get her? A dog. Why? Because besides providing good company, a dog will have to be walked twice a day. Even a short walk is excellent exercise for the elderly. And it's so difficult to walk fish. Cats will scratch. And Musk Ox are simply unhygienic.

5. From Samuel Larry Feldman and the National LTC Network, "When Caring Isn't Enough . . . Meeting the Need for Long-Term Care with Long-Term Care Insurance."

CHAPTER 14
ESTATE PLANNING

MY MAJOR FOR MY MASTER'S in financial planning was in estate planning primarily because I viewed this as one key area that was not being properly addressed by the elderly public. People spend thousands of hours during their lifetime trying to build an estate but just a couple hours, if that, determining what will be done with it. It is a sad situation indeed to deal with a surviving spouse—most often the wife—where the man had adamantly refused to do any proper planning for his family. As Edward Young noted, "All men think all men mortal but themselves." In more colloquial terms, a man perceives the problem as not *when* he will die but *if* he will die. This attitude of immortality also shows up with small businesses that terminate upon death due to no survivorship planning.

Emphasis: Assets or Intangibles?

The general focus of most books and articles on estate planning is the passing of assets and the ability to reduce estate taxes. (Perhaps now this emphasis is of little applicability to middle-income Americans because higher levels of assets can be passed to survivors.) Nevertheless, the real essence of planning should include all the issues of aging such as gifting, charitable strategies, long-term care, health care, Medicare coverage, physician's directives, social security coverage, and death and dying. Additionally, you are dealing not just with the elderly client, but with the entire family as well as other loved ones (even mistresses), businesses, creditors, the IRS and other tax agencies, physicians, hospitals, hospices, and Fluffy the Cat (not a joke—you'd be surprised). You get the idea. Thorough estate planning is far more involved and far more emotional than most people realize.

In fact, the emotional turmoil of estate planning is one of the key elements that is rarely addressed in either books or seminars. The prime emotional turmoil is the psychological devastation and heartache that universally occur when no, or limited, estate planning is done. Incomplete planning takes longer to correct and, hence, causes more strife than a quicker resolution with proper wills and trusts. Because poor planning causes such grief, you would think more people would realize that they need to do estate planning. But that's not so, simply because people do not like to confront disability and death.

A fine example of what can go wrong happened when a relative of mine died at the age of 45 of a massive heart attack. He left a mess because there was no will. I think a great part of his inability to plan for his demise was due to the fact that his entire family had a long history of heart disease and his father died young. The issue of estate planning probably made him visualize a potentially short lifetime (which was certainly true because he did not take care of himself). Everything finally got straightened out, but not without complications. Costs were not insignificant, as the services of an attorney were required. And the surviving spouse had additional emotional stress because of the probate, which was much longer and more involved than it need to have been.[1]

Several of my clients are widows. It was obvious that even when finished, the estate planning could have been better designed in order to relieve the anxiety of a death on the survivor. Estate planning is a twofold consideration; it involves both seeing that assets are passed on to survivors correctly as well as making sure that the grief and anxiety are reduced for survivors. The process can be somewhat involved, sometimes intimidating, and expensive. But, you cannot put a price on tears.

Assets

As of 2003, the tax-free lifetime amount of assets exempt from each estate is $1 million. And it is projected to increase to $3.5 million by 2009. Those figures are somewhat deceptive, for two reasons. First, as of 2011, the law supposedly reverts back to the old restrictive law. Will it? No way! (And I wrote that before the Republicans won everything in the 2002 elections.) I am still not convinced Congress will pass the full exemption—maybe somewhere in between. And that figure might be between $1 million (as it currently exists in 2003) up to perhaps $2.5 million per person. Congress can still institute a tax for those with the largest estates and leave the middle-income person to escape the brunt of estate tax exposure. Of course, that is my educated opinion, and you are certainly entitled to adjust as necessary. Table 14.1 details estate deductions, as stipulated by current tax laws.

Table 14.1 Current and projected estate deductions.

2003:	$1 million
2004:	$1.5 million
2005:	$1.5 million
2006:	$2 million
2007:	$2 million
2008:	$2 million
2009:	$3.5 million
2010:	N/A
2011:	(Taxes repealed) maximum individual rate (gift tax only)

The second issue is that for federal estate tax purposes, we are dealing with a net estate. In simplistic terms, assume you had a house worth

$1.5 million and were trying to figure out what might happen at death. Well, you can't figure it out—or at least shouldn't—without excluding a specific piece of information: your mortgage. Assuming that your house was your only asset and there was a $600,000 loan, you have no estate tax since you are under the current $1 million exemption. ($1,500,000 gross assets − $600,000 loan = $900,000 net asset base for federal estate tax.)

Though I reference this later, it bears noting right now: If you are dealing with probate in California (be sure and check your own state's laws), the value used for probate is the *gross* estate. The difference between net and gross is a huge one. You can pay no estate tax whatsoever and end up with a huge probate fee that could eat up most of your equity. (For the above estate, it is $26,150 just for the attorney plus extraordinary fees, if applicable. If you also pay the trustee, add another $26,150, for a grand total of $52,300.) It is one of the reasons why the costs (say $1500) of a living trust, explained later, may be very viable even where the estate is relatively small in terms of the estate lifetime exemption. For example, a $300,000 gross estate could cost $14,300 or even more in probate fees. If you figure that the net amount after loans was only $100,000, you are being forced to pay out over 14 percent of your assets!

An additional tax item that might be burdensome involves a limited number of states that still impose their own state estate tax. Your own estate attorney will be able to address that issue. Keep in mind that in the future you might actually find more states imposing some fees because of their huge budget deficits.

Increasing Assets

Since you are not dead right now, I assume you have assets that you have put away for growth. Admittedly, the stock market might have crippled you, but, if you had followed the comments I have made about dollar-cost averaging down in Chapter 4, the hit should not have been too bad. Anyway, let's assume that you have a $150,000 net estate now, are 55 years of age, and are trying to figure out what the implications are when you die. As mentioned elsewhere, to do proper retirement planning, long-term care planning, estate planning, and the like, you *must* address how long you might live. You can also work with a number of Internet sites that let you determine your actuarial lifetime by inputting various facts about your lifestyle, age, health, Twinkie consumption, and so on. But for ease of this example, the average remaining lifetime for a 55-year-old male is about 25 years, to which I will add five more years to be conservative. Of course, if you don't take care of yourself and follow a proper diet and exercise, you probably can subtract five years. And I shall also assume a 7 percent before-tax return. So, over a 30-year period, the value of your assets would grow to $860,000, rounded, which is well under the $1 million current estate exemption available at death.

While I told the truth in the above sentence ($1 million estate exemption available at death), I was also very misleading because I did not provide you with the whole truth. That's because you can use your lifetime exemption while you are alive without having to pay estate tax. This topic is discussed more thoroughly later, but the point is, you don't have to wait to die in order to transfer large amount of assets to others without tax.

Also note that I have not accounted for income or long-term capital gains taxes, if applicable, to be paid by the beneficiaries. I am only referring to the net estate left by the deceased—not what is left after taxes for the beneficiaries. I'll give you some quick examples shortly, but suffice to say, the element of basis must be understood by both grantors and beneficiaries before death. You should carefully read the following section on basis so your beneficiaries won't be mad at you after you leave this existence (assuming they are not already mad at you. But I digress...).

Also note if you were married and the combined net estate happened to be, say, $1,800,000, you and your spouse are each entitled to $1 million lifetime exemptions ($2 million total) and the joint gift would have escaped estate taxes once again. (Make sure you note that I used the term spouse. Only legally married couples are allowed to effectively double an exemption allowance.)

Frankly, with the proposed higher estate exemption limits, most readers will be able to dismiss many of the convoluted life insurance trusts for the sake of avoiding, reducing, or paying off estate taxes. That does not negate the possibility of gifts while alive so you can benefit others, but the overriding concern about estate taxes at death should be relatively moot for most middle-income consumers. See how dying is now much easier?

Basis.   Regardless of the estate tax, a critical issue remains: whether your beneficiaries will get the assets you intended. That involves the issue of basis since, even if the assets are distributed in an equal manner, the end result after taxes can leave net assets in no way reflective of the initial intentions. The following short examples should make the point.

Assume you have a 401(k) plan that has $200,000 at your death. It goes to your son, Bob. You have a $175,000 life policy for your daughter, Sue. You have provided nothing else for her. Bob has told Sue about this discrepancy and she has always felt resentful toward both of you because of that $25,000. As a result, there is a strained relationship between Sue and you and between Sue and Bob. You no doubt have heard about this kind of situation many times before. But who really gets what? Well, your daughter gets $175,000 free and clear because that's what happens with life insurance, in most cases. But Bob does not get $200,000 because ordinary income tax will need to be paid on this type of retirement asset. At an overall 30 percent income tax rate, he will pay $60,000 in taxes and net only $140,000. Now, all of a sudden, Bob is mad at Sue and at you for the deception. In essence, all the relations were messed up before death and are even more messed up after. This is not a legacy that anyone wants to leave, but in my experience, it is indicative of at least 75 percent of all wills and trusts leaving varied assets to more than one beneficiary. Table 14.2 illustrates an unequal asset distribution scenario.

Table 14.2 Unequal Asset Distribution

Current allocation with Sue receiving less gross distribution.

	Gross Assets before Tax	Net Assets after Tax
Bob receives 401(k)	$200,000	$140,000 (assuming 30% overall federal and state income tax rate). Bob actually receives $35,000 LESS than Sue
Sue receives Life Insurance	$175,000 Sue thinks she is being short-changed $25,000	$175,000 (Insurance is generally not subject to income tax)

Clearly, leaving equal amounts can actually make the situation worse. Let's assume that Dad increases the life insurance for Sue so the gross amounts before tax are equal for both children. At its face, $200,000 apiece may make both children feel comfortable in that you had provided for equal distributions, or so you thought. The problem is that the situation gets all the worse after death (see Table 14.3).

Table 14.3 Revised allocation where Dad equalizes gross distribution.

	Assets before Tax	Assets after Tax
Sue receives Life Insurance	$200,000 Both may think Dad has been fair because of Aequal@ distributions	$200,000 (Insurance is not subject to income tax). Sue and I go to Hawaii for an extended vacation.
Bob receives 401(k)	$200,000	$140,000 (assuming 30% overall federal and state income tax rate). Bob actually receives $60,000 LESS than Sue. Bob is even more irate, incensed, irrational, angry—with $60 K less than Sue.

Because of the obvious inequality, Bob wants Sue to give him $30,000 so they both are equal in net assets. He will go up to $170,000 and she drops down to $170,000. Do you think it will happen? Not likely. But let's say Sue is amenable to the proposal or even offers it willingly herself. It looks nice, but there is a problem. If she should give Bob the $30,000, only $11,000 (as of 2003) qualifies for the annual gifting. The other $19,000 requires a gift tax report and reduces Sue's lifetime exemption. (Gifting is discussed below.) Even if the lifetime reduction is not a problem, the filing of the report is an onerous and expensive annoyance that everybody would want to avoid.

Dad has left a legacy of animosity and sibling rivalry that can exist for generations. Of course, maybe the ultimate disparity was intentional because he did like one kid better than another. Or perhaps one needed more funds than another, had a sick child, or whatever. If so, all parties should clearly understand the implications of taxation beforehand. But be careful that your intent does not also destroy your family now or after you are gone.

The bottom line is this: A will or trust that does not take the net amounts into account is a poorly drawn instrument. And if you used an attorney or other adviser and you did not see this in writing, go get some of your money back. That professional missed a key element of planning and had a fiduciary duty to inform you of this issue. Since we are on the point of competence, remember that estate planning addresses money now and in the future. The attorney should be completely competent with a financial calculator since it will be mandatory in determining present and future values.

Intangible Estate Planning

So far in this chapter, we've looked at the passing of assets and examined how planning can accomplish that task correctly. However, while the transfer of physical assets is important, the overall action of dealing with one's demise is still fraught with emotional errors and uncertainty.

The use of a formal document (a will, a trust, and so on) should allow a clean break from life in an expeditious and suitable manner. It should also allow and provide for a shortened grieving period for your loved ones because the details have been worked out beforehand. I know that money may be a primary element in many deaths but the loss of a loved one can cause far greater decline in the joy of a beneficiary's life than pure money.

Careful planning that includes medical directives, living trusts with competent trustees, and so forth can lessen the emotional strain. Those issues do not tend to be the thrust of most presentations or seminars on estate planning, which instead focus on the sale of trusts, insurance, annuities, and other products and fee services. These aspects may resolve potential conflicts—certainly the use of medical directives does—but the overriding issue in estate planning should be the human element.

Dying Intestate

Dying intestate means that you die without a will. As a single person, you may believe that the distribution of assets will occur with limited court exposure. Nothing could be further from the truth. First of all, the court will have to do extra work in determining what the assets are and to whom they are to be distributed. For those whose parents are still alive, you also need to remember that they will face the added unnecessary emotional strain of dealing extensively with the probate court system.

If you are married with small children, you have no idea the mess that will happen. Depending on what state you live in, only part of the assets may get distributed to your spouse, since state statutes may call for the allocation of set amounts to the children. In many states, the spouse receives 50 percent of the estate and minor children receive the other 50 percent. Such allocations may require the spouse to file reams of paperwork in order to get the assets redistributed. It will cost a lot, since an attorney will need to file additional paperwork with the courts. And the emotional strain on the survivor will be greater. This is actually what happened when my brother-in-law died. The house went directly to my sister because of titling but the other assets encountered the obstacles above because there was no will. The situation was very messy, the work involved was time consuming, and the additional strain elicited more tears. In short, there is no rational reason not to make at least a simple will. They are not perfect, but they are better than nothing.

Wills

Note that each state has different rules for drawing up a will. You can write a will yourself, though doing so definitely is not recommended: The odds are astronomical that you will make a lot of mistakes. I am also not wild about the forms at stationery stores either. They aren't very complete, and you can almost make as many mistakes using one of those as you could by making up one.

Many books and CD-ROMs provide more "expert" advice for drafting wills. If you are strapped for funds, using one of these might work. But if I had my druthers, I still would opt for using an attorney who truly knows what he is doing. The cost shouldn't be too excessive—say, from $100 to $500, depending on intricacies and the location of the office. City lawyers cost much more, in general, than their more rural counterparts. Many times, it is true that you get what you paid for. But in this case I am referring to a basic will, not like the Bretton Woods Agreement (for you history buffs).

Once you are married, a will is essential. Admittedly, if you are single or married with no children, there may be little reason to think about an early death. But it happens nonetheless. Should you have children, a will becomes absolutely mandatory. They would still have to go through probate with a will, but at least you have limited your family's exposure to exasperation, which they would have had had you done nothing at all.

Be aware: Even if you have a very complete will, so you think, it might not do what you intend it to do or anything at all. For example, assume you have a 401(k), annuity, life insurance, and similar contractual assets that require that you name the beneficiaries. Whomever is on that paperwork is exactly who will get the asset, regardless of what you may stipulate differently in a will or trust. For example, if you put your daughter as the beneficiary of your life insurance policy but then decide later, in your will, to change the disposition to a 50-50 split between your daughter and son, your daughter will receive 100 percent of the life insurance, because the policy remains outside the intent of the will. You have to remember this issue when you set up a will or a trust since your new desires may never be instituted.

Here is another real gem of an issue that you need to address with an accomplished attorney. Assume you want to disinherit your wife (or husband) by unilaterally willing everything to your mistress. Well, under state statutes. the spouse may have rights against the estate for her or his specific ownership of assets. The idea originally was developed under dowry and courtesy (rights in the other spouse's property). While these "rights" have been generally repealed by statute, the essence remains that what you thought was going to someone may never get there. All sorts of issues are involved with wills and trusts—separate property rights, community property, and so on. It's tricky stuff and clearly reflects why an estate planning attorney can be helpful.

Probate

Almost all estates—even estates with living trusts—must undergo some process of probate, which is the court review of the disposition of assets. Probate may not be as aggravating an exercise for the ultimate beneficiaries as sorting through an estate in which the decedent dies intestate, but not by much. It is a time-consuming process and can be costly. Now, it is true that many states allow some small estates to avoid the costs of probate. But the middle-income American consumer will invariably have assets beyond a state's minimum. And then the fees will get you. For example, a $500,000 California estate will costs $11,150 in attorney's fees and another $11,150 by the executor (for a total of $22,300). Many texts say the average cost for probate is about 4 percent of the net estate, though in California it is about 8 percent to 10 percent. So, a $300,000 estate may cost $12,000. But it could be much higher.

Once again I bring your attention to the value of gross and net estate. The federal estate tax is based on *net* estate while the California probate is based on *gross* estate. Check your state's laws to find out whether estate taxes are based on gross or net. Table 14.4 illustrates the differences between gross and net estates.

Table 14.4   Comparison between a $1,000,000 gross estate and $500,000 net estate.

	Estate Tax	Probate Fees with a Will	Living Trust (explained below)
Gross Estate 1,000,000	None	$42,300	No probate fees if done properly—though recognize there are some fees for attorney and CPA services.
Net Estate $500,000 liens= $500,000 net estate	None	It's still $42,300— an 8.5% reduction of the net estate	No probate fees if done properly

Probate fees may be higher than the figure mentioned above due to extra work by the attorney phrased as "extraordinary fees." Some books and journalists talk about the fact that the probate fees are negotiable with an attorney. Are they? Get real! There is no way that a bereaved spouse or other loved one is going to go out and make appointments with several attorneys and negotiate the best price. The statement may be true, but it borders on the absurd. If you want to reduce or negate probate fees, consider a living trust and doing the homework before a death, not after. Postmortem planning is not planning. It's expensive, time consuming. and emotionally debilitating.

Executor, Executrix, or Administrator Fees

The probate fees above reflect attorney fees of $21,150 and trustees fees of $21,150. Most books simply say that this $21,150 executor fee can be disclaimed by the executor-beneficiary so that more money is left to the other beneficiaries. I think that this statement reflects very poorly on the amount of work by the administrator and, certainly, to the added emotional strain in finalizing all elements of a death.

To illustrate, let's assume that there is just the administrator to contend with. He has the right to accept the $21,150 fee, but it would be taxed as ordinary income at, say, 30 percent, for a tax of $6345. But if it was left in the estate and it was under the current $1 million, there would be no tax. Such a deal—the choice is obvious. On the other hand, suppose the current net estate was right at $1,021,150. Estate taxes would be applied at a 41 percent rate and the tax would be $8671. Now it would be better to take the $21,150 out of the estate, since the tax would be lower.

"Disclaim" means that you can actually refuse receipt of assets from an estate because you don't want it or for any other reason. However, you should not have received it first and then try to disclaim. Also, once disclaimed, you cannot pick to whom it will go. Table 14.5 details trustee fees.

The issue of executor fees is seldom as clear if there is more than one beneficiary and where the acceptance or rejection of the executor's fee can cause a lot of animosity. Read on.

Let's say you were the executor and a beneficiary, but there were five other children/siblings/beneficiaries. Now, trust me, the situation changes. First of all—particularly for those who have already been through it—does the amount received by a beneficiary ever make a dif-

Table 14.5   Take or disclaim Trustee's fee

	Administrator/ executor, income tax bracket of 30% overall	Estate Tax at 41%
$21,150 taken as executor fee and net estate under or at $1,000,000	$6,345 ($11,150 × 30%) . But executor could leave money in the estate for tax of $0	$0 Better to leave the fee in the estate
$21,150 left in estate and net estate already over $1,000,000	$6,345.	$8,671 ($21,150 × 41%). Since the $6,345 tax is cheaper, better to take the fee as the executor.

ference? Is there any animosity if one beneficiary gets $5000 more than another? $500? $50? Name your number: It can make a huge difference, not just in the money, but in the attitude of one sibling to another. And any hostility can last for years and years. I have seen this happen.

Because the executor can charge this fee and diminish the pie for the rest, the other beneficiaries tend to load up a lot of impassioned feelings that the executor should do the work for nothing and let the executor fee stay in the estate. The truth is, though, that executors have to do a tremendous amount of work during very difficult times. The emotional strain is extensive—more so, certainly, than the other siblings who are waiting impatiently for a resolution (and their money). And these executors know and feel it. So I think they should be paid. But not necessarily in the manner you think. And a real-life example makes the point.

A client of mine was selected, along with one of her sisters, to be the executor of her father's estate. There were seven children in total. She clearly stated that there was going to be a lot of pressure on her from all sides about the money distribution. I told her she should get paid but that her father should make a statement in the trust that the executor must get paid. That way the "blame" could be placed upon the deceased, not on the executor. Guess what? Her father went ahead and had the trust changed to reflect what he also felt was going to be a difficult endeavor worthy of payment. He also told the other kids. While they still may not like it, they now know exactly what the deceased wanted to have happen, and any ensuing problems or animosity against the executor(s) is decreased considerably.

This is certainly not standard practice in any will or trust documentation I have seen. Nor will the issue come up normally in conversation with your attorney. But I think many estate planning professionals should consider including a provision for an executor's fee in the will or trust. Having one can solve a lot of hard feelings. Of course, it clearly means that there needs to be open dialogue between Dad, Mom, and the kids, and that is certainly not the case in many families. But if the provision exists, the difficulty of death can be made easier.

How to Complete Probate

It takes time to complete the probate. The following is the basic process in one state (California) to show you how probate involves more issues than simply counting up the money, seeing an attorney, and then sending it out.

Basic California Probate Process

1. Write a will.
2. Appoint an executor.
3. Death.
4. Notify the executor.
5. Take steps to secure the deceased's property. (The executor does this, by notifying banks, employers, and others of the death; if necessary, the executor has utilities turned off, cancels newspapers, seals the house, and so on.) The executor does not pay any debts or distribute any property at this time.

6. Make funeral arrangements. (The executor may be involved with this activity.)

7. Prepare a petition for probate. (The executor's attorney prepares the petition, which is filed with a death certificate and the original copy of the will.) At that time, the executor secures a federal tax identification number for the estate.

8. File a newspaper notice. This action is mandatory with probate. This notice tells people of the death and that the will is being probated and that creditors have a fixed amount of time (usually no more than four months) to come forward or be barred from further claim.

9. Mail notices to heirs and beneficiaries. The executor must send a copy of the petition for probate and a copy of the will to every beneficiary or heir.

10. Hold a hearing for probate, usually about six weeks after probate is filed.

    At the hearing the judge will decide on the validity of the will. If the will is valid, it will name the beneficiaries who will take the estate after creditors and taxes are paid. At the hearing, the judge signs "letters testamentary" allowing the executor to sell or change title to the deceased's property.

11. Inventory the estate. Hire an appraiser. File all claims for the benefits due the estate. (These include fraternal or lodge benefits, social security, and so on.)

12. File inventory with the court.

13. Pay creditors. Creditors are usually assembled and paid one month after the time limit is exhausted (therefore at least five months after probate process begins). If there is not enough money in the estate to satisfy all creditors, payments are made in the following order:
    a. Executor's fee, if any
    b. Attorney's fee
    c. Reasonable funeral expenses
    d. Family allowance (usually a fixed sum of money for main-

taining the deceased's spouse and dependent children while the will is being probated.)

   e. Homestead allowance (generally an amount needed to pay the normal upkeep of the home while the will is being probated)

   f. Exempt property: a surviving spouse or children have a right to a fixed-dollar value (the amount varies from state to state) of the deceased's tangible property, such as the car, furniture, paintings, and so on.

   g. Taxes (fiduciary tax on estate's income)

   h. All outstanding medical expenses

   i. All other claims

14. Pay state inheritance tax (not applicable in many states).

15. Pay federal estate tax, if any. This payment is normally due within nine months after death.

16. Petition for distribution of the estate. The executor presents the final accounting to court.

17. File the final notice in the newspaper announcing closing of probate and distribution to heirs and beneficiaries.

18. Hold final hearing: The judge reviews the executor's actions and closes probate.

Note that the process lasts at least nine months. We all have heard about probate taking years and years. And since we are all going to live a long time and stress is good for us, this is not a problem. Right!

Unfortunately, we're still not finished with this issue. In today's mobile society, people may own property in several states. Maybe the property is a vacation home or it could be property left as an inheritance. Regardless, a probate will be required in the state of residence and the states where the other property resides. Now, you have twice the problems and potentially twice the cost. A living trust, addressed below, can mitigate many of these problems.

Lastly, we have the issue of privacy. Do you really want someone to know you left your silk undies to your dog? Of course not. But since probate is a public procedure, everything you do will be known by others. Think about that. You have all sorts of people you have never met reviewing distributions of assets that is none of their business going to people they don't know and probably could care even less about. All sorts of rumors can start that can impact your beneficiaries.

So what does probate provide outside of a lot of time, confusion, money, embarrassment, and extra tears? Perhaps not much. It's not the devil that many call it, and some states make it easier than others. But middle-income property owners may wish to do other types of planning to avoid this scenario.

Now do you see why somebody other than attorney should be compensated for the effort of acting as executor?

Gifting

For most middle-income American taxpayers, *gifting* is a relatively straightforward proposition. The tax code indicates that you can gift up to $11,000 (indexed for inflation) per person per year to anybody. There are no tax repercussions to the recipient and you simply lower your taxable estate. For example, let's imagine you have a $500,000 estate. You want to give 10 people each $11,000 cash. They get $11,000 and your estate is now down to $390,000 ($500,000 − $110,000). No special forms, no tax on your part. Most of the times this transfer is pretty simple. But it does have its bad moments.

The above gift was made in cash, but it can be other assets as well. Let's say it was stock that you had purchased for $5000 many years ago. It's now worth $11,000 and if you sold it, you would have to pay the long-term capital gains tax on the $6000 gain. Instead, you gift it to your niece. She gets the $11,000 stock with the same tax basis of $5000. If she sells it, she pays the tax at a lower tax bracket. It sounds good, and it is.

But here is a little gem you don't hear about. What happens if the asset is held for 20 years thereafter and is then sold for say, $15,000? How much is taxable? (The answer: $10,000.) The problem is that nobody remembers what the tax basis actually was, since there is no require-ment that there be a written statement of the gift transaction. If the IRS audits, who knows what will happen? (Think about the repercussions if the asset was 10 times the value.)

Why bother with the problem? I suggest that when anyone gifts an appreciated asset that they also provide documentation of the tax basis, which in most cases would be the original sales price. (There are more rules if the price has dropped, but we're not covering all the issues here.) Admittedly, you have to keep such documentation for years and years until it is finally sold, but it is a lot better than spending hours of frus-tration with the IRS trying to determine a value 10 or 20 years ago.

What happens when you gift beyond $11,000 per person per year? Now it gets sticky in that you will have to file a gift tax return. You won't have to pay any taxes for a while since all you are doing is reducing your lifetime exemption. Once you have gifted a lot, then gift taxes are applied.

As an example, assume you gifted $26,000 to your brother. The first $11,000 is your annual exclusion but the extra $15,000 requires you to file a gift tax report. Let's also assume that we use a current individ-ual estate tax exclusion of $1 million. What happens is that your life-time exclusion is now reduced by the extra $15,000, to $985,000. In actuality, the drop is neither that significant nor too severe, but you still had to file that darned report. That is an aggravation that most peo-ple would like to avoid. Maybe you can time the gifts differently over a couple years. Or maybe, just maybe, you can take advantage of some unique gifting opportunities.

College Gifting

Let's say the gift was to help your brother (actually, it does not have to be a relative) go to college. Tuition is $22,000, which is certainly well more than the annual $11,000 gifting limit. Guess what? You can gift the tuition amount for the benefit of your brother directly to the college and not incur any gift tax problems. Remember, college gifting covers tuition only. It does not include room and board or books. Therefore, you could gift the $22,000 directly to the school as well as another $11,000 as the regular gift to your brother. Nice.

Let's say that your son or daughter wants to go to a prestigious college 10 years from now (In 2003–2004, Harvard costs over $37,928 for tuition, fees, and room and board.). You want to set aside money in a special kitty that might earn enough to pay for the expenses when your child turns 18. In most states, you now can do so through a 529 plan. These are special state college plans that allow you to gift up to five years at once ($55,000). The plan offers significant tax benefits in that the gains and dividends are not taxed to you currently. Ultimately, the full account is not taxed at all, if it is used properly. You retain control of the account and can change the beneficiaries from one to another and even use the money yourself for your own higher education.

Each state administering the plan has significantly different rules; some even give you a tax deduction for the investment. Plenty of texts and Web sites are devoted to the topic of saving for college, and it is worth the effort to check them out. If you want to save even more money here, just don't have any more kids.

Medical Costs

Can gifting be used to pay off someone's medical costs? Yes, it can. For example, imagine that a grandmother is concerned that the medical bills of her recently injured daughter will financially devastate the granddaughter. The bills are over $61,000, which the grandmother could easily gift to the granddaughter. Nonetheless, the amount would be $50,000 above the current annual gift maximum of $11,000. Not to fear. If the payment for the bills is made directly to the hospital, no gift repercussions apply. Once again, this "gift" does not have to be for a relative. So the grandmother could pay the $61,000 and still gift a separate $11,000, for a total of $72,000 without taxes.

Using Your Estate Exemption Now

If you gift more than the $11,000 currently allowed annually, you use up some of your lifetime exemption. If it stays within this limit, there is no deduction against your lifetime exemption. The point is, the law indicates it is a lifetime exemption, not one that must be used solely at death. Therefore, you can gift your entire lifetime exemption, or any part of it, at any point in your life in addition to the annual $11,000 gift.

To illustrate, assume the lifetime exemption in 2003 is $1 million. You can gift it all plus the annual $11,000 gift ($1,011,000) right now to a singular entity. Or $511,000 to one person; $511,000 to another. Or $261,000 to each of four persons. Or $111,000 to one, $211,000 to another, $73,000 to another, and so on. There would be no gift tax currently owing. Of course, you will need to file a gift form to the IRS, but if you really wanted to gift the asset today, the paperwork might be the only issue.

Now, someone might ask, why would you want to give away that much today? Because you can take a highly appreciated asset out of your estate and place it in the hands of another. For example, let's say you had a $500,000 building whose value was growing at 8 percent annually and you are age 50. If the asset is kept till death at age 85, it would be valued at $7,392,672. If we assume that estate taxes of some type would be levied (say 30 percent), then the tax would be over $2,200,000. In the alternative, if it was given to your daughter today, the entire growth would be out of your estate since she becomes the sole and full owner. Admittedly, one does not know what estate taxes will be in the future. Nonetheless, this is a viable gifting technique that could mitigate changes in the estate tax law later on.

Titling

Several types of property titling can help you avoid probate. The reason you can avoid it is that the property is directly titled so that it can pass to the ultimate beneficiary upon your demise. Such contractual entities include life insurance, annuities, 403(b) plans, 401(k) plans, IRAs, and other properties where you can use titling as community property, joint tenancy, tenancy by the entirety, and tenants in common.

Let's consider your life insurance. You need to have a beneficiary designation on the application. When you die, and you will, the asset can go directly to the beneficiary without the court's intervention—and, as mentioned, bypassing any other changes in a will. (If you want to change the beneficiaries, contact the life insurance company directly for a Beneficiary Change form.) The life insurance is still added to the total net estate for estate tax purposes, but they at least bypassed the expensive and potentially messy element of probate.

For example, if your net estate is $700,000 and the life insurance policy of $500,000 is in your name, and you are single, the total estate is now $1,200,000. So now you do have estate tax, because you're over the current $1 million exemption limit. Let's be careful out there. Don't let a valuable asset like life insurance lose part of its value to estate taxes if that can be avoided.

Let's review other titling opportunities. I'll also show you some aspects that are completely detrimental to proper planning. Unless indicated otherwise, the owner is single in the following examples.

Joint Tenancy

Probably the most well known way to title and pass assets to another is *joint tenancy*. Generally it means that if you have a number of people owning a property, then whoever lives longest is the last owner. In between, the other owners cannot sell, gift, or otherwise transfer their interests to anyone else. Obviously with most rules, some exceptions apply, but this is close enough for our concerns here. This form of ownership is also valid for married couples. While it is an apparently straightforward method of passing assets, joint tenancy can have severe problems when using it for nonspousal situations (and in some spousal situations, as addressed in "Community Property").

Let's say you own your home and would like to pass it on to your son. You can simply record a new deed with him as joint tenant. You die and, since the property is already titled under contract to your son, the property is transferred without the necessity of probate. (It is still included in your estate, for estate tax purposes.) This arrangement looks great on its face. Even the IRS will give you the benefit of the doubt in that it was not a gift at the time of the change in ownership but merely a titling to facilitate estate transfer. (You then won't have to file a gift tax report, unless a true gift was intended.)

Nevertheless, joint tenancy has big drawbacks. That's because, regardless of whether the property was a true gift or not, your son (or whomever) is on the title as actually owning part of the property. If he should go into bankruptcy, be liable for a judgment, or whatever, guess what the court or creditor could do? They could attach the property with a lien simply because he was on title.

But let's just say your son was simply a jerk. He could potentially take out a mortgage on the property and not make payments. He could gift his interest to someone else. And, heaven forbid, he gets a divorce from that hussy you never liked and she gets the interest as part of the divorce. None of this is in your best interest.

What is the lesson of the story? You must carefully consider all the repercussions before putting anyone on title simply to bypass the issue of probate. It's better to have the property and pay a probate fee for a distribution through a will than to lose the property, or have it tied up in court, just to save a few thousand dollars.

There are other issues with joint tenancy, as well. Consider a married couple in which each spouse has $1 million and property is titled as joint tenancy. When the first dies, the surviving spouse automatically receives the deceased's estate and now has $2 million. If the survivor then dies before any other planning takes place, the estate will be taxed, since it is $1 million over the current lifetime exemption. That puts the estate in the 49 percent bracket, and the taxes would be $780,800. Not good planning. Actually, it stinks because proper—and relatively simplistic—planning could reduce the exposure to $0. This works the same as an unlimited marital transfer, addressed below.

Tenants in Common

In this case, let's say that 25 of us own a property where we each have an undivided interest. I own 4 percent, John owns 11 percent, Mary owns 6 percent, and so on. The difference between *tenants in common* and joint tenancy is that we each can sell, assign, gift, will, or transfer our interest to anyone else at any time. Therefore, there could be brand-new owners tomorrow, unlike joint tenancy, where no one changes.

Community Property

Community property is a unique form of ownership between married couples in eight states (Arizona, California, Idaho, Louisiana, Nevada, New Mexico, Texas, and Washington). It doesn't work the same in every state, and Louisiana has special rules all by itself, so you need to do some of your own homework. Generally, however, unless property has been set aside as sole and separate property, the spouses own everything 50-50 regardless of who bought what or when.

Community property also allows a full step up in basis at the date of death versus a one-half step up under joint tenancy use. Because that is rarely understood, I offer the sample situation given in Table 14.6. (You have to understand basis, if you buy anything of substantial value in your life.)

There are no extra taxes for retitling a joint tenancy property as community property, at least in California. And for the vast majority of good marriages, the benefit for the surviving spouse is obvious: less tax.

Keep in mind: You can hold property exclusively in your own name (see the following section "Sole and Separate Property"), if it is desig-

Table 14.6 Community Property and Joint Tenancy for Married Couple

(Community Property not available for non-married entities)
$250,000 rental property purchased 10 years ago, now worth $500,000

Community Property	Man	Wife
Property initial basis $250,000	$125,000	$125,000
Husband dies, Property value $500,000		
Basis for surviving spouse (full step up in basis to the value at the date of death)		$500,000
Taxable amount		$500,000 value minus updated basis of $500,000= $0 tax

$250,000 rental property purchased 10 years ago, now worth $500,000
Joint tenancy does not allow full step up in basis

Joint Tenancy	Man	Wife
Property initial basis $250,000	$125,000	$125,000
Husband dies, Property value $500,000		
Basis for surviving spouse (50% step up in basis at the date of death)	Basis for spouse for this one-half of asset goes up to $250,000	Surviving spouse retains initial basis of $125,000
Total basis for surviving spouse is $375,000		$375,000

(continued on next page)

Table 14.6 Community Property and Joint Tenancy for Married Couple
(continued)

Joint Tenancy	Man	Wife
Taxable amount		$500,000 value minus updated basis of $375,000= $125,000 taxable. At a 20% long-term capital gain tax rate= $25,000 tax

nated as such and none of the monies are commingled with community property assets. You will need to discuss this matter with an attorney to be clear on the proper documentation.

Sole and Separate Property

Spouses can retain assets in their own name and do nothing to transfer funds to the other spouse at any time, including death. But having
significantly different sums in each account, as you would with *sole and
separate property*, can cause some unnecessary estate tax consequences.

To illustrate, assume two people marry for the second time, and the
husband, age 75, brings in net assets of $3 million. He marries a woman,
age 35 with just $500 to her name. (Yes, I know this is an extreme sit-
uation, but just think of what happens in Hollywood and it all makes
sense. Does Anna Nicole Smith ring a bell?) Assume neither of them
has children. Or they don't like them. Anyway, if no planning is done
and the husband dies in 2003, the estate tax would be $945,000 on the
$3 million.

Illogical and unnecessary! Proper planning before death could have
transferred $2 million to the wife and, potentially with the new tax laws,
it could accumulate with no estate tax until she dies. He would have
been left with $1 million and used his current $1 million exemption.

(Yes, it is also possible to transfer the entire $3 million to the wife.) And she would have had years to do other planning that would be more acceptable than sending an unnecessary $945,000 check to the IRS.

Unlimited Marital Transfer

The most simplistic method to transfer the assets to the other spouse, regardless of the value of those assets, is in using the *unlimited marital transfer* deduction. Any spouse can transfer any amount of assets to the other—even before death—to the other spouse. (If you are a noncitizen, separate and messy estate planning rules apply. Become a citizen—it's much easier.) There is no tax for such transfer. (Once again, this is for married spouses. Friends, children, and same-sex unions do not apply.) The best part of such transfer is that there is no probate on the first to die. That's a heck of a savings in cost, time, and emotional turmoil, but you need to recognize that, assuming no other planning, you simply end up with more money for a potential probate hassle at the second to die.

Let's look at a simple example (see Table 14.7). If the husband died with $300,000 of assets and it was passed, under the unlimited marital

Table 14.7 Unlimited Marital Transfer—Limited Assets

Husband with $350,000 of assets.		Wife with $150,000 of assets
Husband dies and uses unlimited marital transfer.	$350,000 is transferred to wife	
No estate taxes since under the $1,000,000 exemption.		Wife now has $450,000
		If she dies with under $1,000,000 of assets, no estate tax. But probate may still apply.

deduction, to his wife, who had $150,000 of assets, her total is now $450,000. There is no estate tax on the husband's estate simply because there was nothing in his name at death. And if the wife's estate stayed under $1 million when she died, the tax issue is effectively moot since it is under the lifetime exemption for this study, or $1 million. But let's look at the added values beyond that due to this same type of transfer.

As regards estate taxes, the transfer of funds to the surviving spouse may be okay if the total assets are less than $1 million net for the last to die. But if the assets are more than that amount, estate taxes start at 41 percent. For example, if the deceased passed $700,000 upon death to the surviving spouse who already had $700,000, then there is the potential of having a $1,400,000 estate that would incur current estate taxes. (Remember, that the $700,000 could have been passed just as easily with the use of joint tenancy and so on.) Table 14.8 illustrates a transfer for estates worth more than $1 million.

Table 14.8 Unlimited Marital Transer—Assets over $1,000,000

Husband has $700,000 in net assets. Husband dies. No estate tax since nothing in account.		Wife has $700,000 in net assets
	$700,000 transferred to wife	Wife now has $1,400,000
		Wife dies. Assume lifetime estate deduction is $1,000,000. Estate taxes are $167,000 on the $1,400,000. Possible probate on $1,400,000.

Why does this happen? Why didn't the first to die, say the husband, get the use of his $1 million exemption and avoid the extra taxation later on? Because he did not elect to use his election; he chose the unlimited marital transfer instead (or direct titling) and therefore lost the use of his exemption. As such, the marital transfer can look great for the first death but you need to be aware of added costs and difficulties for the second to die—absent other planning. But if proper planning is done, most of the middle-class consumers could avoid probate and avoid estate taxes. Read on.

Tenancy by the Entirety

Tenancy by the entirety is available for married couples in about half the states and works the same way as joint tenancy in that, upon death, the surviving spouse automatically receives the rest of the property. You do avoid probate but the estate tax implications are the same as with the unlimited marital transfer. The last to die could be impacted by large estate taxes and significant probate. Of course, you don't have to do this; you can retain ownership in your own names with sole and separate ownership. However, as stated, that doesn't necessarily solve the estate planning either. My point is that you need proper planning to limit the problems due to estate taxes, unequal distributions, and emotional problems.

Once again, I refer you to a competent estate planning attorney for more particulars. The information in this chapter is relatively straightforward, but the ramifications can be extensive if other legal issues are involved such as numerous creditors who have a claim on the estate.

Appreciation

To know what type of planning may be necessary, how a will or trust might work for the beneficiaries, you need to have some reasonable idea what the assets will be in the future. Some of this planning may become moot with new tax laws—nonetheless, other laws and issues are bound to impact an estate and you need to know what a potential financial and tax impact might be in 10, 20, 30, or more years.

To illustrate, let's assume that a couple are both 55 years of age and have assets currently valued at $400,000. Do you see the problem yet? If you take those assets and assume no other additions or subtractions, a 7 percent average annual return on investments, and a life expectancy of another 30 years until they're about 85 years old, the ending value is over $3 million. Yes, 7 percent might be a tad too high for your acceptance, but simply adjust the parameters at your discretion—interest rate, lump sum, and time frame—for your own situation. Table 14.9 details the appreciation of assets.

Table 14.9 Appreciation of Assets

Current Value	Return, yearly compounding	20 Years	30 Years	40 Years
$100,000	7%	$386,968	$761,225	$1,497,446
$300,000		1,160,905	2,283,677	4,492,337
$500,000		1,934,842	3,806,127	7,467,229
$1,000,000		3,869,684	7,612,255	14,974,457

As stated, the new tax laws may allow a complete offset of estate tax. But our huge federal deficit may force some changes later on and you should therefore analyze an estate that would need formal planning. So, let's say that an estate size of $4 million was left to a surviving spouse. She died and the estate tax, under current laws, would be about $1.5 million. Would you want your ultimate beneficiaries to write the IRS a $1.5 million check? That's more than a 37 percent reduction of your estate. Actually, it will probably be *much* more.

How's that? Well, most people don't have $1.5 million lying around just to pay bills. The money is invariably tied up in assets that will have to be sold relatively quickly, since payment to the government is normally required in nine months. The result is apt to be a fire sale of assets—probably including illiquid ones like real estate—and the net received might be far less than normally expected. The loss due to taxes could easily eat up more than 50 percent of the entire estate. It's not exactly a happy ending to your life. So let's look at various basic planning strategies and ones that can reduce the tax exposure.

Trusts

As stated, a will is a formal document that indicates to whom assets are to be transferred (and much more, depending on the complexity). But it requires probate for most estates—and certainly for the average middle-class consumer. The basic provisions for trusts are relatively simple methods of avoiding probate while including all the elements of a will and more.

Actually, while a trust can help reduce estate taxes and eliminate most of probate, those assertions are not its true claim to fame. A trust is an excellent asset management tool since it defines, in appropriate detail, what is supposed to happen, when, and by whom if a particular situation(s) should befall either or both trustees.

The paragraphs that follow describe some of the most popular types of trusts.

Revocable Living Trusts

Most people are familiar with the term *living trusts*. They are trusts that are set up while you are alive and allow you to manage assets in effectively the same manner as though they had been retained in your own individual name. A *revocable living trust* is one that can be changed at any time and in any manner by the trustee(s) of the trust. That's who you become as the "owner" of the trust you established: the trustee. You do not have to set up different social security numbers; all the income will be accounted for the same way and taxed the same way because the trust is revocable.

The difference with the trust is that you will buy and sell everything under the trust's name—say, the Smith Family Trust. That is an inconvenience in some ways but offers the advantages of no probate and, specifically, that the document decides what will happen and how upon incapacity or death. That's the real bonus. Remember this key point: A trust is a great management tool for what can go wrong. It can save some taxes for larger estates, and a plus is the ability to avoid probate. But it's the management element that people should address first and foremost.

In the basic use of a trust, the husband and wife (generally) want to use as much of their lifetime exemption as possible. It is simply not a transfer of all assets to the surviving spouse. As indicated previously, a husband or wife could transfer all monies to the survivor at death with the unlimited marital transfer, but then there can be estate taxes at the second to die. But with a trust, the first to die may simply have his or her, say, $1 million go into an irrevocable trust when he or she dies and the survivor retains the rest of the assets. Let's assume $2 million of total net assets to see how this works. Table 14.10 illustrates this concept.

Notice how simple this was. There was no estate tax since it was possible for the husband to use his lifetime exemption by setting up the irrevocable trust upon his death.

Also notice that there was no probate because the trust already owned the assets. This is a key point requiring further commentary. When the revocable trust is set up, the assets need to be retitled and identified as part of the trust assets. For example, your house needs to be retitled and recorded as becoming part of the Smith Family Trust. Your stocks and bonds need a change of ownership so that the revocable trust already owns them. That way, when you die, they can move directly to the irrevocable ownership and bypass probate. If you do not retitle these assets before you die, they still can get into the trust (testamentary trust), but the transfer will have to go through probate. That process is illogical, time consuming, potentially expensive, and emotionally charged. But this situation happens a lot. The trustees (that means you) think the attorney has done it, you didn't have time, you forgot, and so on. You must be sure that the assets are transferred to your revocable trust before you die in order for the trust to be set up correctly.

The *irrevocable trust*, depending on how it is set up, can provide income, support, and maintenance, and even a 5 percent additional payment or principal each year. The point being that the deceased's irrev-

Table 14.10   Revocable Trust with $2,000,000 of Net Assets

Husband dies	2,000,000 total assets; 50% ownership or a transfer of assets to make ownerships equal	Wife
Irrevocable Trust = $1,000,000 Minus $1,000,000 lifetime exemption = $0 taxable estate		$1,000,000
No probate since assets were already ATitled@ to go to irrevocable trust		Wife dies
		$1,000,000 assets Minus $1,000,000 lifetime exemption = $0 Estate tax
$1,000,000 or whatever trust is then worth goes to beneficiaries—say their children.		$1,000,000 or whatever wife's assets are then worth goes to beneficiaries

ocable trust can and does provide an ongoing benefit to the survivor while at the same time having the ability to use the $1 million lifetime exemption. This way, when the last survivor dies, he or she has only $1 million to declare and that can be offset by the $1 million exemption. Hence, there are no estate taxes at all for either estate. And at that point, the beneficiaries of both trusts are now able to receive their distributions. Wasn't that simple? Sure, we could add all sorts of technical jargon, extra ways of using trusts (spendthrift trusts, for example) under various conditions, and a bunch of other details. Irrevocable trusts can get complicated. But the diagram and the notes should get you to an attorney with the confidence that you understand the fundamentals.

Trustee Selection

Most people select friends and relatives as the successor trustees for trusts that require continued financial services. That can be a disaster if they are not knowledgeable about investments—and few people truly are. Further, I have run into so many bank and other type of "institutional" trustees that are incompetent it defies logic. In one specific situation with a client, he had two to three different trustees and supervisors each year for a three-year period from one of the largest banks in the United States. The portfolio, left by his mother in trust, was handled ineptly at best. That said, there are good trustees and the selection can be limited in scope by reading Chapter 3.

Depending on the size and complexity of the trust, it might be viable to use co-trustees, such as a competent personal friend along with a professional trustee. Even that is no guarantee against incompetence, but a trust protector might be. Read on.

Trust Protector

Articles and personal experience have clearly shown that the selection of a particular trustee may not be beneficial to the beneficiaries over time. The trustor may have believed that the original trustees were professional, and they might have been. But time changes much. An astute trustor may designate an individual—preferably separate from the beneficiaries, to avoid a potential conflict of interest—to oversee the trust on a regular basis. If the *trust protector* determines that the fees are now too excessive, the trustees incompetent, the beneficiaries would be better served by another trustee, or whatever, this individual has the right, through the original trust agreement, to change these parameters without necessitating a formal court petition.

Additionally, the trust protector can change the terms of the trust, if necessary. For example, assume there was to be a distribution of assets to a beneficiary at age 35. However the trustee found out that she, at age 34, was now in a commune. Her funds were apt to be given to the religious cult and lost. The trust protector could reallocate the funds over her lifetime instead, or until such time as he believed her capable of using the funds objectively.

Or maybe a beneficiary needs extra money now for an operation.

The trust protector can serve a myriad of duties. I would suggest that every trustor seek further review of this area with proper counsel and definitely implement a trust protector.

Will with Trusts

You might think that having a living, revocable trust would completely negate the need for a will. Au contraire. For some small property in an estate, pourover wills are required for both the husband and wife. They are designed to transfer miscellaneous small personal items, such as jewelry, fishing gear, and so on, to the trust for subsequent distribution. Yes, such assets do require probate. However, the amount of such assets is small—or they should be—and should stay under the radar screen of most states. For example, California does not charge fees for estates under $100,000.

Additionally, a will is the only place where a father and mother can designate who will be the guardians of their children in case they both die.

QTIP Trusts

Qualified terminable interest property (QTIP) trusts are generally designed for second marriages. For example, let's assume the husband is older—age 65—with children from his first marriage. He marries someone much younger—say, 40—and we'll assume she has no children. They have children together. He is concerned however, that when he dies, his first children could be disinherited if he left everything to his new wife. So he sets up a QTIP trust for the children from his first marriage.

Normally, the QTIP trust is set up so that when the husband dies the benefits go to the surviving spouse in the same manner as the husband's irrevocable trust. Upon the wife's death, however, the assets in the trust will go to his first children, not to any children they had together nor to any children she might have had or spouse that she might have married after his demise. The wife, in any case, will get the assets that he passed directly to her. The husband just doesn't want to forget his first children (and they sure don't want to be forgotten). All in all, a QTIP trust is pretty straightforward in the way it works.

Here's how it works: Let's assume that the estate is worth $2 million, all the property is the husband's, and that he has two children from his first marriage. He is now 65; she is 40. (I should be so lucky.) They have kids of their own. He sets up the trust to leave $1 million to their kids but he is unwilling to leave her the other $1 million outright because she may not leave any of that to the children of his prior marriage(s). So he leaves her $500,000 outright on his death but puts a separate $500,000 into a QTIP trust. She is able to get income, support, 5 percent of principal, and so on, so she does receive something of value. But upon her death, the $500,000 goes to his first children and there is nothing she can do about it, assuming she wanted to. Table 14.11 illustrates how a QTIP trust works.

This basic scenario can have a million different variations: Maybe there are three prior marriages for him; two for her; each has children from these libidinous unions. Too, let's say that she has money she brings to the marriage. So they can each set up regular trusts for the children from the second marriage plus a number of other QTIP trusts to be sure the kids from previous marriages get something, no matter what. In theory, this setup appears to be fine and there really isn't too much to it—except that it won't work in many cases. Why? Because the

Table 14.11   QTIP Trust for the Benefit of Prior Children

Husband Dies	2,000,000 total assets	Qtip trust for benefit of husband's former children	Wife
Irrevocable trust = $1,000,000 Trust can provide benefits to the wife and the remaining assets at her death go to their children.		$500,000. Trust can provide benefits to the wife and the remaining assets at her death go to his children.	$500,000

new wife may not be much older than his first children. By the time she dies, his own children may have already died waiting for her demise. In such cases, the QTIP is better replaced by life insurance or direct gifts when the older husband dies.

The distribution of assets can make a huge difference in the legacy you leave. It's not just the amount, but the timing as well. If you make your kids wait until they are 80 or older before anything gets to them, you can bet they will be saying some not-too-nice things about you.

Physician's Directive and Health Care Proxy

A trust will almost undoubtedly include a *physician's directive* and *health care proxy* to determine who has responsibility for you and how you wish to live and die. This is a very critical area that needs its own focus.

Each state tends to have its own specific wording for these documents. The following is an example of the text used in New York: "By appointing a health care agent, you can make sure that health care providers follow your wishes. Your agent can also decide how your wishes apply as your medical condition changes. Hospitals, doctors and other health care providers must follow your agent's decisions as if they were your own. You may give the person you select as your health care agent as little or as much authority as you want. You may allow your agent to make all health care decisions or only certain ones. You may also give your agent instructions that he or she has to follow. This form can also be used to document your wishes or instructions with regard to organ and/or tissue donation."

You may need a separate trustee to act in this regard. That is not as simplistic as it appears. Many people may add their spouse as the "logical" choice—just as you may have done with your living trust. But does your spouse have the same belief system as you do? Beyond that, and most importantly, can your spouse steel him- or herself- to effectively pull the plug when he or she is so emotionally devastated? I have asked that question of many people. Some are concerned that the spouse, or other loved one, would not feel comfortable about this difficult decision. Therefore, I have been asked to be the trustee in such cases. Sure, it might be hard to do this, but, quite honestly, I am a firm believer that people have the right to determine how they live (within reason) and to die the way they want (within reason).

Do these agreements work? Will physicians and hospitals pay attention to them? Generally yes, but you should validate the issue before you enter a hospital. That said, the physician's directive or similar documents have won a lot of acceptance during the last five years. If you put in a reasonable amount of homework and investigate physicians who are willing to carry this out, you should feel comfortable that your desires will be properly respected and initiated when the time comes.

Make sure you have discussed these documents in full with your spouse, trustee, children, and so on, as well. I did have a client whose husband fell off a ladder and hit his head. He went into a coma that would have left him in a vegetative state. He never wanted that and his attorney had the proper documents drawn up. His wife said that taking him off life support was the hardest decision she ever made. By the same token, we both knew exactly that it was the right decision, it's what he wanted and, subsequently, it made the decision much easier. And she never had to look back and second guess.

Your attorney will include these documents with your trust. If you have a will, there are plenty of sites that provide the correct contract for your state. Do make sure you do this.

Estate Planning Attorneys

Let's look at why you shouldn't use just any ol' attorney for your estate planning needs. You may have noted that I have a law degree. Whoopee. I am not an attorney (I need my integrity). But in the same context I can tell you that neither the degree nor passing the bar would have given anyone the insight necessary to know what really goes on with proper estate planning. Legally, just about any attorney can offer wills, trusts, and other estate documents. But there is a huge difference between those attorneys who have received a formal estate planning designation in their state (though I know some states have no such designation) or those who have some other specifically related background.

Admittedly, getting an estate attorney might be a moot issue for small and simplistic estates, but my experience has shown that few things are really that simple. It may cost you more to use such experts, but it probably will be worth the effort and expense to locate those with advanced education.

Note that once again, I am not necessarily referencing experience per se. Someone with 20 years in the business might have simply taken one years' worth of experience and then repeated it 20 times. I want something more than time in the business. I want advanced knowledge and formal insight.

As a repeated caveat to your selection, the attorney (actually anyone dealing with money) must have personal competency with a financial calculator. Remember, they are dealing with money that not only exists now but will accumulate into the future. In order to properly plan for this increase, they must know the impact of taxes, inflation, growth rates, actuarial lifetime, and more. The ability to calculate the impact of these elements is mandatory. Estate planning requires expertise and insight far greater than completing some forms. If they cannot use a calculator, I'd opt out of any involved documentation that includes an analysis of present and future values. In other words, find someone else.

Summary

The material presented here should give you a better insight as how an estate plan might work upon death. Recognize, however, that a major consideration is to reduce some of the anxiety and emotional distress that would arise with no or improper planning.

You probably will need a formal document prepared by an estate planning attorney, and I hope this insight will make the process more understandable and expedient. It might even make it cheaper, since an understanding of what is needed can shorten the time frame for preparation of the documents and some attorneys might give you credit for that (though don't hold your breath).

Notes

1. The attorney the widow hired was not the best. She could have spared herself the extra stress of dealing with less-than-ideal legal "help" by doing more work up front, reducing the need to attend to details later. That's the whole point to planning.

CHAPTER 15
ARBITRATION AND LITIGATION

*I*F YOU HAVE EVER BEEN WRONGED by a broker or agent, chances are you feel frustrated, mad, and stupid, among other emotions. And the sad fact is, there may be little you can do to rectify the situation. No matter how you cut it, the odds are generally stacked against you of getting all of your money back—or even part of your money. And if you don't use an experienced attorney to help fight your case with you, the odds are lesser still. A General Accounting Office study in 1992 noted that clients represented by attorneys won in 58 percent of the cases. Furthermore, those clients represented by an attorney were 1.6 times more likely to receive an award in excess of 60 percent of their claim than those investors who attempted to represent themselves. That statistic, however, can be misleading since you still have to figure how much of a percentage of the award would be cut to the attorney (probable a minimum of 25 percent up to around 40 percent). Additionally, few cases may ever be brought to arbitration or mediation to begin with since the amount may be too low for an attorney to bother with. A lot of cases under $50,000 never end up on the statistical radar in the first place. I know many readers/victims will concur with that assessment.

An Overview of Arbitration and Litigation

Through my Web site, I have received hundreds of emails from consumers who have been victimized on all sorts of issues. I have served as an expert witness in court and in arbitration settings. I have also acted as arbitrator for many years where I was the one securities representative out of the three-member panel—the other two being independent individuals such as CPAs, attorneys, and retired judges.

As it turned out, as an arbitrator, I tended to "side" with the prosecution in many cases. Why? My decisions were based in no small part on my awareness that the securities, insurance, and planning industries are not played on a level playing field. The industry practices are so far beyond the grasp of general consumers—and the sophisticated ones as well—that they can rarely comprehend where they stand unless and until a major problem is exposed. For example, the $120 billion fine levied against some of the major brokerage firms because their analysts said to "buy" an investment while at the same time, internally, saying the product wasn't any good should give the investing public some idea that they were primarily used as a commodity. A more simple answer is that stated in my introduction: the fundamentals of investing have never been taught to brokers or agents. But the industry has accepted a fiduciary duty to do what is right and suitable—hence I hold them to those standards. That the professionals have had only a single class in securities or, at the most, the equivalent of a single semester of college preparation in planning does not release them from the knowledge, duty, competency and integrity demanded of a true professional.

Clearly, the industry has violated its most basic duty to consumers. That is bad enough, but the situation worsens when you try and get back lost money. That serious roadblocks exist on the path to recouping such losses is clear to those who have already been involved in litigation in their lives. People may lie in depositions, court, and just about any other place where the truth is demanded—especially where money is the issue. Judges and juries can and do make mistakes. Some are just plain stupid. That's just the way things are.

Of course it can all work perfectly, but my point is simple: If you want to avoid the litigation with securities and insurance, reread Chapter 3 and make sure you hire someone with the appropriate background who can do the job well in the first place. (Bad news, though: There aren't many.) The search for a qualified professional to help you will be difficult. But if you do so, the results will be far more worthwhile than if you just accepted the marketing hype and misconceptions offered by any brokerage firm (commission or fee) or by anyone who proffers planning designations as evidence of expertise. Always keep in mind that, no matter what advertising or marketing say to the contrary, agents, brokers, and planners are usually woefully undertrained to provide the level of competency that you would expect from, say, your doctor.

Compared to the study and work required by a physician, most of the people in the financial industry do not have specialized education in their fields. They don't have degrees in economics, business, or finance—and almost certainly no degrees in the very work they do (securities, planning, and insurance). There is no "residency" overseen by true financial professionals; what training there is generally is overseen by salespeople. In fact, there is no residency period at all to establish a formal practice. (Actually, they practice on you!) Continuing education is generally a rehash of old or simplistic stuff at best.

Essentially, no ethical standards must be adhered to, regardless of what you might hear to the contrary. Standards are promulgated by the planning organizations, but usually someone is found guilty of an ethical violation only when and if he or she has been found guilty of a legal one.[1]

Why It Goes Wrong

Why is so much money lost through unsuitable investments and inappropriate and unknowledgeable advice? Money, pure and simple. You have the money. They want it. And, for the most part, consumers have been willing to part with their money solely on unsubstantiated competency. The rationalization by investors who lost money—"But I thought I could trust him" or "She seemed so nice"—gets real old real fast. Many used that as their sole reason for following the improper advice. The only people worthy of trust are those who have a solid background, have been properly trained, and aren't just mere salespeople or hucksters. But they are few in numbers.

Consumers also lie and misrepresent their position—and should be held responsible for such actions. Some people tend to think they have the insight to figure out what to buy via some discovery on the Motley Fool site by chatting with a bunch of auto mechanics, nuclear physicists, mailmen, history teachers, and so forth. Such arrogance and ignorance is generally an offset of potential awards for testimony for arbitrations and other litigation.

Nevertheless, the industry is required by law to provide suitable investments. The supposed higher degree of knowledge and expertise is at the broker and firm level. They market this expertise and trust consciousness. They are therefore held accountable as fiduciaries in doing so. If industry members want to be treated as experts, they have to also accept the underlying responsibility.

Because of the highly effective industry marketing, consumers do not have much, if any, insight into allocation, correlation, and the rest of the fundamentals. They believe the perceived elements of competency and trust that are highlighted in every industry ad. Even if consumers have done more scrutiny, it is highly debatable that anyone, outside of those who have actually taught the securities licensing classes, would categorically know that the fundamentals are not taught to brokers and never have been. The firms are aware of this situation and certainly don't reveal it to the public.

Will such positions change? I seriously doubt it. Nonetheless, the SEC and NASD need to provide much more broker and arbitrator education. I wrote to them about this issue on numerous occasions. I also wrote to the CFP Board, requesting that their officers comply with their own ethics standards. Almost every effort I attempted for professionalism met with dismal success. For example, here is the comment that I got from a source at the NASD when I tried for education of arbitrators: "The [brokerage] firms will never allow the fundamentals be taught because it would slow sales." This is an absolutely true statement and, from a business perspective, I certainly understand it. But it says nothing for education, practical application, or, certainly, the elements to address suitability and fiduciary duty.

In terms of the extensive effort to get the CFP Board of Standards to enforce their own ethics code, I actually filed a formal complaint against the Board of Standards for violating their own standards (2000). The board's attorney (1995) and an incoming president (2001) stated that they will not enforce an ethical violation unless it is preceded by a legal one. If you check their violations for the last 5 to 10 years, you will clearly see the pattern. True, the board is a nonprofit organization that is limited in its capacity, but it should so indicate. That said, you are not "nonprofit" and need to be protected from activity against common sense when an egregious action occurs.

As such, the elements of suitability, ethics, and fiduciary responsibility by the industry will rarely be upheld as a canon for the consumer.

You need to recognize this inherent difficulty. The comments put a true perspective on the uphill battle you face before a sale of securities or service. Should the purchase or service go wrong, you will face difficulty in presenting the case before arbitrators, attorneys, boards, and so on, who either have little understanding of real-life securities or planning applications or really have not cared to find out. And, you may find only limited effort or assistance from the various organizations if the issue at hand does not dovetail with their direct interests.

That's not to say that the use of an adviser with the greatest background and years of experience is a guarantee of success. It's not that attorneys cannot and do not make exceptional legal presentations. Nor does it mean that arbitrators may not make difficult legal decisions nor do the best job they may be capable of doing. And, it wouldn't be fair to say that all organizations are so singularly myopic that you cannot get assistance in the very egregious activities associated with complaints and litigation. However, the tools needed to address the issues from a fundamental real-life application to suitability, fiduciary duty, and so forth, are stained from inception and often can lead—and, in fact, have led—to incomplete, inaccurate, and grossly contorted judgments.

Types of Cases and Statistics

During the high-flying 1990s, when almost nobody had a clue as to what they were doing, I had limited work as an expert witness in financial cases. As long as an account went up, few people even thought, knew, or cared about the underlying risk and other associated problems, specifically suitability. Once so many people started losing big bucks, however, they began to realize that substantial sections of their accounts were based on gambling in an unsubstantiated areas, most often in technology, and their accounts were improperly diversified, if at all (and many still aren't). You can see from Figures 15.1 and 15.2 how the claims have increased, starting in 2001.

Per the NASD 2002, just a little over half of cases heard by NASD arbitrators were decided in favor of investors. In fact, NASD Dispute Resolution President Linda Fienberg has noted that 70 percent of arbitration claims are settled before a decision is reached. (There are no statistics indicating who got what, why, or what the terms of the settlements were.) When a case isn't clear-cut, arbitrators often "split the baby," giving the broker, perhaps, 60 percent of the responsibility for any losses and the investor the other 40 percent. Punitive damages are handed out infrequently: They are awarded in just 2 percent to 4 percent of all securities arbitration cases. (Punitive damages are generally awarded against the defendants for (very) egregious actions.)

Figures 15.3 and 15.4 illustrate NASD arbitration cases in mid-2002.

New case filings through December

2003	2002	2001	2003 vs. 2002
8,945	7,704	6,915	16%

Number of cases closed through December

2003	2002	2001	2003 vs. 2002
7,278	5,957	5,582	22%

Turnaround time* (in months) through December

	2003	2002	2001	2003 vs. 2002
Overall	14.6	13.7	13.0	7%
Hearing Decisions	17.4	16.5	16.6	5%
Simplified Decisions	6.1	7.6	9.2	–20%

*The *timing* of the arbitration process is heavily influenced by Code of Arbitration Procedures, time limit parties, and the panel.

Figure 15.1 Summary Arbitration Statiwstics December 2003.

Year	Cases	Year	Cases
1990	3,617	1997	5,997
1991	4,150	1998	4,936
1992	4,379	1999	5,508
1993	5,421	2000	5,558
1994	5,586	2001	6,915
1995	6,058	2002	7,704
1996	5,631	Through December 2003	8,945

Figure 15.2 Arbitration cases filed.

Unless the panel awards attorneys' fees (which may not happen), your lawyer will typically collect about 33 percent to 40 percent of any award or settlement. (You *must* use an experienced securities attorney, though one will be hard to come by. Trying a substantial case by yourself will be fraught with errors and frustration.)

Type of controversy*	1999	2000	2001	2002
Margin calls	104	284	375	366
Churning	565	473	784	824
Unauthorized trading	915	611	884	930
Failure to supervise	1,097	1,270	1,968	2,633
Negligence	1,329	1,867	2,275	2,522
Omission of facts	474	476	692	1,176
Breach of fiduciary duty	2,093	2,489	3,458	4,236
Unsuitability	1,311	900	1,524	2,644
Misrepresentation	1,482	1,321	1,895	2,623
Online trading**	55	214	155	95

*Each case can be coded to contain up to four controversy types. Therefore the columns in this table can be totaled to determine the number of cases served in a year.
**Online trading was first tracked in 1999.

Figure 15.3　Controversies involved in arbitration cases.

Year	Cases	Year	Cases
1990	4,019	1997	5,880
1991	4,037	1998	5,484
1992	4,375	1999	4,767
1993	4,230	2000	5,473
1994	4,484	2001	5,582
1995	5,779	2002	5,957
1996	6,331	Through December 2003	7,276

Figure 15.4　Security types involved in arbitration cases.

Even if you do win, will you get paid? A General Accounting Office (GAO) study of arbitration awards handed out in 1998 found that 52 percent of arbitration awards weren't paid, and 12 percent weren't fully paid. (In early 2003 that percentage was up to 13 percent because some firms have simply gone out of business.)

Associated Issues

Most investors opening new accounts with a brokerage firm are required to sign a statement that any disputes must be submitted to an arbitration panel—and not a court—through the local National Association of Securities Dealers, The New York Stock Exchange, or similar venues. Its intent is to provide a fair hearing that is faster and cheaper than going to court and hearing the case before a jury. Unfortunately, the costs associated with arbitration are escalating and the time span for getting to a resolution is growing to well past a year. As such, arbitrations are taking far longer and are far more involved in legal tactics than ever before. Now, that may or may not be a credible perception of all cases but my personal experience with arbitrations dovetails with that position.

Regardless of the legal maneuvering, the real drawback issue for plaintiffs (this means you) is the fact that the usual three-member panel may have, and often will have, limited understanding of the real-life applications of the issues that are presented before them. Further, some may be loath to hear a presentation that includes fundamentals that invalidate what they may have done for years. A discussion of diversification by the numbers (wherein you need at least 50 stocks for proper diversification) is apt to be anathema to arbitrators who have traded stocks for years under the belief they could beat the statistical average.

Even with this factual material and real-life application, arbitrators may still not and often do not agree with what should have been done. The fundamentals given in the situation presented may have been very new, variant, or both, to what the industry has proffered. So, the arbitrators are apt to conclude a case upon their own supposed insight to stock trading and other esoteric issues inconsistent with suitable practice.

Not just arbitrators have traded individual securities inconsistently and unknowledgeably—pretty much everybody has. But if the arbitrators, acting as judges, have been unaware of, or were incapable of, or reticent to, an understanding of the ways to determine the numerical or emotional risk, they are apt to be unable or unwilling to recognize the perils of a nondiversified portfolio. At an arbitration hearing, they may not accept any facts altering their historical belief system.

Per attorney Dan Solin, author of *Does Your Broker Owe You Money*: "The makeup of these tribunals tends to be older men who are very set in their ways and unaccustomed to dealing with anything that they have not heard many times before. It could take a serious effort on the part of a number of investors and attorneys [and experts], and a protracted period of time, to convince some of these tribunal members that since the rest of the financial world has long since accepted these theories [of investing], they should do so as well." (If you are going to attempt arbitration, buy his book before you even start the process.)

The exception that I take with his comments is that the theories of modern portfolio theory, diversification (by the numbers of course), standard deviation, and so on, have not been taught at all or certainly in their real-life application. More importantly, even when these fundamentals are offered to those that should make an effort to understand, this knowledge generally goes no place. These are not idle comments. There have been many attempts—securities arbitration reform by the NASD in the 1990s and others, before and after—all culminating in nothing. So, the effort to convince arbitrators and others who think they already know everything is far more difficult that even Dan Solin intimates.

On the other hand, members of a jury will have far less experience in dealing with such complexities and should be more open-minded to a clear-cut and direct explanation of risk and reward (as long as the statement stays relatively simple.) A solid presentation of facts to a jury of peers would be more consistent with justice. Most of your peers would not have been actively trading stocks nor would believe they have the capability of doing so. They would be more receptive to what should have been done. Furthermore, many of the jurors would have undoubtedly gotten cold calls from brokers, annuity pitches from insurance agents, and so on. Undoubtedly, a few of them took flyers they wish they hadn't.

If you have the possibility of using the court system and a jury, I would suggest you discuss this option at length with your attorney. You very well may have a better chance for restitution by going through the court system than by going through arbitration. (Though it tends to be more costly and can take years through the appeal process.) Of course, that begs the issue that a full and proper case based on the fundamentals is actually presented, which is not necessarily a given with the often-limited knowledge of said fundamentals by attorneys and experts.

No matter the legitimacy of using knowledge and real-life application in arbitration, it might backfire big time. Arbitrators may take personal affront to such a presentation, no matter how well it is handled. And you can be assured that the defense attorneys will attempt to discredit not only the facts but the presentation itself. If the plaintiff's attorney and expert witness are not totally in sync with the facts and the best way for them to be submitted to the arbitrators, the case could be lost. The truth is a great defense, but it does not work all the time.

Another issue is the extensive amount of time that it is now taking before a case is heard. Claimants must realize that the legal system—which includes arbitration—is apt to wear you down emotionally. It may do so until you accept next to nothing in an award or simply walk away because you cannot bear the stress. The personal and emotional toll is extensive. I always counsel victims that they need to steel themselves to months and months of various legal requests for documentation along with a bunch of useless ploys in the game between firms. And this includes name calling and character assassination. It can be an extremely grueling and mentally debilitating experience.

It is irrelevant if you have the greatest case since O. J. Simpson (okay, wrong analogy). The brokerage's attorneys will normally tell you through your attorney that your case is unwarranted, the client authorized the trades, monthly statements were sent, you were sophisticated because you read a magazine once and you knew where a book was (no joke), the account gained in value (minuscule or otherwise, even if for the wrong reasons), and so forth. Going to court or an arbitration

CAVEAT INVESTOR

It really is tough to try and answer questions from either the defense or plaintiffs if no one really cares about the fundamentals and part of the case is effectively dismissed. I have been involved with attorneys and arbitrators who not only did not have a clue to diversification or the fundamentals of investing but didn't want to learn either.

In one case, the arbitrators elected not to hear any testimony at all since they stated that they already "knew" the complexities of the subject better than I did. The plaintiff, a totally unsophisticated 55-year-old high school graduate with no work history (she lived off an inheritance) was stated by her broker to be a sophisticated investor who fully grasped the commodities investments she had been lulled into buying. And some hedging. And other clearly objectionable and unsuitable investments. This was a no brainer arbitration that ended up being heard by some with no brains. Very sad.

In another major arbitration, the attorney never took the time with me to review the broker's notes, which contained statements regarding standard deviation that were incorrect. (I was not even told that there were two other experts he hired to testify nor, certainly, what they were covering.) The client won $500,000, but the amount would have been greater had the issue of risk been definitively addressed.

In yet another upcoming case, a discussion with a CPA/attorney went nowhere in addressing the huge risk of the holding of a singular security. Simply because a stock may have provided good dividends for years in no way offsets the violation of diversification.

This is really tough stuff to present.

hearing is not an easy endeavor without some bloodletting, so be prepared accordingly. Actually, most people never get that far anyway.

Many years ago in a conversation with a firm conducting arbitrations, we estimated that probably only 3 percent to 4 percent of all the people who have a valid claim actually pursue it past a conversation with their broker or maybe a letter to the broker's supervisor. Dan Solin notes, "thousands—maybe millions—of investors who are not suing their brokers have valid claims that their brokers have either made unsuitable investments for them or encouraged them to invest in unsuitable investments."

Most people don't want to admit their losses or be put into an arena where their ignorance or stupidity is identified over and over. While they are not able to handle the financial devastation, they are even less willing to handle the added emotional deterioration with so many people they never met hearing how badly they "screwed up." The psychological element of finding out you put your trust in someone who had little expertise can be psychologically devastating to the point of inaction.

Case in point: Several years ago I counseled one woman who had taken almost a full hit on a $40,000 investment. Even though she had an attorney, the brokerage firm worked her over well. While, on one hand, she wanted to fight and show them what they had done wrong, it was apparent that, as time wore on, she was becoming more depressed and anxious. When they repeatedly offered just $14,000 to settle, despite her attempts to up the ante, she finally caved in well before arbitration. The emotional turmoil over five months was more than what she had anticipated or could accept.

This situation happens a lot, since the psychological element definitely will come into play with the vast majority who wish to go forward. You just need to be aware going in what will transpire. In another case, an elderly plaintiff suffered his second stroke two days before the hearing. Coincidence? I think not. It was the strain of the case. In another, the plaintiff's attorney suffered heart problems because of the intensity and strain of the upcoming case and had to postpone the hearing for two months.

Even if a claim gets to arbitration, the delaying and shameful tactics still go on. In one instance, I had to fly to New Orleans in November 2002 for a supposedly short hearing. The defendants offered legal pleadings that we thought had already been addressed in prehearing conferences by her attorney. From 9:00 A.M. to 4:00 p.m., not one shred of evidence was heard. The plaintiff, an unsophisticated woman who had waited a long time to be heard, made this comment: "Yesterday was a new experience for me. It was a long-awaited opportunity to resolve this distressing situation. Imagine my surprise when most of the day seemed to be mainly spent in arguing whether we were supposed to be there! I thought that was already established. To see those stacks of binders and boxes of papers and to hear the visiting lawyers say basically 'It's not fair. We're not prepared.' was amazing, to put it mildly. It seems like the idea might be to make things take so long, be so hard and be so complicated that regular people will just go away. I don't think that is the American way. I hope not."

The same thing might happen in court, but the public has been led to believe that arbitration is a short process, far less complicated, and certainly less expensive than a court hearing. As mentioned earlier, if there is a possibility of having a jury trial, I would consider it, since it is my opinion that a jury of open-minded, nonbiased citizens would be more receptive to a factual presentation of the fundamentals than would arbitrators.

Initial Steps to Arbitration

If you do decide to pursue a loss, the first step is to contact the broker. You can do so by phone. Perhaps a simple mistake has been made—extra shares erroneously purchased, for example. A situation like that is not usually a problem and it can be rectified quickly. When you are dealing with a situation that is more involved, you should still start with a preliminary phone call. Maybe there will be some resolution. Sometimes the broker clearly feels responsible and may admit to an error. On the other hand, the broker may also present a sob story so you will feel sorry for him and simply avoid any further controversy. In either case, I have actually seen many investors—particularly if the broker was a friend—actually eat the losses rather than make the broker feel any worse. *Really.*

But if you decide to pursue resolution, whether the broker admits guilt or not won't make any difference, because the broker has no authority to give you back any money. Assuming this is the case, you may want to decide to write a letter to the firm—normally to the broker's supervisor—outlining the scenario. Once in a while the supervisor may reply directly, but a letter normally will be sent up to the firm's attorneys who will subsequently reply with a standard retort. They'll very likely say that your case is unwarranted, the client authorized the trades, monthly statement s were sent, you were sophisticated, the account gained in value (minuscule or otherwise), and so forth.

You are urged to use caution if you decide to attempt to do any of this activity before hiring an attorney. When you send anything of consequence in writing to the firm without formal review by a professional, you may state information about yourself or your conduct that could be construed negatively and this can really backfire in formal arbitration. Anything in writing almost always has far more relevance to a case than oral testimony.

I am not saying that you should lie or intentionally mislead in any statements you make. But there are ways of saying things—and then *there are ways of saying things.* Per Solin: "If you are going it alone, you should not send any complaint letter until you have had an expert analysis done. Any statement you make in a complaint letter prior to the time when a careful analysis of account records has been done can come back to haunt you when they are used against you at an arbitration tribunal by counsel for the brokerage firm."

Assume that you use an attorney. (Again, doing so is highly encouraged and absolutely mandatory for large cases.) You should expect a long, drawn-out process of failed negotiations right up to the arbitration date. If you look at the situation from a purely business aspect from the brokerage firm's point of view, the strategy may be, and often is,

CAVEAT INVESTOR

The statute of limitations can result in claims being denied or reduced to a minimum . Generally speaking, you are barred from presenting a claim if you do not do so within a certain period of time from the transgression. Some arbitrations hold to three years, others to six. The length of time depends on the state in which the wrong was committed, the strength of arguments by plaintiffs and defendants, and, lastly, the whim of the arbitrators as to whether they will hear a case irrespective of the supposed legal restrictions. Many claims will be limited, if allowed at all, by this statute.

The impact of the statute of limitations negatively affects a large number of filings. But, clearly, it does so more for the elderly who really take a beating with incompetent agents and bad products. Perhaps the wrong didn't really become noticeable for a long period of time. (Cases with limited partnerships and some life insurance polices come immediately to mind.) If the wrong involves poor financial planning (incorporating many areas, disciplines, and individuals), the impact might not be noted for years. Further, efforts to find an expert to prepare the report might take months, and months might elapse before the report is completed. In any case, the elderly are more apt to wait out the situation longer before acting, be more trusting of supposed restitution by an agent, and so on. So a lot of money will never be received by an aggrieved party.

Because the entire legal, securities, planning, and insurance systems and industries have never really allowed the real-life fundamentals to be taught to their personnel, this area of limitations should be amended to reflect the reality of time with many of the products and activities.

used to get you to accept a low offer at some point prior to arbitration, right up to the day of arbitration.

Ethics aside, does the ploy work? You bet! Few people can handle the continual onslaught of negative commentary for that long, and many opt out by accepting a low-ball offer. I have always told people that the undertaking is as much an emotional endeavor as it is a financial trial and they simply have to steel themselves to the system in order to prevail.

Assuming you are willing to take the case further, you will need to contact the NASD and get their forms and pay their fees. There is a lot that goes on and it will normally take quite a while before you get to tell your story.

Summary

The element of arbitration is often far removed from reality. Because of that sad fact, you have few opportunities to receive monies lost when you have been wronged. You are dealing with a flawed system; you need to recognize how the game is played and react accordingly.

Follow the steps above and try to use an experienced attorney who is well versed in the process. Steel yourself to the emotional difficulties and the time to fruition. The process can work very well for the most egregious actions. But it is not a perfect settlement whenever there are the subtleties of testimony that are reviewed by entities with imperfect knowledge and little real-life insight to application.

If you have been wronged, try to get your case submitted as soon as possible. Otherwise, part of your claim may be denied before the case is ever heard.

If American consumers want to limit their exposure to having things go wrong, first they will have to learn to pay a lot more attention to who they are using. The wholesale reliance on referrals and other such noninvolved effort has led to the purchase and use of products and services no professional would allow.

Notes

1. I have reviewed the statistical history of the CFP Board of Standards violations for many years to corroborate the statement. Almost every violator has already been found guilty of an infraction by the NASD, the courts, and so on.

Index

About the Author

Errold F. Moody has more than 30 years experience as a financial consultant and personal financial planner. He is the founder of the popular and acclaimed website www.efmoody.com, ranked among the best by *USA Today*, *BusinessWeek*, *Forbes*, AOL and others. In addition, he publishes a monthly newsletter, *Moody's Review*, which cover all topics in the financial arena. Frequently called as an expert witness on brokerage and financial issues, he has taught and written extensively in the field. He is a former instructor at the University of California at Berkeley, University of California at Irvine, the University of San Francisco and numerous community colleges. Dr. Moody also is a former instructor for the Dearborn Financial Institute and Securities Training Corporation where he taught securities courses for the Series 6, 7, 22, 24, 26, 27, 52, 62 and 63 exams. He has also been an arbitrator with the NASD and the Pacific Stock Exchange. He still conducts insurance continuing education training for AD Banker. He has conducted numerous seminars for a variety of organizations including the American Association of Individual Investors. Moody has been published and quoted in a variety of major media, including the *San Francisco Chronicle*, *Smart Money*, *The Wall Street Journal*, *Mutual Funds Magazine* and most national newspapers. He is a Certified Financial Planner, registered investment adviser, mutli-state securities adviser, California Life and Disability Insurance Analyst, real estate broker and B-1 general contractor. He holds an M.S. in Financial Planning as well as a BSCE, LLB, MBA and PhD. He is also one darn good fisherman.